Kanadische Studien zur deutschen Sprache und Literatur

Etudes canadiennes de langue et littérature
allemandes
Canadian Studies in German Language and Literature
herausgegeben von
Armin Arnold · Michael S. Batts · Hans Eichner

Nr. 19

Sponsored by the Canadian Association
of University Teachers of German

PETER LANG
Bern · Frankfurt am Main · Las Vegas

Michael S. Batts

The Bibliography
of German Literature:
An Historical
and Critical Survey

PETER LANG

Bern · Frankfurt am Main · Las Vegas

© Peter Lang Ltd., Publishers, Berne (Switzerland) 1978
Successor of Herbert Lang & Co. Ltd., Berne

ISBN 3-261-03026-7
450 copies

Printed by Lang Druck Ltd., Liebefeld/Berne (Switzerland)

Acknowledgements

This work has occupied me for several years and could not have been completed without assistance from various quarters. The collection of the library of the University of British Columbia served me well, and additional materials were supplied through the good offices of the Inter-Library Loan Service. In the initial stages I also made use of the collections at the University of Toronto and of the Newberry Library. It was the British Library, however, that served me best and I render grateful thanks to that Library and its staff both for the service I received and for permission to reproduce certain illustrations.

I received financial assistance from the Committee on Research of my own university and from the Canada Council to enable me to visit the libraries mentioned above and to defray the costs of producing the manuscript. To Miss Beryl Morphet I am indebted for the preparation of the final typescript and for proofreading.

The book has been published with the help of a grant from the Humanities Research Council of Canada, using funds provided by the Canada Council

Abbreviations used in the text

"Aber nur die Bibliographie, diese Statistik aller Wissenschaften, enthüllt unparteiisch das Material zur Erkenntnis des menschlichen Geistes"

Emil Weller

Contents

Introduction

The term bibliography has acquired such a broad range of meaning in English, and this range is so different from that of the German *Bibliographie* that I feel impelled to preface any explanation of the aims of this book with a brief discussion of the different forms of bibliography and the relationship between them. The *Concise Oxford Dictionary* (116) still gives precedence in the fourth edition (1954) to the gloss "History of books, their authorship, editions, etc." as does Webster (496) whose definition in the third edition is considerably more refined than in the second edition, although without any basic change in priority. Popularly, however, the term has come to mean solely a list of (usually printed) works of any kind, and this view receives support in many works such as, for example, the *Random House Dictionary* (409) which gives precedence to the gloss: "complete or selective list" on any given subject.[1] It is not surprising therefore to find in the *Encyclopedia of Library and Information Science* (148) the grudging admission that the term is applied by the layman only to bibliographic compilation.[2] "A bibliography" is in fact not infrequently merely a listing of works cited in a book or essay.[3]

Common usage is thus much wider but at the same time much narrower in scope, and the casual employment of the term in place of the more precise "list of works cited" or some such similar term is understandably anathema to the purists, the true bibliographers. For them one branch of bibliography is indeed concerned with the listing of works, but in a very particular form; and it is only one branch on the family tree of bibliography. Broadly speaking, there seem to be only two main branches of bibliography, the one dealing with the *enumeration* of extant works with common characteristics, the other with the *particular characteristics* of books as physical objects. The source of popular usage is easily recognizable in the former of these two divisions, and in Germany this aspect is often recognized as the primary, if not the sole, form of bibliography.[4] The latter has been subject to numerous and at times conflicting

---

1   A similar statement is to be found in *The American College Dictionary* (14); the *World Book Encyclopedia* (513) defines bibliography first as "a list of books or articles about a subject," adding that "the term bibliography can also mean a list of books that an author has written" and that "one type of bibliography ... describes books as well as lists them."

2   The article on bibliography is by Roy B. Stokes (II, 407–19)

3   Cf. John Ferguson (160): "a treatise on almost any subject nowadays is not considered complete if it does not furnish a 'bibliography' of the literature, both as evidence of the author's industry and as a help to the student" (p. 5).

4   Joris Vorstius (492), for example, refers to the definition of bibliography "wie üblich als die Lehre von den Schrifttumsverzeichnissen," and goes on to say that in its *broader* sense it includes also "Bibliothekslehre ... soweit sie sich mit der Verzeichnung und Erschließung der Bücherbestände befaßt." The use of the term in its widest sense as "das gesamte Buchwesen" Vorstius rejects outright (p. 4).

descriptions. What John Ferguson (160) described in 1900 as "technical book description" as opposed to "enumeration of books treating of a subject" (p. 6) has evolved in recent decades into a complex system of related sub-disciplines.

One of the greatest of contemporary bibliographers has attempted on numerous occasions to define the boundaries of his discipline, and a paper read to a joint meeting of the Bibliographical Society of the University of Virginia and the Bibliographical Society of America may serve as an example. In that paper, published under the title "Bibliography, Pure Bibliography, and Literary Studies," (82) Fredson Bowers maintains that bibliography is a "far too general term" and therefore distinguishes *in addition to* enumerative or compilative bibliography the following categories: historical bibliography, analytical bibliography, descriptive bibliography, and critical or textual bibliography. Since the third and fourth categories are considered to be dependent upon the second, we arrive at the following outline:

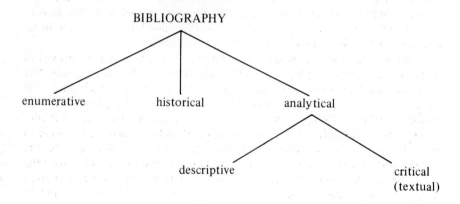

BIBLIOGRAPHY

enumerative   historical   analytical

descriptive   critical (textual)

It would not be appropriate here to enter into a criticism or even a detailed description of these distinctions. Suffice it, that by historical bibliography is meant in general the history of books and printing (Stokes defines it [note 2] as the "broad understanding of the milieu of the book"); and by analytical bibliography is meant the study of *individual* books as physical objects in order to determine precisely "all the circumstances of the book's manufacture and history" (Stokes). The results of this enquiry are applied in description and textual criticism.

These are the special forms of bibliography, and they have been described in order to emphasize what will *not* be the concern of the present work. Bibliography in the title of this work refers only to *enumerative* bibliography — bibliography apparently in the common sense of the word, except that it too has a narrower, a more academic definition than the one generally accepted. The three essential features of enumerative bibliography are that the works enumerated have one or more common characteristics, that the listing is complete, and that it is in some kind of logical arrangement. It is not of course easy to prove that a listing has failed to omit any single item, and clearly few lists have achieved or will achieve this perfection. The intent must, however, be there. As for the common characteristics, these may be of virtually any kind, except that of location. That is to say, a number of books may have a common content, a common size, a common appearance, or a common source, even common ownership; these are characteristics which are permanent. But a listing of books in a common location — most obviously a library — is not a bibliography, but a catalogue. The order too may vary widely and may be either simple or complex, for example, by year of publication or based on a detailed analytical subject classification. Many definitions of the various kinds of bibliography have been made over the three hundred odd years since the term was introduced, and these cannot be surveyed here. For the purpose of this work the term bibliography is used in the enumerative sense and means *a complete and organised listing of all works having one or more characteristics in common other than their location.*

This definition, simple as it may sound, raises immediately one very obvious problem. Bibliography in this specific sense is something relatively new. How then can one speak or write of bibliographies in earlier centuries? The simple, and I hope reasonable, answer is, that one must apply the modern standard with due regard for the historical situation, that the desire for strict accuracy must be tempered with an understanding of the times. If there were at certain times no bibliographies in our sense, then surrogate forms must be accepted or records sought that may serve to provide the kind of bibliographical information relevant to the time. These bibliographical sources may not fall strictly within the terms of the definition given above, they may even be excluded from it, as in the case of library catalogues. They will also inevitably not be solely or even primarily concerned with "German literature." They must, however, be accepted in a work such as this faute de mieux. It is therefore inevitable that the "bibliographical sources" surveyed in the early part of this work are not infrequently general in nature and far from being bibliographies in the true sense of the word. They are, for example, at the beginning European in context and "universal" in scope; but they are the only works available. Only as time progresses — and the survey will proceed as far as possible strictly chronologically — is it possible to narrow the scope of the study both geographically and from the point of view of subject matter. The focus of works sharpens only slowly, and it is not until after the Enlightenment that it is possible to restrict consideration exclusively to Germany and later than that before it is possible to limit one's self to "pure" bibliographies and concentrate on those directly related to literature. With the development of formal and highly specialized studies in vernacular literature the focus finally shifts from primary to secondary literature, i.e., from literature to criticism.

Above all the purpose of this work must be kept in mind. As we move further away from our past and the pace of progress (apparently) increases, the landmarks behind us become fewer; only the outstanding ones remain visible. Whatever the difficulties of comprehending the literary works of the past, such difficulties are compounded by our lack of knowledge of the background from which these works grew. It is not enough to know something of the personal life of an author, of the political situation of his time, or of the economic state of his locality. One must also know something of the literature of the time, literature in the broadest sense of the word. This aspect of history is unfortunately often neglected, but what could be more relevant for an understanding of a literary work of any period than the literature which existed or was created concomitantly with it? This is not to suggest that our aesthetic evaluation of literature is wrong; there is no intention of suggesting that Walther von der Vogelweide is not a "greater" poet than Dietmar von Aist, or Goethe a "better" novelist than Sophie La Roche, although from a sociological standpoint the literature of lesser quality may possibly be a more significant indicator than the greater works. The main problem from a bibliographical point of view is that the lesser works, against which the greater ones should be measured and understood, disappear from view in the course of time. The totality of literature at any given time is something that can only be reconstructed through recourse to reference sources, to bibliographies.

Looked at from this point of view, then, it becomes evident that enumerative bibliography has a significance far beyond its function as a source for literary studies. Just as a bibliography in the field of literature records the state of the art in that field, so other bibliographies do the same for other fields. The sum of bibliographical sources at any given period is therefore a summary indicator of the cultural climate of that period. It can even be argued with some justification that bibliographies give a more accurate picture of the culture of a period than the few great works — whether these are works of art, music, literature, or science — that have come to be accepted as representative of that time. However, it must also be admitted that there is a danger in this viewpoint, a danger similar to that inherent in accepting any work of literature as representative of the *Zeitgeist* of any period. Bibliographies, although in theory committed to objectivity and completeness, are equally subject to the influence of current attitudes and may therefore reflect these in their selection and presentation. Not that their evidence should be discounted for this reason; on the contrary it suggests that bibliographies have a *two-fold* function in cultural history.

The definition given above of enumerative bibliography is "typical" for the present time. Ebert (143) by contrast, writing in the early nineteenth century, regards *selection* as a prime function of the bibliographer and rejects the idea of universal (i.e. complete) bibliography as "unverkennbarer Schwachsinn" (p. v). The complete bibliography as a form is therefore as characteristic of contemporary culture as the works which it lists (which may of course not be contemporary at all). In earlier centuries, when completeness was not considered essential or was interpreted quite differently, the nature of the selection and the method of organisation and presentation are significant indicators of the cultural climate of that time. Bibliographical sources of all kinds are therefore a not unimportant thread in the tangled skein of intellectual history. Through their development and the development of the "discipline" of bibliography per se they reflect the changing perspective of thought, while their contents (bearing in mind always the contemporary definition of bibliography) collectively record the broad spectrum of culture at any given point in that historical process.

The first purpose of the present study is therefore to provide a succinct historical survey of the bibliographical sources available to those who study the history of German literature in all its aspects. Obviously, it is not possible, probably it is not even desirable, to do more than indicate the *nature* of the bibliographical sources; at all events there is no intention of entering into a detailed discussion of their relative value, for they are all we have and cannot now be altered or replaced. By indicating, however, the different kinds of bibliographies, their scope and nature, and the manner in which they develop through the years, it is hoped that the secondary purpose will be achieved of documenting at least in broad outline the development of the concept of the bibliography as such and its relationship to literature. The first five chapters are therefore historical and largely uncritical. The third and rather more problematical aim of the final chapters is to examine *critically* the current state of bibliographical sources in order on the one hand to determine the extent to which they may be considered to measure up satisfactorily to contemporary expectations and on the other hand to suggest the direction in which future bibliographies might most profitably be developed.

In the process of describing bibliographical sources through a thousand years of German literature it is inevitable that a large number of titles must be cited, many of which are of considerable length. In order to avoid the inconvenience of innumerable footnotes and the expense of repetition only the essential bibliographical information is cited in the text. Fuller, if not full, details of all bibliographies and other works referred to will be found in the numbered, alphabetical list of works cited. Numbers in parentheses in the text and in footnotes refer to this list.

Chapter 1

Bibliographical sources in the period before printing

During the centuries preceding the invention of printing bibliographies in the true sense of the word did not exist except in rare instances and then only in rather special forms. Since also our records from this period are fragmentary and incomplete, historical study of the literary production of the Middle Ages faces two distinct problems, namely, the critical analysis of works that have been preserved, and the establishment of the nature and extent of works that have been lost. These two problems are not unconnected insofar as literary works are sometimes valuable sources of information as to what other works might have existed and what their reputation might have been; but the distinction is nonetheless a valid one, for the major portion of the work involving extant manuscripts falls within the field of analytical and descriptive rather than systematic bibliography. Manuscripts preserved in the major libraries today represent without doubt almost all that has escaped the manifold dangers of fire and flood, destruction and decay, and it is highly improbable that more than an occasional fragment will be brought to light in the future. It is therefore the function of analytical, descriptive, and critical bibliography to analyse these extant manuscripts, to establish by comparison their inter-relationships, and to re-establish through the elimination of corruptions and lacunae the original form of the text. *Systematic* bibliographies for this period are based upon edited and printed texts, that is to say, upon the fruits of descriptive and critical bibliography. As modern reference works these will be discussed later.

When studying the literary works of the Middle Ages in their own context, it is impossible to ignore the fact that they represent only a part of the literary output of the period. Exactly how large a part this may be is disputed, estimates varying very widely. Certainly it would seem that at least as much and probably far more has been lost than has been preserved, including some works highly regarded in their own time; but convincing statistical data cannot be adduced, largely, it would seem, because too much has been lost. It is worth noting for comparison that Wing's bibliography of books printed in England between 1641 and 1700 (509) contains approximately 70,000 items; in a later publication Wing lists approximately 4,500 "ghosts" (508) or works which seem no longer to be extant although there is convincing evidence of their having existed. The number of copies of any one book printed is exceedingly difficult to establish or even estimate, and it is true that many works were probably not printed in the maximum allowable number which was raised by the Stationers' Company from 1,250/1,500 at the end of the sixteenth century to 1,500/2,000 in 1635[1], but there were at least many hundreds of copies of each work. Despite this, then, 6 % to 7 % of printed items from a period as relatively late as the latter part of the seventeenth century have been to all intents and purposes lost. Moreover, this figure does not include those works — and there must have been some — for which we have no record at all. In the medieval period manuscripts were produced in only very small numbers and the proportion of works lost will naturally be very much higher. Since any historical appreciation of the period must take the totality into account and not just the part that has been preserved, the question arises as to the nature and extent of contemporary bibliographical sources which may be employed to fill in, as it were, the background.

The relatively few works which may be termed bibliographies in the period before printing are exclusively in Latin for the simple reason that all "scientific" writings were written in that language and "non-scientific" works were not cited in bibliographies. The one traditional form of bibliography, and one that proved, moreover, influential for many centuries, is the bio-biblio-graphical handbook, of which St. Jerome's *De viris illustribus* is perhaps the best known example (274). Such a work listed great men of the past, and the compiler's particular interest often led him to restrict himself to certain groups of people. Jerome's interest, for example, is primarily religious; a similar list by Walter Burley (born 1275) is entitled *De vita et moribus philosophorum.*[2] Particular attention is paid to *writers,* however, and their works are indicated, even though often in general terms, that is to say, by the subject on which they wrote rather than by distinct titles. In one form or another this type of bio-bibliographical work continues to the present day, a recent example being the extensive *Bio-bibliographisches Literaturlexikon Österreichs von den Anfängen bis zur Gegenwart* (66). The emphasis in the Middle Ages was primarily biographical and historical but after the advent of printing came to centre more and more on specific groups, on individual monastic orders, professions and so forth[3].

In the absence of specially designed bibliographies, particularly in regard to contemporary literature, one of the major sources of knowledge about books written and read during the Middle Ages are the catalogues of the larger libraries of that period. Unfortunately book collecting was almost exclusively the domain of the church, and its interests — while by no means as narrow as is sometimes supposed — certainly did not extend to vernacular literature.

---

1 See the Register of the Stationers' Company in Arber's Transcript ii, 43, 307, 883; iv, 22; v, liii.
2 In the 1472 edition (Augsburg: Koberger): *Libellus de vita et moribus philosophorum;* also consulted was the German translation *Das buch von dem Leben und Sitten der heydnischen maister* (Augsburg: Anton Sorg, 1480) (104–6).
3 See, for example, the work by J. Tritheim cited below.

Extensive collections were made of biblical works and of the writings of the Fathers of the Church, of commentators and theologians, even of heathen philosophers and scientists; and great efforts were made to preserve the accuracy of these texts (at least of scriptural texts). To medieval monasteries a great debt is also owed for the preservation of classical literature, which was evidently appreciated and even imitated for its own sake and not solely as an exercise in the process of learning the language. But nowhere, no matter how great the interest in literature per se, be it classical or medieval, is there any respect for works in the vernacular. Latin was the tongue of the Church and the Church was universal. Anything worthy of preservation must therefore be written in Latin or, more rarely, in Greek or Hebrew. What was not written in these languages could be and often was cast aside. This point cannot be stressed too much, for so strong was this tradition that Latin remained the dominant language both for literature and for bibliographical and reference works long after the invention of printing, in fact into the late eighteenth century. The "emergence of German as a literary language" — to use the title of a book by Blackall — (67) preceded in fact by many years the general use of German for scholarly writing, and even some of the early scholarly works in German are provided with titles in Latin, as are, for example, the bibliographies by Draud, discussed in the following chapter.

Although a not inconsiderable number of library catalogues have been preserved,[4] the number of vernacular works listed — at least in these records — is small. These catalogues present, moreover, numerous difficulties. Since the medieval library was primarily a place for study, the classification of books was only a rough, practical one, devised to allow the reader to have works in a given area of study close at hand at a given place. This simple plan was confused by the common habit of binding together not only related but also diverse works in one volume. The catalogue ought therefore to be — among other things — a finding list for works which might be bound in with others, whether or not on the same subject. This was of course recognized by cataloguers, and in the catalogue of books from St. Riquier, for example, there is the note "Omnes igitur codices in commune faciunt numerum cclvi; ita videlicet ut non numeruntur libri sigillatim, sed codices, quia in uno codice diversi libri multoties, ut supra notatum est, habentur; quos si numeraremus, quingentorum copiam superarent."[5]

Such catalogues as have been preserved are, however, often inventories, that is to say enumerative lists of books for the purpose of identification. They may therefore be deceptive, because often only the first work in any given volume is cited, this being sufficient to identify the book. Even if incipit and explicit are

---

4 Listed in, for example, G. Becker, *Catalogi Bibliothecarum Antiqui* (Bonn 1885), T. Gottlieb, *Über mittelalterliche Bibliotheken* (Leipzig, 1890), and so forth.
5 Edward Edwards, *Memoirs of Libraries* (144), I, 301.

given and these can be identified, this does not mean that another work may not have been contained between those identified. Not unless a full description is given, or unless it can be determined from the presence of multiple references to identical catalogue numbers that an analytical catalogue has been drawn up, can it be supposed that the full contents of the library are known.

In this connection vernacular works fare far worse than those in Latin and other languages. To begin with they are normally listed last of all in the general order of things; to find a list beginning even with classical literature, as does the late twelfth century catalogue (by Rutger) of books in the library of the Benedictine monastery of Michelsberg, is rare.[6] One must assume that the energies of the cataloguer may well flag by the time he reaches this section of the library, even if he were not directed to pay less attention to these works. At all events they receive summary treatment. A volume of religious works will often be cited with author, title or other content note, incipit, explicit, and so forth; a volume of Latin literature will have at least the author or some other indication of contents; but the most one learns to expect of these catalogues in regard to items of vernacular literature is an unwilling acknowledgement of their existence. The twelfth century catalogue of books at St. Martin de Tournai lists "libri gentilium poetarum,"[7] the Durham cathedral catalogue[8] "libri anglici," and a brief list of books (1426) in the Cistercian monastery at Heilsbronn (status superioris camerae) contains an entry "et libri theutonici volumina X."[9] On the rare occasion when some indication of the contents is given, as in the fifteenth-century library, small though it is, of the Abbot of [the Benedictine monastery of] Michelsberg ("Libros Abbacie"), there is inevitable frustration in the face of such entries as "Historiam ducis Ernesti, alias Schiltberger, *cum aliis contentis*" (italics added).[10] Rarely then in these and similar catalogues is there any indication of the nature of the contents of the books mentioned.

Catalogues of the libraries of ecclesiastical institutions therefore provide very little in the way of direct evidence about vernacular literature. The most that can be said is that they provide considerable evidence about the history of libraries and thus some insight into cultural developments. Knowledge of the existence of vernacular literature must be assumed in these institutions, but the authorities were interested neither in preserving these works nor even in

---

6 *Mittelalterliche Bibliothekskataloge Deutschlands und der Schweiz* (354a), III, iii, 366ff. Hereafter cited as *MBDS*.
7 Léopold Delisle, *Le cabinet des manuscrits de la bibliothèque nationale* (Paris, 1874), II, 492.
8 Frequently referred to, for example in Dorothy May Norris, *A History of Cataloguing and Cataloguing Methods 1100–1850* (London, 1939), p. 14ff.
9 *MBDS*, III, ii, 216
10 *MBDS*, III, iii, 382.

recording them. And vernacular authors are as totally ignored in the catalogues as they are in bio-bibliographies. It is only with the growth of larger secular libraries late in the Middle Ages, that is to say, about the time of the invention of printing, that there is any body of detailed evidence as to the nature of the vernacular literature which was read at the time. The reasons for the growth of these libraries cannot be discussed here; among them are both technical factors, such as the multiplication of manuscripts and greater wealth, and intellectual reasons, such as the weakening of influence of the Church and a greater level of literacy. What is important for the moment is the fact that the desire to acquire books and the size of collections demanded that records be kept.

As an example of early records of a library containing secular works, reference can be made to the collection of the Counts of Öttingen.[11] The earliest list of this library is very brief and dates from about 1430. It demonstrates all the typical aspects of such lists, that is to say, it describes the book rather than analysing the intellectual content ("Item aber ein steigbůch, ist gemalt und mins jungen hern gewesen"), and contains little that is of interest to literary historians. A later list from 1466/67 is much more extensive. Here there are numerous religious and secular works and also practical handbooks in a confused jumble. Again the information which is sometimes added is of a personal rather than intellectual nature, but an effort is made to include all the contents of a volume. The *Renner,* for example, is bound with other works: "Ein bůch genant der Renner, dar inn sind auch vil stuk her Wolffrands von Eschenbachs lieder, von dez weisen manß ler, von des sunß lere, von dez torochtten vaters lere, von dem krieg von Österrich, von dez Neithartz lieder," and so forth. Or the author gives something of the origin and contents of the material: "Ein bůch von Otten von Dennmeringen, ein důmherr zů Metze in Luttringen hat ditz bůch gemacht von welsch und latein zů tewtsch gemacht, daz set von fremden landen" and so forth. All in all it would seem that the library contained a varied selection of popular German medieval writings, about half secular and half religious. Although there are regrettable lapses into vagueness such as "Ein bůch von allerlay lieder" the information for the most part enables the work to be identified. Additional information which relates to illumination and binding indicates the value set upon these works for their outward form.

This list and others like it date, however, from the time in which great changes were taking place in the book trade through the invention of printing. It is therefore necessary to consider what other bibliographical sources there might be in addition to library catalogues, sources that might also be used for earlier periods. Obviously enough, catalogues cannot be the only documents relating to libraries. Books have always been objects of trade and have been copied and re-copied, loaned or stolen, lost and found. Records of transactions

11 *MBDS,* III, i, 157–61.

concerning books must therefore have existed, and one of the commonest forms is a list of books loaned.[12] The Öttingen library has a list of works on loan which dates from about 1462, and many such lists are to be found with the catalogues of monastery libraries even in earlier times. Other kinds of source are lists of works transcribed (especially in monasteries and by scribes famous for their art), bound or to be bound, acquired, lost, donated, and bequeathed. In Germany such sources are again very few for secular works. There is nothing, for example, to equal in interest the fascinating list of French romances bequeathed by the Earl of Warwick to Bordesley Abbey in 1359[13]. Not, that is, until immediately after the invention of printing, at a time when bibliophiles were still anxious to augment their collections with manuscripts rather than with printed books. But the possibility exists that at least in this area some records may still be found.

One such *Buchnarr* was Jakob Püterich von Reichertshausen, justly celebrated in histories of literature for his *Ehrenbrief.*[14] This lengthy epistle was directed to the Archduchess Mechthild of Austria, a woman with an extensive library and a considerable reputation for learning, who had sent Jakob at his request a list of the 96 works she owned so that he might compare her list with his. Her list is lost, but in his poem Jakob names from her collection the 20 or so works[15] he does *not* know and then adds for her benefit a list of his own books. The full list of his library, which he says he is also sending (164 in all), is also lost, but what we have is valuable insofar as it names more than 30 of his apparently *favourite* works, thus giving us a fair indication of the kind of works considered by a man of his taste to represent the best in medieval literature. It should be noted that his chief interest is in chivalric literature; of these works he may give us a complete list.[16] This is, in other words, an early example of the type of bibliography known as a "best books" list. In addition one gains interesting insight into the *relative* knowledge of (or

12 Curiously enough, one of the earliest book lists in Germany, that of the Diocesan library of St. Kilian in Würzburg, indicates that some of its works were out on loan (Elias Avery Lowe, "An eighth-century list of books in a Bodleian MS. from Würzburg and its probable relation to the Laudian *Acts,"* *Speculum,* 3 [1928], 3—15).

13 Printed in F. S. Merryweather, *Bibliomania in the Middle Ages* (London, [2]1933), p. 283—5.

14 Written in 1462 when he was 62; he claims to have collected books by hook or by crook for over forty years. The "Ehrenbrief des Jakob Püterich von Reichertshausen . . ." is edited by A. Goette (Strassburg, 1899); a facsimile edition was published in Weimar (1920) by the Gesellschaft der Bibliophilen (194, 407).

15 The exact number will vary depending upon whether one considers "five Lancelots" as one or five works. By taking this as five and a later citation as containing three works, Scherer reaches a total of 23 (W. Scherer, *Die Anfänge des deutschen Prosaromans und Jörg Wickram von Colmar* [Strassburg, 1877], p. 16—18).

16 The list is usually considered to be of his favourite books. However, in stanza 119 Jakob plainly says: "Puech der ritterleichen / der hab ich, frau, nit mer."

interest in) literature shown by book collectors in Bavaria and Baden. Jakob is quite adamant about his selection, maintaining that there are not only many poor works but also many poor editions (copies); he claims, for example, to have rejected as unfit 30 manuscripts of the *Titurel:* "wol dreissig Titurelen / hab ich gesehen; der kheiner nit was rechte" (142, 6–7). The first part of his list gives only secular works, and these are more or less in the order of excellence which would be assigned today, with the exception of the first work, the [*Jüngerer*] *Titurel.* The works of more religious character follow in second place and constitute only a quarter of the total.From the list it is evident that Jakob had no interest in lyric poetry and inclined toward epic works of a chivalric and "romantic" rather than heroic character. Not all the works are identifiable with certainty.

In stanzas 85 and 86 of his *Ehrenbrief* Jakob recalls the poetical peccadiloes ("vier lied und rede dreie") of his youth and begs Mechthild to excuse the fact that his talent has not increased with age. Whatever may be the judgment about Jakob's poetic ability, the listing of one's own compositions, albeit in this case in overly brief form (none of the works is known), is not an uncommon practice and as such provides a further category of bibliography, namely autobibliography. The origin of the practice of listing one's own works, no matter what form this may take, does not necessarily lie in a desire for self-advertisement. It may rather be for purposes of protection, that is to say, an author may publish a list of works which are genuinely his in order to prevent spurious works from being circulated under his name. Such was common practice throughout the Middle Ages and was the reason for the list of works compiled by Gennadius of Marseilles among others. His and St. Jerome's example may have encouraged the Venerable Bede to conclude his *Ecclesiastical History of the English Nation* with a summary description in classified order of the works he had written (43). Probably the most ambitious undertaking of this nature is the compilation by Hans Sachs in 1567 of a list of his 4,275 Meisterlieder and 1,773 poems and plays.[17]

A variant form of the autobibliography is the kind of list found in literary works where the author refers to his previous compositions. These can be valuable as in the case of Chrestien de Troyes, who begins his *Cligés* (114) with the lines:

> Cil qui fist d'Erec et d'Enide,
> Et les comandemanz d'Ovide
> Et l'art d'amors an romans mist,
> Et le mors de l'espaule fist,
> Del roi Marc et d'Ysalt la blonde,

---

17 Printed in his *Werke* ed. A. v. Keller (repr. Hildesheim, 1964) v. 25 and 26 where there is also an interesting list of the books owned by Hans Sachs. The first *printed* autobibliography is probably that of Erasmus referred to below.

> Et de la hupe et de l'aronde
> Et del rossignol la muance,
> Un novel conte rancomance . . . .

Although Chrestien is without doubt the best known poet in courtly France even his fame has not saved all his works for posterity. We have, for example, no trace of the story of Mark (and Tristan) and Isolde. The same can also be said of other writers.

This desire to catalogue one's own works, useful though it may be to the historian, is perhaps not without its dangers, since the possibility exists that a poet might be led to list works of others with his own or to insert works planned or purely fictitious. It is probably also connected in some degree with the catalogue of authors, which was a literary genre in its own right, and this type of work provides a final category of "systematic" bibliographical listing. The origin of the catalogue as a literary device (of people, places, and so forth),[18] lies in the literature of ancient Greece and Rome, and in the form that the catalogue takes in the Middle Ages the stress is still on classical authors. The idea is clearly that of establishing a literary canon just as the Church had established its canon of scriptures and Fathers of the Church — although for rather different reasons. The lists represent the authors or works that were read and studied in schools, and as such they are significant forerunners of the guides to study in various disciplines which are in later centuries a fruitful source of bibliographical information.[19]

An early example of such a catalogue of authors may be Alcuin's poem on the library at York, for, although he claims to be recalling what authors the library contained, his list is essentially one of "standard" authors as used in teaching. He states that the library contained the major works in Greek, Latin, and Hebrew and lists then forty in all (no Hebrew authors), roughly divided into Fathers of the Church, ending with Aldhelm and Bede, and secular authors as follows:

> Quae Victorinus scripsere Boëtius atque,
> Historici veteres, Pompeius, Plinius, ipse
> Acer Aristoteles, rhetor quoque Tullius ingens.
> Quid quoque Sedulius, vel quid canit ipse Iuvencus,
> Alcimus et Clemens, Prosper, Paulinus, Arator,
> Quid Fortunatus, vel quid Lactantius edunt.

18   Even also works which one knows as in the list of works in the repertoire of the storyteller. See *Widsith* in *Anglo-Saxon Poetry* tr. R. K. Gordon (London, 1962).

19   I have come across no useful studies of this genre other than those cited by E. R. Curtius who has some discussion of this topic and gives the authors listed by Walter and Conrad (see below) in his *Europäische Literatur und lateinisches Mittelalter* (Bern, [4] 1963) p. 58ff.

> Quae Maro Virgilius, Statius, Lucanus et auctor,
> Artis grammaticae, vel quid scripsere magistri;
> Quid Probus atque Focas, Donatus Priscianusve,
> Servius, Euticius, Pompeius, Comminianus.[20]

This is a quite unexceptionable list. Later in the Middle Ages the lists become much longer and more confused, as classical writers receded into the distance and medieval authors grew more prominent. The classification also becomes confused, as authors could be categorized as Christian or heathen, ancient or modern, by genre and by form.

One of the largest and most interesting lists is that compiled by a German schoolmaster, Hugo of Trimberg, at the end of the thirteenth century. His *Registrum multorum auctorum* (251) comprises 80 authors as compared with the 21 of Conrad of Hirsau in the early twelfth century and 10 of Walter of Speyer at the end of the tenth century.[21] In his expanded version Hugo, who depends heavily on Conrad, reverses Conrad's order and lists the more difficult writers first and the easier ones last. He also excludes some rather well known figures such as Terence, due to his desire to restrict his catalogue entirely to authors writing in quantitative metre. Aside from this, the most interesting point about his work is the addition of numerous medieval Latin writers so that they make up approximately half of the total. The organisation is as follows. Hugo divides the authors into three groups or *distinctiones:* "Ethici maiores," "Katholici auctores," "Ethici minores." Each group is subdivided into two parts, but the subdivision is not very helpful except in the first group where the classical and medieval authors are separated. Each author is named, his work is cited by title and by incipit, and the material dealt with in the work is usually briefly indicated. In this way the works are readily identifiable and a clear picture is given of what was known to a well educated teacher of his period. By comparison with earlier writers and the sources that he mentions, it is evident that Hugo has done much of the research himself and is in fact quite familiar with the works he lists. In other words he gives a short verse history of metrical Latin writers.

Although most of these writers and their works are familiar also to us — although judgment as to their value would vary — it is interesting to note that at the conclusion of his work Hugo also lists his own works:

> Scripsi quidem rithmice   Registrum Auctorum,
> Deinde versifice   Lauream Sanctorum,
> Postea Solsequium   quod agyographorum

---

20 Lines 1547—56 from the *Versus de Sanctis Eboracensis ecclesiae* in *Monumenta alcuiniana* (5). An inaccurate English rendering in Norris (note 8).
21 See Curtius (note 19), and Leslie G. Whitbread, "Conrad of Hirsau as Literary Critic," *Spec.,* 47 (1972), 234—45.

Dat clericis prosaice	noticiam rumorum.
Preterea prosaice	et rithmice multarum
Compilavi codicellum	quendam litterarum.
Sed primitus Theutonice	scripsi quater binos
Libellos, tres ad seculum	quinqueque divinos.
Nunc in hoc opusculo	lassum pedem sisto
Rogans et in domino	nostro Jesu Christo.

Hugo is here claiming to have written before this time eight works in German and a similar statement appears at the beginning of his *Renner* (252):

> Vor het ich siben büechelin
> In tiutsch gemacht, und in Latin
> Fünftehalbez, daz ist war.
> Daz halbe wil ich lazen beliben
> Und wil daz zem ersten schriben (25–9)

The *Renner* is, however, the *only* German work of his that has come down to posterity. Assuming that Hugo is accurately reporting his literary output, this is a very small proportion indeed.

Somewhat later in the Middle Ages a vernacular form of author catalogue, possibly influenced by Latin models, finds its place. One such example, perhaps the best known example in German literature, is that contained in the *Tristan* poem of Gottfried von Strasburg (199). The poet inserts in place of what should have been the usual lengthy description of the ceremony of knighting the hero an extensive discussion of the major writers of his own and the preceding generation, ostensibly because he lacks the requisite skill to describe adequately the ceremony of the accolade. He analyses the qualities and characteristics first of the four epic poets and then of the leading lyric poets. Although his judgment coincides almost exactly with that expressed in twentieth century textbooks, it is surprising that he names as one of the great epic poets a certain Bligger von Steinach – of whose narrative work not one single line has been preserved.[22]

A similarly enthusiastic reference is made to Bligger by Rudolf von Ems a generation or so after Gottfried. In the course of a dialogue with Frau Aventiure, the "muse" of epic poetry, in Book II of his *Willehalm von Orlens* (418), Rudolf expands Gottfried's catalogue of writers and brings it up to date listing twenty or thirty epic writers from the time before Gottfried up to his own time.

Such relatively systematic surveys are extremely useful despite their often cliché-ridden form. They remain, however, too rare; more often the allusions to past or to contemporary writers or works are tantalisingly brief or incompre-

---

22 On Bligger see *Deutsche Literatur des Mittelalters. Verfasserlexikon* ed. W. Stammler, I, 248 and V, 100.

hensible. Literary cross references as they might be termed are not in themselves "bibliographical" sources and it could be argued that a discussion of them belongs more under the heading of textual bibliography. Their importance at least for medieval literature cannot, however, be ignored — nor may their ambiguity. Such cross references occur in almost all works and in some quite frequently, and they are an essential part of the evidence on which textual criticism is based. In particular they are used — as in the case of Gottfried's alleged references to Wolfram in the passage mentioned above — to establish chronological relationships. Such allusions need to be treated with extreme caution since their relationship, in particular the question of priority where there are references back and forth, can rarely be established without reference to additional, usually external, factors.

In summary it may be said that there are three broad categories of contemporary bibliographical sources for our knowledge of medieval literature: bibliographies per se; library catalogues and related documents; and literary sources, either distinct works or parts of works. A clearcut distinction is not always possible since a given source, for example an autobibliography, may contain features of more than one group. Of these broad categories bibliographies proper contain information of only peripheral interest for German literature and are generally speaking bio-bibliographical reference works chiefly related to ecclesiastical affairs and authors of antiquity. Library catalogues also provide peripheral rather than direct information about German literature during the earlier and middle centuries of the medieval period. Substantial value is not provided until very late in the period, concomitant in fact with the development of printed books. Direct knowledge of the broad spectrum of literary production in the vernacular depends therefore almost entirely for the Middle High German and earlier periods on references, systematic or casual, made within the texts themselves.

Chapter 2:

From the invention of printing to the Thirty Years' War

The immediate effect of the introduction of printing by movable type was a sharp increase in the numbers of books produced and a reduction in their cost. It is true that there had been a steady increase in the numbers of manuscript copies of individual works since the end of the fourteenth century, an increase due in part to efforts at what might be termed large scale commercial reproduction in the place of the earlier casual one-from-one type of copying. A well known example of "mass-production" of MSS is that of the scriptorium of Diepold Lauber.[1] The illustration opposite is of an advertisement issued by him around 1450.[2]

Manuscript copyists could not, however, compete with printers using movable type and the number of manuscript books dwindles rapidly through the latter half of the fifteenth century. Nevertheless their existence may not be entirely ignored until late in the sixteenth century and bibliographies of the period sometimes include but do not necessarily discriminate between manuscript and printed works (as Constantin does, for example; see below).

For the scholar of the period the importance of the printing press lay in its ability to produce books more quickly and more cheaply. This meant that he was able to acquire a larger collection than would have been the case before the advent of printing. At the same time it meant that there was a much wider choice of books than hitherto, and the need therefore soon developed for bibliographies of various types. One may in fact say that by 1600 almost every conceivable type of bibliography had been attempted in one way or another.

The book buying public remained, however, a relatively small section of the community. Apart from ecclesiastical and similar institutions and the nobility, books were primarily collected by professional men, such as doctors and lawyers, and by scholars; all of whom depended in the main upon their own resources rather than upon those of an institution. This scholarly community was international in character, perhaps never more so than during this period of the so-called Renaissance. Because this was a European movement and a revival of interest in classical antiquity, the common languages of discourse and writing were the classical languages, primarily Latin. Although there are the first signs of what are in effect nationally oriented bibliographies, the vernacular is rarely used and vernacular writings are rarely mentioned.

---

1 See the supplement (volume 5) to *Die deutsche Literatur des Mittelalters. Verfasser-lexikon,* ed. Karl Langosch (Berlin, 1955).
2 Reproduced from *Der deutsche Buchhandel in Urkunden und Quellen,* ed. Hans Widmann (Hamburg, 1961), I, 15.

Item welicher hande bücher man gerne hat, groß oder clein,
geistlich oder welßlich, hübsch gemolt, die findet man alle by
Diebolt louber schriber. In der burge zü hagenow
Item das groß buch genant Jesta romanord vnd saget was zü ... geschicht
vnd saget von den ... do got gewandelt het vnd saget ouch von den keisern ...
ffome vnd von den ... was wunders sie getriben haue vnd von ...
geschriben die die römer gemaht haue vnd ist mit den figuren gemolt. Item ...
cristi. Item die ppiin alten gemolt. Item ein gerymete bibel. Item der ritter her
wigoleis gemolt. Item wolff dietherich gemolt. Item das gantze passinal der
heiligen leben winterteil vnd sumerteil zwey grosse bücher. Item op ...
vnd ewangilien durch das Jar allen tag mit glosen vnd von den heiligen
vnd Jungfrowen. Item wilhelm von orliens gemolt. Item her ... vnd ...
vnd küng artus gemolt. Item der heiligen drie künige buch gemolt. Item ...
gemolt. Item siben meister bücher gemolt. Item bellial gemolt. Item der ...
ritter. Item die grosse Troye gemolt. Item des hertzoge von isterich gem ...
Item die hymelstrasse genant der Welsche gast. Item die zehen gebot mit ...
Item von eime getruwen ritter der sin eygen hertze gap vmb ein ...
frowen willen. Item isopus gemolt. Item quite bewerte artzenie ...
... Item ... Item pfaffe ... vnd sust cleine b ... bücher
Item ... Item ... Item des ritter vnder dem zuber. Item ... loß bücher
Item der selen trost. Item von dem ritter sant alloxius. Item ...
Item der künig von franckenrich. Item ein keiserlich recht buch. Item ...
Item schachzabels gemolt. Item von sante gregorius den sinder. Item ...
gemolt. Item ein salter latin vnd tütsch vnd sust anders ...

The first German bibliographer, the father of bibliography as Bestermann (45) calls him, Johannes Trithemius (from Trittenheim on the Mosel), offers an example of this national interest. Born on February 1st, 1462, Tritheim studied in Trier, Holland, and Heidelberg. By chance rather than by predilection he entered the monastery of Sponheim in March 1482, took his vows at the end of that year, and was elected abbot on August 15, 1483 at the age of only 21. He believed that the study of religious writings was an essential part of monastic life and, apart from his own studies and homiletic writings, laboured to build up a comprehensive library. He himself was devoted to the study of all areas of the humanities and sciences.[3] By the year 1505 the monastery library is supposed to have contained two thousand volumes and it attracted many visitors including such notable scholars as Konrad Celtis and Johannes Reuchlin.

Tritheim himself was no mean scholar and not only corresponded with many other scholars but also travelled widely and was well received in high places, including the court of Maximilian I. Whatever the judgment may be about Tritheim's religious and historical (or pseudo-historical) writings, there is no doubt about his devotion to bibliography. Using the standard bio-bibliographical form he continued the tradition of St. Jerome and his successors with his *De scriptoribus ecclesiasticis* and compiled also an extensive biographical-historical work on the Benedictine order: *De viris illustribus Ordinis S. Benedicti.*[4]

Of much greater interest for the literary historian is, however, his *De viris illustribus Germaniae*[5] in which, encouraged by his equally patriotic friend J. Wimpfeling, he lists the accomplishments of leading intellectual figures from Germany's past. This work as it appeared in 1495 lists 303 persons including such familiar literary figures as Notker of St. Gall, Otfried of Weissenburg and Hrotsvith of Gandersheim. A lengthy article is devoted to his friend Wimpfeling (lxv[v]–lxvi[r]), and the following excerpt will indicate the rather stereotyped nature of the biographical details.

> Iacobus Vimpfelingus Sletstatinus presbyter in ecclesia Spirensi: vir in divinis scripturis eruditissimus: et in secularibus litteris egregie doctus: theologus. philosophus. orator. et poeta celeberrimus: qui primum Erffordie deinde Heydel-

---

3 The only comprehensive modern study of Tritheim is by Klaus Arnold, *Johannes Trithemius (1462–1516)* (Würzburg, 1971).

4 Both are in the *Opera historica*, 2 volumes, ed. M. Freher (Frankfurt, 1601; repr. Frankfurt, 1966). Tritheim also wrote a more historical account of the Carmelite order, *De origine, progressu et laudibus Ordinis fratrum Carmelitarum*, which is contained in the *Opera pia et spiritualia*, ed. J. Busaeus (Mainz, 1604).

5 The title of the original edition is *Cathalogus illustrium virorum germaniā suis ingeniis et lucubrationibus omnifariam exornantium* (1495/6), British Library, IA 389. It is included in the *Opera historica*, p. 121–83.

berge philosophiam et sacras litteras publice docuit: magnamque eruditionis sue gloriam acquisiuit. Vir inquam undecunque doctissimus: ingenio subtilis: eloquio disertus: qui et metro excellit et prosa. Scripsit utroque genere multa prae clara volumina: quibus nomen suum longe lateque divulgavit. E quibus extant subiecta . . .

Following this are thirty-six lines listing Wimpfeling's works; the article concludes:

Vivit adhuc in civitate Spirensi. Annos etatis habens. quinque & XL sub Maximiliano imperatore. Anno dñi qñ hec scripsimus. Mill'. CCCC. XCV. Ind'. Xiñ.

In including also himself and listing his own works, Tritheim continues the tradition of autobibliography, hastening too to add the not uncommon caveat that, should he have written anything contrary to the teaching of the Catholic faith, this should be considered as recanted.

In conclusion, it is worth noting that Tritheim wrote a little tract entitled *De laude scriptorum manualium*[6] in which he proclaimed the virtue of handwriting without wishing in any way to detract from the practical value of printing. It is clear both from this writing and from his activities as a writer and collector of books, that Tritheim fully appreciated the value of the art of printing. However, he claimed that strenuous manual labour was unsuitable for those in monastic orders since it would detract from their energies for divine service. A much better employment is the copying of manuscripts for this is not merely a practical function and − since he stresses the importance of copying religious works − to the greater glory of God, but it also gives the copyist food for thought in what he writes. In passing it may be noted that Tritheim points out that by no means all books get into print, and even if they do, printed works may only last 200 years or so, manuscripts a thousand or more.

After Tritheim's pioneer work it was nearly a hundred years before another such embryonic national bio-bibliography appeared. In 1581 Cornelius Loos published a short work entitled *Illustrium Germaniae scriptorum catalogus* (322)[7] containing relatively lengthy articles on a number of figures. He limits himself to entirely orthodox writers of his own century, 89 of them in all. Included among these is Tritheim to whom over six pages are devoted, of which the following are the first nine lines:

---

6 1494, Hain *15617; *Opera pia et spiritualia,* p. 714−64. Newly edited with German translation by Klaus Arnold (Fränkische Bibliophilengesellschaft, 1973); Latin-English edition by Roland Behrendt, O. S. B. (Lawrence, Kansas, 1974).

7 An earlier work often cited, the *Illustrium Germaniae virorum historiae aliquot singulares . . .* by Hieronymus Ziegler (Ingolstadt, 1562), is purely biographical.

> IOANNES TRITHEMIVS, in villa Trittenheim Treuerensis dioecesis, natus. Est
> autem illa sita ad Mosellam non incelebrem Inferioris Germaniæ (vt.Cæs. Comment.
> nec ita vetusta æstimatio) fluuium; qui se Confluentiae in Rhenum exonerat. Illinc
> ortum, Ioan. Lucienberg. I.D. in suo Thesauro Poëtico, ex Conrado Celtisz. Car.
> Od. 28. ita meminit.
> Talis Mosellae natus est vuidas etc.

The list of Tritheim's works occupies two and a half pages and ends "& alia"!
Although various attempts at national bibliography were made in other
countries, beginning with Doni's *La libraria* in Italy in 1550 (137), there were
no further efforts in this direction in Germany. The recording of book
production took another path and it was not until the latter part of the
eighteenth century that specifically nationally oriented bibliographical works
re-appeared.

As the bio-bibliographical approach was traditional, it was natural, given
the international nature of learning at this period, for bibliographies to develop
along the lines of disciplines rather than along national lines with the inevitable
problem of heterogeneity. The most respected subject areas, medicine,
theology, and law therefore soon developed specialized bibliographies with a
basically biographical orientation. These are only of peripheral interest for the
literary historian, but they do provide important background information on
the lives of influential figures, that is, they may be used for information about
persons cited in literary works; and they indicate in some degree the state of
the art as practised at the time. Among the earliest such works are Symphorien
Champier, *De medicine claris scriptoribus,* 1506 (113)[8] and Otto Brunfels,
Catalogus illustrium medicorum, 1530 (96); Giovanni Nevizzano, *Index
librorum omnium . . . in utroque iure,* 1522 (376); and Jakob Zannach,
Bibliotheca theologica, 1591 (515). Israel Spach, a professor of medicine in
Strasburg, published in addition to a medical bibliography (449) a work
entitled *Nomenclator scriptorum philosophicorum atque philologicorum,* 1598
(450).

This last work includes both printed and manuscript "publications" by
5,490 authors and it covers a wide variety of fields, since the terms philosophy
and philology had still a general rather than particular application. The authors
are listed within subject divisions alphabetically by first name and there is an
index both of authors and of "Locorum sive rerum." Here are two examples.
Under "poetae sacri" we find — "Otfridi Evangeliorum liber. Bas. 71 in 8.
veteri sermone Francico" (p. 162), and under the heading Poetae comici" —
"Germanici" we find: "Nicodemi Frischlini Wendelgarda Francof. ap. Wendel.

---

8 Paschalis Le Coq's (Gallus) *Bibliotheca medica,* which had appeared in Basel in 1490, is
  a lengthy biographical listing of famous medical practitioners. Works are named in many
  cases but often without any indication of when or where they appeared.

Hom. 89. Phasma. Grypsvualdiæ. 93. 8" (p. 213).[9] Spach's work is also noteworthy for including a number of bibliographies under the heading "Bibliothecarum scriptores." There we find the above-mentioned Doni, Gennadius, Symphorien Champier, Tritheim, Zannach and others, in all about 30 works. In passing we should note a less successful work of the same period, namely Johann Jacob Frisius's *Bibliotheca philosophorum classicorum authorum chronologica . . .* published in Zürich in 1592 (167). After the chronological sequence ending with the year 1490 and before a brief listing of recent authors Frisius lists a few general and particular bibliographies (p. 53). His work is not infrequently cited by later bibliographers.

Spach's technique of citation may strike us as somewhat primitive, in particular the brevity of titles, but he does assemble a great amount of information useful to the literary historian and he does provide both subject and author indexes, something which many later compilers neglect to do. His attitude towards bibliography is perhaps also worth citing as exemplifying the approach of an enlightened bibliographer of this period. After referring to his medical bibliography, Spach promises another one, "simili scopo ac proposito." He then continues:

> Scripserunt quidem varii varia de variis materiis sub variis ac diversis titulis & inscriptionibus: Eorum tamen in hac mea recensione potissimum facta est mentio, de quibus mihi constitit aut constare potuit, ubi vel euulgati, vel tantum adhuc manu exarati sint, ac reperiri queant. Typis quoque excusa sunt saepe levia quaedem scripta, ubi nec autoris nec typographi annotantur nomina. Est etiam proletariorum scriptorculorum & famosorum libellorum infinitus quasi numerus: qui tamen cum tanquam noctue noctu tantum volitent, lucemq́; ipsam verè fugiant, nec ut hîc insererentur operae praecium duxi. Alia autem de causa magna ex parte non apposui eos, qui aliorum scripta de una in aliam transtulerunt linguam: qui disputationes conscripserunt philosophicas (hae enim peti facilè possunt â singularum Academiarum typographis) Ephemeridum quoque & Prognosticorum Mathematicorum (Practicas vulgò vocant) in singulos annos scriptores (desideranti nāq; habere prostant in satis bona copia) Particulatim quoque ea scripta non iudicavi esse recensenda, quae sub universalioribus continentur: ut Physices praecepta eius, qui integram tradidit doctrinam totius Philosophiae: Optices E.G. qui Mathematices & c. Simplicem autem institui autorum enarrationem, absque encomiis seu eulogiis appositis, cuiuscunque vel regionis vel religionis fuerint, vel etiam quo idiomate sua conscripserint. Integros librorum titulos non adscripsi, haud certè subterfugiens laborem, sed ne in magnam molem liber exscresceret, & ut pecunia modica parari posset. In his tàm variorium ac multorum numero scilicet 5490. autorum consignandis scriptis, multa fateor, & quidem ingenuè ac libenter fateor, me fugerunt: multa & te (fortè) fugiunt. Multa minùs commodum locum obtinere videbuntur. Nemo sine crimine non modò viuit, sed ne scribit quidem. Optimus ille, qui minimis urgetur. Cogita & te hominem esse, quare & te latere multa posse; tum & te errare posse.

---

9 *Frau Wendelgart* was published in German, *Phasma* in Latin.

As might be expected, the first personal bibliography after those of religious figures, and in fact the first full, analytical, personal bibliography, was devoted to a medical man. Gessner, the great universal bibliographer of whom more will be said shortly, published in his preface to the third Froben edition (1562) of Galen's works (170) a bibliography of Galen which was a model for its time. The work is highly detailed and logically organized, being arranged as follows: editions of Galen, divided into Greek and Latin and lost works, and commentaries on Galen classified by biography, chronology, anti-Galenists and so forth; this is followed by a classified list of Galen's individual works and an alphabetical index to all editors, commentators etc. This bibliography covers in all 36 folio pages of close type.

Galen had in his own time compiled an autobibliography under a title (latinized as) *De libris propriis liber,*[10] and this tradition was now carried forward, the first autobibliography to appear in print as a separate item being apparently that of Erasmus of Rotterdam who published in 1523 his *Catalogus omnium Erasmi Roterodami lucubrationum.*[11] The *De propriis libris* was first published separately according to Gessner in Basel in 1531, the first complete edition of Galen having appeared only six years earlier.

The biographical approach to bibliography was clearly natural to the time and it reflects an interest in a group or class of people rather than a group of books. This was therefore also the approach to subject bibliography and although it inevitably entailed some admixture of irrelevant material since not all lawyers wrote only on law and so forth, yet it was only slowly superseded. Even such special categories as J. P. Foresti's list of notable women *De plurimis claris scelestisque mulieribus,* 1497 (163) or the numerous lists of banned books, are based upon common factors other than the contents of the books. One might suspect of course that the banned books would all be heretical or anti-religious writings, but a brief glance at some of these very interesting compilations shows immediately that there was a wide variety, to us an astonishing and incomprehensible variety, of reasons for anathema. A number of indices from this early period have been gathered together and printed by

---

10   The same title, *De libris propriis,* was used by Jerome Cardan, who cites the example of Galen and lists 52 of his own works. This list is included in the volume entitled *De Sapientia libri quinque* (111).

11   ... *ipso autore cum alii nonnullis.* There is no imprint and the 36 pages are unnumbered. The "colophon" reads "Basileae, tertio Calend. Febru. An. à Christo nato MDXXIII." According to Graham Pollard and Albert Ehrman, *The Distribution of books by Catalogue from the Invention of Printing to A.D. 1800* (Cambridge, 1965), p. 159, an earlier list was printed in 1519 by Thierry Martens at Allost. I have not seen this.

Reusch.[12] The following is an excerpt from a "placat" of the Emperor Charles V, September 22, 1540:

> "... In den eersten, dat niemant, van wat state ende condicie hy zy, en sal moghen onder hem hebben, vercoopen, gheven, draghen noch lesen, preken, instrueren, sustineren ende defenderen, communiceren ofte disputeren, heymelicken oft openbaerlicken, van de leerijnghen, schrifturen ende boucken, die ghemaect hebben ofte souden moghen maken Martin Luther, Jan Wiclef, Jan Hus, Marcilius de Padua, Ecolampadius, Ulricus Zwijnglius, Philippus Melancthon, Franciscus Lambertus, Joannes Pomeranus, Ottho Brunfelsius, Justus Jonas, Joannes Puperi ende Gorcianus oft andere authueren van haerlieder secte ofte van andere heretyke ofte dwalende secte, ghereprobeerd van der kercke, nocht oock de leerijngen van haren adherenten, fautueren ende complicen, nochte die Nieuwe Testamenten gheprent by Adriaen van Berghen, Christophorus de Remunda ende Joannes Zel. Phrases Scripturae divinae. Interpretatio nominum Caldeorum. Epithome topographica Vadiani. Paralipomena rerum memorabilium. Historia de Germanorum origine. Commentaria in Pitagore poema. Commentaria in phisicam Aristotelis per Walcurionem" etc. (p. 25).

One of the first specifically subject-oriented bibliographies in Germany is contained in a short work on agriculture published by Johann Camerarius the Younger in 1577. The work is entitled *De re rustica*... (109) and contains at the end a "Catalogus scriptorum Rei Rusticae, & Herbariae, tam veterum quam recentium: qui in variis linguis aliquid scripserunt." The list runs to 14 pages and is ordered alphabetically by the author's first name within language divisions. There are few bibliographical details. An entry for Gessner appears, for example, thus: Conradi Gesneri Epitome germanicum de quadrupedibus, avibus & piscibus, Tiguri in folio." In the later edition of 1596 (110) the bibliography is considerably longer (pp. 201–35).

The most important development in sixteenth century bibliography was undoubtedly the tendency toward universality. The concept of universal bibliography arose about a century after printing first began and has not been entirely abandoned even in the twentieth century.[13] However the term has not always meant the same thing and some comment is therefore necessary before Gessner's work is discussed. When sixteenth century scholars spoke of books and literature, they did not think of the total output of the presses. They meant works of quality, scholarly and scientific works, the writings of the

---

12 Franz Heinrich Reusch, *Die Indices librorum prohibitorum des sechzehnten Jahrhunderts* (Nieuwkoop, 1961). The earliest separate publication of the Roman index would seem to be that of 1557 *(Index auctorum et librorum, qui tanquam haeretici, aut suspecti, aut perniciosi, ab officio S.R. Inquisitionis reprobantur, et in universa Christiana republica interdicuntur).* The list is alphabetically ordered and divided into banned authors, banned books by named authors, banned anonymous works.

13 See, for example, E. Garfield, "World Brain or Memex? — Mechanical and intellectual requirements of universal bibliographical control" (176).

church fathers and theologians, philosophy and classical literature. They did not normally consider any part of the steadily mounting number of vernacular works. These were automatically excluded because all serious writing was in Latin. It is therefore not, at least in reference to the sixteenth century, a contradiction to call Gessner's great work a universal bibliography even though its title reads: *Bibliotheca universalis, sive Catalogus omnium scriptorum Completissimus, in tribus linguis, Latina, Graeca & Hebraica.* [14]

Conrad Gessner was born into a poor family in Zürich on March 26, 1516 and he remained without any substantial financial status all his life. Supported partly by relations and friends he studied botany and medicine among other things and taught first in Lausanne and Basel before returning permanently to Zürich. Here he taught and practised medicine until his death in 1564. [15] Gessner seems to have done little in the way of original research, outside perhaps medicine, but he had a genius for gathering together and excerpting all previous writings on any number of subjects. He made great efforts to obtain accurate information both in person and by correspondence from all possible sources in order to fill in gaps which he discovered. In other words his work was largely compilatory in nature but systematic and directed toward completeness and accuracy. His enquiring and critical mind, combined with his systematic approach to the collection of material, led him to see relationships and explanations of physical phenomena which had not been evident before. Apart from his bibliographies, he wrote many works, on botany and medicine, for example, and even one on linguistics, entitled *Mithridates* (190). His best subject bibliography is probably that on zoology, [16] but of greatest interest for the literary scholar is his massive universal bibliography.

Apart from not being universal in the modern sense of the word, Gessner's *Bibliotheca universalis* is also not in the strict sense of the word a bibliography. Although the vast majority of articles lists particular works of individual authors and relevant bibliographical details, there are numerous entries which are of a purely factual nature or which merely refer the reader to a source. In many cases the references are to figures that appear or are cited in the works of others. Included are even familiar literary figures such as Lancelot and Tristan.

---

14 This work together with the appendix and the epitome (of Simler) was recently reprinted (Osnabrück: Zeller, 1966). A brief appreciation of Gessner's published writings as a whole is contained in *Conrad Gessner 1516–65, Universalgelehrter, Naturforscher, Arzt. Mit Beiträgen von Hans Fischer, Georges Petit, Joachim Staedtke, Rudolf Steiger, Heinrich Zoller*, ed. Max Hofmann (Zürich [1967]). Included are numerous facsimiles from Gessner's works.

15 Gessner provides an autobiography to the date of writing in his bibliography (p. 179^v–183^r). The first biography of him was published by his friend Josias Simler in Zürich in 1566.

16 For Gessner's work in natural history generally, see the article in Hofmann (note 14) and the literature cited there.

These entries read as follows: "LANCELOTUS quidam historiam scripsit fabulosam, & historiam amatoriam: sic enim invenio citari: nec scio an una sit, aut diversae historiae" (475^V). "TRISTANNI cuiusdam (barbari scriptoris, ut videtur) historia amatoria fabulosa extare fertur" (620^V). Strictly factual entries occur such as the following: "GOTHARDUS, nomen proprium viri apud Germanos, significat robustum in deo, quod Hebraeis Gabriel ..." and the subsequent entry is a good example of the brevity with which Gessner not infrequently contented himself: "GOTHARDUS Alemannus scripsit super Institutis" (277^r).

With all the inevitable imperfections of such a compilation — inaccurate or incomplete information (especially in regard to imprint etc.), unevenness of treatment and sometimes uncritical dependence on previous work — Gessner's bibliography is a vast source of information about those writers of the past and present who were known to his contemporaries, and about what was thought of them. The all too brief and frequently repetitiously formulated biographical details should not hinder our appreciation of the bibliographical information. Herewith, for example, the first portion of the entry for Rotsvitha of Gandersheim:

> ROSVIDA nobilis mulier in Saxonia nata, in Gandeshemensi coenobio, quod non longe ab Hildeshem distat, sacromonialis, miro ingenio et doctrina claruit & in utro scribendi genere admirabilis. Ad virgines enim sacratas castitatem et continentiam hortando Latino sermone conscripsit, Comoedias sex ..." (4 of a total of 8 lines).

An appendix to the *Bibliotheca universalis* appeared in 1555 (186) and contained approximately 4,000 entries. At the same time an *Epitome* (189) was prepared by Josias Simler (reissued in 1574 under the title *Bibliotheca instituta* [445]), in which abbreviated versions of articles from both the original and the appendix were printed, the latter being distinguished by an asterisk. There are over 4,000 names cited in the index to this work and a total of approximately 9,000 entries. All three works are in the traditional form of alphabetical order by first name but contain indexes by surname.

Before either the *Appendix* or the *Epitome* had appeared, Gessner had begun to work on a subject index to his bibliography. This was to be organized in 21 parts of which nos. 1–19 appeared in 1548 under the title *Pandectae* (191), and no. 21 (theology) in 1549 under the title *Partitiones* (192). The twentieth section which was to have been devoted to medicine, never appeared. The organization of the index is complex but not overly difficult and the following scheme will exemplify it. The 21 *Libri,* "De grammatica et philologica," "De dialectica," etc., are divided into sections entitled *Titulus.* Book 4, for example, is headed "Tituli libri IIII. de poetica" and begins with "I De poetica in genere" and "II De fabulis." There are eight *Tituli* in this book, of which the seventh is, as in many but not all cases, further subdivided: "Titulus VII. De poematiis: cuius partes sunt 4. 1 De satyris, 2 De Sylvis, 3 De hymnis, 4 De elegiis." References are then made to the authorities on the subject, sometimes with chapter or page numbers. In larger sections with each letter of the alphabet clearly set off, the order is usually purely alphabetical. An alinea is used to divide longer sections either within *Tituli,* or parts of *Tituli,* or to indicate the letters of alphabetical order. Abbreviations, especially in titles, are copiously used and there are numerous cross references. At the end of the 21st section (*Partitiones . . .*) there is an "Index communis in libros xx pandectarum," i.e. to 1—19 and 21 with approximately 4,000 entries.

After Gessner there are only two other works before the Thirty Years' War which may be considered as general, if not universal, subject bibliographies. These are the *Bibliotheca theologica,* 1614, *philosophica,* 1616, *historica,* 1620 of Paulus Bolduanus (76—78) and the *Bibliotheca materiarum* of Johannes Molanus (355). Although the latter's work was not published until 1618, the author had died in 1585 and his work will therefore be treated first, having been scarcely altered before it was published (by Andrew Schott). Molanus was a theologian and compiled his list of books, as he says in his sub-title: "Docentibus, Concionantibus, ac Scriptoribus pernecessaria." It is consequently not surprising that there is a strong theological and Catholic emphasis. His collection is not, however, by any means restricted to theological matters and there is a very considerable number of secular works, listed under specific subject headings, as, for example, at the beginning:

> Abagarus, Aballardus, Abbas, Abel, Abraham,
> Abramias, Absolutio, Abusus, Academiae,
> Academici, Acedia, Acceptio personarum, Accidentia,
> Aceptali hæretici, Actio, Adagia sacra, Adam etc.

Since the work is subject oriented there is no author index and only an "Index vocabulorum materialium."

The work of Bolduan is rather different in so far as he "limits" himself in each of the three volumes to a specific area, although the term philosophy is used in the widest sense. Instead of a unique alphabetical listing, Bolduan divides the field into broad areas, basically according to the traditional classes of the liberal arts, and then sub-divides again into smaller groups before resorting to alphabetisation. There is an especially long section on music, and here as in other sections many German works are listed along with the more scholarly Latin works, e.g. in Venationes/Jägerkunt and Aucupia/Vogelbücher.

Finally, before leaving the field of universal bibliography for the time being, mention must be made of Constantin's *Nomenclatur insignium scriptorum* (118). In the sub-title of his work Constantin promises an index to Gessner, but does not provide it. Instead he puts forward a list of what seem to him the most significant works in all fields — therefore the phrasing of the title — *insignium.* Whatever may have been the bases on which other bibliographers selected their authors (rather than books), they were not by and large critical of what they listed. By publishing a list of what he considers the best books on any given subject, Constantin ushers in that much-maligned form of bibliography (or non-bibliography as the purists would have it), namely the select(ed) bibliography. Obviously this idea was not entirely new since bibliographers before him had selected, Tritheim, for example, the *illustrious* men of Germany, but the process was rather different. With Constantin, it seems, begins in Germany the idea of making a conscious and critical choice between works across all subject areas. The following is the outline organization as it appears at the beginning of his work:

Grammatica	Linguae	
Historia		
Poesis	Commentarii	
Rhetorica		
Dialectica	Ars memoriae	
Philosophia	Logice	
	Physice	
	Ethice	Gnomice
	Politia	
	Oeconomia	
Mathematica	Arithmetica	
	Musica	
	Geometria	
	Cosmograph.	Geograph.
	Astrologia	
	Astronomia	Genethiologia
	Optice & Optrice	Divinatio
Sancrosancta theologia	Cabala	
	Chemeia vel Alchymia	
Medicina		
	De metallis	
Jurisprudentia		
Mechanica	Ars militaris	
	Architectura	
	Pictura & scalptura	
	Agricultura	
	Venatio	
	Aucupium	
	Piscatus	

Statica et Metrica i. de pōder. & Mēsur.

Idyllia. i. opuscula   vt $\begin{cases} \text{De re Aulica} \\ \text{De re Nautica} \\ \text{De re Culinaria} \\ \text{De arte Natandi} \\ \text{De re Vxoria} \end{cases}$

Stromata, Encyclia & Catholica: illa varias res, hæc disciplinarum orbem continent.

An asterisk indicates supplement, works in Greek are indicated by g, manuscripts by m and books in the royal library by F (= Fontainebleau).

Selection or compilation by would-be bibliographers is not the only basis for book-lists in the sixteenth century. As in the period before printing, recourse must be had to less formal sources. One kind of source which is of great importance is the list of the publisher's production or the bookseller's wares. As early as the fifteenth century printers had printed lists of works available, usually in a very, and for us regrettably, abbreviated form, but as time went on these lists took on another character. Printers could not afford the time and expense of travel to distant places when, as is obvious, the local population could absorb only a small part of their production. The habit therefore developed of printers' purveying not only their own productions but also those of presses elsewhere with whom they had entered into agreement. Also non-printers entered into agreement with one or more printers/publishers and sold books under various forms of financial agreement. The earliest form of advertisement – as in the case of manuscripts – was the single leaf, but booklets soon appeared and were significant enough to be included by Gessner in his *Bibliotheca universalis:* "Typographi bibliopolae plaerique, praesertim quibus instructior librorum supellex est, tabulas et indices librorum à se impressorum aut venalium habent, quorum nonnulli etiam libellis excusi sunt: ut . . ."[17] Some have been preserved from the 1540s and a detailed list of these and the earlier broadsides may be found in Pollard (401). The facing illustration is a broadsheet advertisement by Anton Sorg dated Augsburg, 1483.

Although publishers did travel and send agents on travels, they also regularly attended major fairs themselves. There they not only sold and exchanged books, entered into financial arrangements, and settled accounts, but often met and discussed possible projects with promising authors.

Documents relating to the activities of booksellers exist in various forms, from official acts and contracts to descriptions by travellers of visits to bookdealers. Occasionally, valuable information may be gleaned from these documents. One of the most interesting to be published is the *Mess-Memorial* of Michael Harder, which contains complete accounts of his sales during the Spring Fair at Frankfurt in 1569 (219)[18]. The most interesting point about his

17 *Pandectae,* XXI, 21ʳ.
18 *Mess-Memorial des Frankfurter Buchhändlers Michael Harder, Fastenmesse 1569,*
    ed. Ernst Kelchner and Richard Wülcker (Frankfurt/Paris, 1873). Whether or not Harder

From Konrad Burger, *Buchhändleranzeigen des 15. Jahrhunderts in getreuer Nachbildung* (102) sales – which were considerable – is that they consisted primarily of editions of popular literature and practical handbooks, dating from the previous twenty years or so. That is to say, he was not selling the works listed in the current Fair Catalogue. The illustration on p. 43 is an excerpt from the facsimile edition.

During the sixteenth century the Frankfurt fair came to be the most important book trading centre for all of Europe, and it therefore became of paramount importance for publishers, dealers, and buyers to know what would be available. One of these publishers, namely Georg Willer of Augsburg, hit on the idea of issuing a list of all works offered at this fair (341). From 1564 on he published in autumn and spring a list of new books offered for sale at Frankfurt and available through him. Since the Frankfurt fair had international status, this catalogue was in effect an international bibliography of books new and forth-coming (to use a modern term). It goes without saying that the number of foreign items is small; also the listing of German works is incomplete, being comprised in the main of "serious" works of which Willer had had notice. From 1568 on Willer printed this catalogue in Frankfurt and extended both his coverage and his information. His catalogue developed from a listing of works available through him to a genuine attempt at a complete listing with names of publishers. In other words his catalogue became a profitable enterprise in itself and was no longer primarily an advertisement of his wares. On page 44 are the title-pages of the first two catalogues (autumn 1564 and spring 1565).

In order to maintain some degree of control over the publications offered for sale at the fair and to forestall trouble from the imperial censors, the city council of Frankfurt decided in 1598 to block private catalogues and to issue an official one – the *Ratsmeßkatalog*. This also helped to prevent announce-ments of books not yet – and perhaps never to be – published, to cut down on pirated reprints, and so forth. Despite the steady decline in importance of the Frankfurt fair through the seventeenth century catalogues were issued regularly until 1749.[19]

Other publishers attempted to print their own Fair catalogues at the end of the sixteenth century, but none was successful other than Henning Grosse who began his venture in Leipzig in 1594, having previously published catalogues of his own publications as far back as 1587 (204).[20] Grosse's catalogue was based

was a bookseller and whether or not these books were simply sold by him on behalf of the heirs of the Gülfferich publishing house is irrelevant here. See Heinrich Pallmann, *Sigmund Feyerabend, sein Leben und seine geschäftlichen Verbindungen* (Frankfurt, 1881). There are some details of production and sales. For an early description of Frankfurt and its book fair see James W. Thompson, *The Frankfurt book fair: the Francofordiense emporium of Henri Estienne* (Chicago, 1911).

19 Pollard/Ehrman list the various catalogues to 1627 (p. 81). A reprint of the entire series has been undertaken by Bernhard Fabian; so far only *Die Messkataloge Georg Willers* I and II (1564–80) have appeared (Hildesheim, 1972–73).

20 I have not seen a copy of any catalogues as early as this (Pollard/Ehrman, p. 105).

Mehr ausskauff Matthes Harnisch [17]
Den 31. Martij: faham 69.

2	Albertus magnus	12½	25
2	Esslandts artzney	12	24
4	Eulenspiegel	17	68
4	Bauwmpractick	6½	26
j	losar und Maller	29	29
2	Narrenschiff	20	40
2	Pontus	19½	38
3	Knabenspiegel	10	30
3	Grobianus	11½	34½
3	wuchertausch...	6	18
3	Spieltausch...	6½	19½
3	Softausch...	7½	22½
3	Ehrtausch...	6	18
3	Fluchtausch...	7	21
3	Jagtausch...	16½	49½
3	Bausch...	15	45
3	Gesindtausch...	8	24
2	Tristrant	16½	33
3|	Fortunatus	14½	43½
2	Esopus	47	94

Herbst 69   das gelt 5 ß
Zalt 5 R   ... 1479
Rest er noch 2 ₰ 19 ß 4 ₰   Summa ist 4 ₤ 14 ß 5 ₰.

NOVORVM LI
BRORVM, QVOS NVNDINAE
autumnales, Francoforti anno 1564.
celebratæ, venales exhibuerunt,

CATALOGVS.

Ad exterorum Bibliopolarum, omniumq́ rei Li-
terariæ Studiosorum gratiam & vsum
compti, & venales expositi:
AVGVSTAE,

IN OFFICINA LIBRARIA
Georgij Vvilleri, ciuis & Bibliopolæ Augustani;

Inserti sunt his nonnulli, ijdemq́ perpauci vetu-
stioris editionis libri, ob raram eorum & insi-
gnem vtilitatem commendabiles, & iam
multoties à doctis viris
expetiti.

ANNO A SALVTIFERO VIR-
ginis partu, M. D. LXIIII.

LIBRORVM
NOVORVM, QVI
Francofurti ad Mœnum, nundinis Quadragesi-
malibus, anni à Christo nato 1565. expositi, uenales exhibebantur,

CATALOGVS.

In communem Studiosorum, & exterorum Bibliopolarum gratiam & vsum typographicis formu-
lis excusus, & in lucem emissus.

AVGVSTAE

Prostant in ædibus Georgij Vuilleri, ciuis, & Bibliopolæ Augustani.

Verzeichnus der newen Bücher/welche
zu Franckfurt am Mayn Fastenmeß dises
1565. Jars in offenlichem kauff sein
fürgelegt/ vnd feyl gehabt
worden.

on the Frankfurt listing but was more carefully prepared and much more extensive despite his attempt rigidly to exclude works announced but not published. Grosse came into conflict, however, with another publisher, Abraham Lamberg, who had obtained the right to publish this material, but discussion of this point leads to an altogether different topic which will be treated below. By 1600 the combined catalogues of Frankfurt and Leipzig listed over 1,000 items.

Willer's catalogue was printed from 1585 on by Nicolas Basse and this enterprising printer conceived the idea of cumulating the semi-annual issues of the Frankfurt fair catalogues. In 1592 the first such cumulation was issued in Frankfurt under the title *Collectio in unum corpus* ... (32), covering the years 1564–92 (Spring). The items are listed under broad subject areas alphabetically by author, or by title for anonymous works – Protestant and Catholic theology, Law, Medicine, History, Philosophy, Poetry, Music. The foreign works are similarly listed but under rather narrower headings. The Latin and German history sections have a considerable number of subject cross references, e.g., "Cometen in gemein. Such Johan Pretorii," "Heinrich Pantaleon. Such. Heldenbuch," etc.

Basse had the usual ten year copyright for this work and no sooner had it expired than a new cumulation appeared. This publication is primarily the work of Johann Cless, who had died in 1599. His material was brought up to date somewhat and published in 1602 with the title *Unius seculi eiusque virorum literatorum monumentis ab Anno Dom. 1500. ad 1602* (115). Despite the claim of the title this bibliography in fact lists only works from Basse's *Collectio* together with those printed between 1592 and 1600/1601. Some pre-1592 works have been omitted where new editions had appeared, but generally speaking it is a poorer work, showing signs of having been prepared from Cless's manuscript by a hasty and incompetent continuator. It is divided into two main parts, viz. I Latin, French, Italian and Spanish works and II German works. Authors are entered alphabetically by first name under the usual discipline headings.

In the meantime Grosse in Leipzig had also published a cumulated catalogue covering the years 1593–1600. This was the result of his dispute with his competitor Lamberg who had succeeded in obtaining sole rights for the publication of the fair catalogues. Grosse hit on the idea of publishing a cumulation and then following this up with a series of *Continuatio(nes)*. It seems evident that he envisaged cumulating these too after a further five year period, but by 1603 had already reached an agreement with his competitor. The agreement consisted largely of Lamberg's retaining the privilege of printing the Frankfurt catalogues for Leipzig, but printing also a run of the same – with a different title page – for Grosse. After the expiry of Lamberg's copyright in 1619 Grosse held the sole rights.

There was one further attempt at a cumulated index to German book production, perhaps the most interesting venture before the eighteenth century. In 1610 and 1611 Georg Draud put out three volumes entitled *Bibliotheca exotica*, *Bibliotheca classica* and *Bibliotheca librorum germanicorum classica* (138–41). These volumes contain not only the cumulated listings of the fair catalogues from 1564 to 1610 but also works not listed in the catalogues and many works from before 1564. Draud attempted in fact to cover the period which had been misleadingly given on the title page of Cless's *Elenchus*. Moreover, he made a valiant attempt to organize the much larger number of works in such a way that the bibliography would be genuinely convenient for scholars interested in specific subject materials.

Draud organized the works in his *Bibliotheca exotica* first by language and then by subject. Within these subject areas, e.g., "Libri theologici, iuridici, medici," etc., works are listed alphabetically by author surname. Anonymous works are appended in a second alphabetical listing by title. In the much larger *Bibliotheca classica* and *Bibliotheca librorum germanicorum classica* (works in Latin and German; the word *classica* in the second work means "classed"), Draud retained the major divisions by disciplines but ordered the material within these divisions by subject. For each work he selected as specific a subject entry as possible, using wherever feasible a word or words from the title. In cases where a work was entered under a word not taken from the title, a cross reference from a title phrase may be made to this word. The Latin volume, for example, begins with the following entries:

> Abbreviaturae linguae sanctae. Vide Grammatica.
> Abelis historiae. Vide Martyres.

Under "Grammatica" there is to be found Georg Weigenmaier's *Tractatas abbreviaturarum omnium sanctae linguae* and under "Martyres" we find a work by D. Lud. Rabus entitled *Historia de S. Abele*. In the case of synonyms or subjects too specialised in meaning he provides a cross-reference to the appropriate heading, e.g., under "Analogia sacramentarii" (following some entries) we find: "Vide etiam Coena Domini" and "Analogia Christi vide Passio"

This is how Draud describes his procedure in the preface to the *Bibl. germ.*

> ... daß dieselbige so wol für Ungelehrte als auch für Gelehrte, so viel müglich, seyn, und inen einen richtigen Weg zu jeder Materien zeigen wirt, also und dergestalt, daß nicht allein ein jedes Buch in die Claß und Stell, dahin es gehörig, gesetzt ist, sondern da etwan eins oder daß ander (wie dann der mehre theil) ein solch frontispicium und Titel hat, daß nicht jederman, unter welche Claß solches gehörig, ästimiren kan, weiß aber zum wenigsten, wie es mit eins, zwey oder drey Worten in gemein genennet wirdt, und dasselbige nur demnach es zur einen oder der anderen Facultet gehörig ist, nach anweissung des Alphabets auffsuchet, ime alsdann wo solches zu suchen remissive zum augenschein gezeiget wirdt.

In order to enable the user to locate the work of individual authors, Draud provided both volumes with an author index.

A second and enlarged edition appeared in Frankfurt in 1625 (140) with a slightly simplified organisation. Some related entries are put together and additional entries made, so that the groups are larger. Under Heldenbücher, for example, in the 1611 edition there are eight entries plus a cross reference and the note "Such auch Ritter Thaten." Under this heading there are three entries and the note "Such auch Kurtzweilige Historien." Here there are twenty-three entries and the note "Such auch in Allerhand Künsten/Amadis." This section, "In Allerhand (Allerley) Künsthen," has not only an entry for *Amadis* but also a heading: "Kurtzweilige Geticht und Geschicht," where there are 23 entries and seven references. In the 1625 edition this whole section has been absorbed into the "Historische Bücher" where there are now for "Heldenbücher" 16 items and the note "Such auch Kriege." The "Kurtzweilige Geticht und Geschicht" now appear in this section with a total of 92 entries and 4 references. The total number of works has in other words increased, but the number of headings and cross references has been reduced. Under the letter H there were, for example, in the 1611 edition 20 headings with 42 cross references in 5.5 pages; in the 1625 edition this has become 18 headings with only nine references but filling 9.5 pages.

The fair catalogues are of course far from being a complete listing of all works published, and more will be said of this at the beginning of the following chapter. They do, however, cover a large proportion of the book production of the time and as such are exceedingly important. Their value as bibliographies, and not just as lists of new books, was soon recognized, and they were extensively used both in Germany and abroad. An English bookseller named John Bill, for example, produced an English edition of them between 1617 and 1628.[21] These catalogues served in effect as national bibliographies and their format, semi-annual publication etc., have remained virtually constant to the present day. Attempts at national and local bibliography had been made elsewhere, but these had not proved successful or even influential. Doni had published *La Libraria,* a listing of Italian publications, in 1550 and there was an early example of local bibliography in Poccianti's *Catalogus Scriptorum Florentinorum* in 1589 (400). The only work which approaches being a local bibliography in Germany is the *Catalogus singularis, omnium librorum, qui in electoratu et ducatu Saxoniae hoc semestri typis excusi sunt. . .* published by Lamberg in 1604 in order to protect Saxon booksellers from the demands of the Imperial Book Commission.

Having considered the work of the bibliographers and the publishers it only remains to consider the book-buyers, those who collected and sometimes also

21 See *Cambridge History of English Literature* (New York: Putnam, 1910), IV, 460–61. A detailed discussion in Pollard/Ehrman, p. 86ff.

disposed of books. As was said at the beginning of this chapter, the invention of printing from movable type made more books available to more people. Although some collectors steadfastly clung to manuscript copies, they were soon an insignificant minority and large libraries of printed books became common among scholars during the period of Humanism and especially after the Reformation, when the religious quarrels were being fought out in book after book and broadsheet after broadsheet. As yet there was apparently, however, no great interest in cataloguing these collections and making them known, presumably because they were primarily for the *use* of the owner. Book lists had been made as a form of inventory in the monastery, for example, at the change of a librarian, and in the case of a private person, this could occur at his death or at the sale of his books. Later on such catalogues take on increasing importance, but none is as early as the sixteenth century.[22] There are, however, two catalogues of secular institutional libraries which date back this far, namely those of Leiden and Augsburg.

The Leiden catalogue, published by Petrus Bertius in 1595 (315), classes books by "faculties," viz, Theology, Law, Medicine, History, Philosophy, Mathematics, Literature, and within these classes the books are assembled by size. Supplementary lists contain the titles of books donated and written by members of the faculty. An idea of the relative size and importance of language and literature studies may be gained from the fact that the section entitled "Litteratores et qui ad linguarum cognitionem pertinent" contains only 23 items.

The catalogues of the Augsburg city library begin with the *Catalogus graecorum librorum manuscriptorum*, 1575 (23) and David Hoeschel's *Catalogus graecorum codicum*, 1595 (22). The former is unpaged and lists only 126 items in 11 pages. The later work contains a much greater number of MSS in 58 pages, and numerous pages are left blank in the copy used, presumably for additions. A general index of works both printed and manuscript was then published (by Georg Henisch) in 1600 in a rather strange, tall (30.5 x 9.5 cm) format (21). This lists books of the "lower" (p. 5–78) and "upper" (p. 81–556) libraries together with the books "in armario" (p. 557–9). Works are arranged by size within the usual subject divisions and there is an alphabetical index of authors which contains approximately 3,700 names. As an example of the scope of the library it is worth noting that the major works of Tritheim are listed (there are 6 page references to him in the index), but his work on German authors is not among them.

---

22 With the exception of the list compiled of books at Cambridge university and included in John Caius, *Historiae Cantabrigiensis liber primus* (London, 1574), p. 85–87. A list of the books at Franeker university (founded 1585) dates from 1601 (164).

Before concluding this chapter it would seem appropriate to refer briefly to the existence, if only in embryonic form, of union catalogues.[23] By the end of the sixteenth century several attempts had been made to gather into one unified catalogue the titles of works held in a number of libraries. Simler, for example, in his 1574 revision of Gessner's *Bibliotheca universalis* claims to have made use of Martin Dresser's compilation of the libraries of Saxony and Thuringia: "A Dressero . . . accepimus catalogum librorum Mss., qui partim apud ipsum, partim in publicis quibusdam bibliothecis Misniae et Turingiae servantur. . . ." (p. 491). This relatively restricted undertaking was for the time being the last of a number of abortive efforts reaching as far back as the end of the thirteenth century. At that time a rudimentary union catalogue of the holdings of monastery libraries in England had been made, apparently by the Grey Friars. This *Registrum anglie de libris doctorum et auctorum veterem* survives in a MS from around 1400.[24] This and the somewhat later *Tabulae septem custodiarum* were expanded by John Boston in the fifteenth century to form the *Catalogus scriptorum ecclesiae*[25] and the latter work was then utilized by John Bale for his *Scriptorum illustrium maioris Brytanniae catalogus* published at Basle in 1557 (31).[26] Lehmann has also described a late fifteenth century MS which lists works in many libraries of the Lower Rhine area; not all the abbreviations for the individual libraries could be elucidated. And finally, in 1532 a large compilation based on the lost work of a predecessor encompassed the holdings of libraries of the Low Countries, Northern France and Northern Germany. According to Lehmann the catalogue comprises 1) an alphabetical list of approximately 2,000 authors with biographical and bibliographical references, 2) a list of saints' lives, 3) a lengthy list of anonymous works. A somewhat later compilation by Wilhelm Carnificus and Johann Bunderius, to which references were made through the first half of the seventeenth century, seems to have been entirely lost.

From the foregoing it is evident that, whatever may be said about the art of printing or the trade of bookselling, in bibliography at least almost everything that could be done had been tried by 1600 or soon after, much of it in Germany. The traditional form of bio-bibliography had burgeoned into bibliographies of individual writers, of professional groups and of the whole of the scholarly world. There was a universal bibliography and a list of best books, a bibliography of German writers and one of notable women; there were

23 For the following see Paul Lehmann, "Alte Vorläufer des Gesamtkatalogs" in his *Erforschung des Mittelalters: ausgewählte Abhandlungen und Aufsätze*, vol. 4 (Stuttgart, 1961), 172–83.
24 On the *Registrum anglie* etc. see Ernest A. Savage, *Notes on the early monastic libraries of Scotland* . . . (Edinburgh, 1928)
25 See Thomas Tanner, *Bibliotheca Britanico-Hibernica* . . . (London, 1748).
26 First published according to the British Library catalogue at "Wesel" in 1548 by Theodorich Platen; edited by R. L. Poole and M. Bateson (Oxford, 1902).

subject bibliographies and broadly classed library catalogues. Authors had listed books they had written, printers had made lists of the books they produced, booksellers had made lists of books currently available to them; and the city of Frankfurt had laid the foundation of national bibliography in its *Meßkataloge*. Form bibliographies, that is lists of books of particular size, shape etc., had not yet made their appearance, but something of the kind was present in the numerous lists of banned books.

In all of this the tradition of considering the class of author rather than the subject of the book was still strong, but it was weakening. This is indicated not only by the early approach to subject bibliography by Gessner, but by the interest shown in subject organization and classification in general. Gessner's scheme was influential and his authority is cited by later "classifiers" such as Florian Trefler in his *Methodus* (479). Classification per se is no direct concern in this study, but it becomes an increasingly important aspect of bibliography as the disciplines fragment and proliferate and the subject bibliography consequently becomes an essential foundation for research.

Chapter 3:

From the Thirty Years' War to the middle of the eighteenth century

A great deal of research has been devoted to the history of books and printing from the time of Gutenberg to the end of the sixteenth century. Since, however, the modern period of bibliography does not commence until the eighteenth century, the period between 1600 and 1700 is still a largely uncharted area. To establish the nature and extent of works published in this period is therefore perhaps more difficult than for either earlier or later periods. To a not inconsiderable extent the difficulties derive from the Thirty Years' War — from its causes as well as from its effects — and from significant changes in the nature of book production and trading. Some knowledge of these factors is therefore essential to an understanding of the bibliographical problems which exist.

By the end of the sixteenth century the importance of the Frankfurt book fair had already begun to diminish. Interest in religious matters had led to the production of a vast quantity of highly polemic, primarily sectarian literature, and to a sharp reduction in what must be designated, for want of a better term, belles lettres. Since much of this literature was not only in the vernacular but often of purely local or national import, it was of no great interest to foreign booksellers. At the same time presses outside Germany continued to develop rapidly and to supply more and more of the local markets, as the use of the vernacular in published writing increased. During the course of the century the proportion of works published in Latin steadily decreased and even in Germany they never again outnumber works in German after the year 1690.[1]

An additional factor influencing German book production was the decline of the system whereby books were exchanged between booksellers, rather than bought (or taken on credit) in order to be sold, as had been the case in the very early days. The large number of publishers and the variety of their products in content as well as in quantity and quality made such a system very cumbersome. Publishers of good quality works were unwilling to exchange their productions for works of inferior quality, while booksellers were virtually compelled to print in order to be able to effect an exchange. Exchange across national borders was especially difficult.

These general developments affected the trade as a whole. In Frankfurt itself the deciding factor was the existence of a form of censorship. The

1 See Gustav Schwetschke, *Codex nundinarius Germaniae Literatae bisecularis* (Halle, 1850).

Imperial Book Commission, which had been set up by Maximilian II in 1569 (Kapp/Goldfriedrich I, ch. 10), had gained the right to exercise some restriction on the trade through its presence at the fair, although the city, regretting its earlier mistake, at first circumvented genuine censorship to a great degree. Gradually, however, the influence of the Commission came to be felt more and more. It favoured of course Catholic writers and attempted to hamper Protestant authors and publishers, despite the fact that Frankfurt was essentially a Protestant city. During the Thirty Years' War, which in any case disrupted normal trade relations, the Commission gradually gained the upper hand and virtually forced publishers to abandon their support of the Frankfurt Fair and to turn exclusively to Leipzig.

From a bibliographical point of view the gradual demise of the Frankfurt Book Fair through the influence of the Imperial Book Commission had important repercussions. In the first place the fair catalogues became less representative of the whole of German book publication (and also of course of European publications), and reference must therefore also be made to the Leipzig Fair catalogues. In addition to those publishers who no longer attended the fair, there were those who failed to list some or all of their publications for one of a number of reasons. They might fear that the book would be unpopular with the authorities, or that it might actually be censored. Or they might hope to avoid having to supply the requisite number (at times quite high) of "legal deposit" or inspection copies by failing to list works. Publishers were on the other hand required to furnish the Commission with lists of their publications and these records provide in some cases supplementary evidence of their output.[2] And in addition to those who stayed away for such and similar reasons there were many, especially foreigners, who were not willing to risk travelling during wartime.

The contents of the *Meßkataloge,* valuable as they are, cannot therefore be taken as a reliable summary of all that was published at the time. There were regular complaints that works were listed prior to publication and then perhaps never published at all. That this practice was common knowledge is made evident by the comment of the English bookseller James Allestrye (July 18, 1653): ". . . it is a very usual thing for the booksellers of Germany to send the titles of books to be put in the catalogue before they are printed, so that at present they are not to be had."[3] However, statistics based upon the *Meßkataloge* — such as those by Schwetschke[4] — have relative if not absolute

---

2   See Gunter Richter, "Die Sammlung von Drucker-, Verleger- und Buchführerkatalogen in den Akten der kaiserlichen Bücherkommission," *Festschrift für Josef Benzing,* ed. E. Geck and G. Pressler (Wiesbaden, 1964), pp. 317–72.

3   A. Growoll, *Three Centuries of English Booktrade Bibliography* (London, 1964 [New York, 1903]), p. 15–16.

4   See Schwetschke (note 1) and Theodor Bestermann, *A world bibliography of biblio-graphies* (Lausanne, [4] 1965).

validity. Bearing all the above-mentioned factors in mind and also the fact that numerous small "jobbing" printers produced many trade books for strictly local consumption without ever considering sales further abroad, it is clear that, for example, the figure of only 307 works published in 1635 (Schwetschke, p. 90) does not by any means represent the total output of all presses for that year, although it may truly indicate the low-water mark in German book production.

The Thirty Years' War clearly had a devastating effect on the publishing trade; capital, labour, and commercial exchange were all restricted, and foreign publishers, particularly the Dutch with their better methods of production and novel sales techniques, were not slow to take advantage of the situation. Books were still being written and read of course; perhaps more important for us is the fact that the desire existed to collect books not merely haphazardly but systematically, so that many of the great private libraries became established in the seventeenth century. One might say in fact that, bibliographically speaking, the major feature of the period is the growth of private libraries (alongside public libraries) and also of an interest in the methods of building, organizing, and utilising these collections. It is probably also important that the desire to display books, to exhibit them along with other objects acquired, encouraged careful arrangement and may even have led to the preservation despite the wars not only of many works but of entire libraries. One cannot do better therefore than begin this period with an indication of the bibliographical information provided by publications relating to these libraries.

In 1627 there appeared in Paris a work on building library collections which rapidly became something of a classic. Although one cannot escape the suspicion that the elegance of the style has almost as much to do with its success as the profundity of its thought, there is no doubt that Gabriel Naudés *Advis pour dresser une bibliothèque* was extremely influential (367). In 1644 a second edition was published and it was included in the same year in Louis Jacob's *Traicté des plus belles bibliothèques* (261). In Germany characteristically, it was translated into Latin and included in 1703 in the second volume of the second edition of J. J. Mader's *De bibliothecis . . .* (329).[5] An English translation made by the diarist John Evelyn (371) was presented by him to Charles II in 1661 (see the diary entries for Nov. 16 and Dec. 3). The original version was most recently reprinted in 1963.[6]

Although this work is primarily of interest to historians of library science rather than to bibliographers, it is worth noting Naudé's approach to such matters as collection building, as a background to the understanding of libraries of the time. His aim was the development of a rounded collection, that is, one

5 P. 71ff: "Gabrielis Naudaei Parisiensis Dissertatio de instruenda bibliotheca . . ."
6 This is the edition cited here, published by VEB Edition, Leipzig. There are numerous other editions and translations.

that contained the best works in all branches of knowledge and did not neglect to include works the content of which was unacceptable (e.g., heretical or outmoded), provided that such works had been influential. In other words he wanted all sides to be represented in any critical areas. This catholicity of taste, or perhaps better, this unrestricted breadth in book collecting, is something that characterizes private libraries of this period in sharp contrast to the libraries, primarily of public and ecclesiastical institutions, in earlier centuries.

Also noteworthy is Naudé's attitude toward bibliographies. He is aware of their existence since he refers in passing, for example, to "Neander, Cardan, Gessner,"[7] but he is evidently of the opinion that existing catalogues are a more important if not the chief source of bibliographic information. Early in his work he stresses the necessity of familiarity with the catalogues of all kinds of collections, both large and small. From these we can not only know what exists; also "ils nous peuuent instruire des liures, du lieu, du temps & de la forme de leur impression" (25f.). Such references to the usefulness of library catalogues together with the advice to establish and improve one's collection by acquiring and amalgamating with it other whole collections, make it evident that Naudé is not keenly interested in bibliographies per se. Such an attitude is of course a reflection of the distinction between the bibliographer who attempts to list all works in any field and the collector who only wants the best, and it is this basic distinction which is to lead later to new forms of bibliography (on Naudé's introduction of the term "Bibliographia" see below).

Naudé himself was a highly respected librarian and among numerous other works he produced a catalogue of the Cordes collection, *Bibliothecae Cordesianae catalogus,* which was published in Paris in 1643 (370). This work, which is not indexed, lists approximately 8,000 titles divided into a number of subject divisions or disciplines. With some variations such divisions remain standard for most catalogues for many decades to come. In this instance there are the following sections. Biblical writers, theology, bibliography, chronology, geography, history, biography, military science, civil law, canon law, philosophy (including mathematics and medicine), political science and literature. It is noteworthy that the admittedly short section "Bibliothecarii" follows immediately after theology. Thirty seven works are listed, including such varied items as Gessner's *Bibliotheca universalis,* the Bodleian catalogue, and bibliographies of the works of monastic orders (p. 132—4). One characteristic of this catalogue which is fairly soon to be generally abandoned is the

---

7 Michaelis Neandri *De bibliothecis deperditis ac noviter instructis* in J. J. Mader, *De bibliothecis atque archivis virorum clarissimorum . . .* (Helmstedt, 1666), p. 37—53 (also in the second edition referred to above). Girolamo Cardano, physician, philosopher, etc, is perhaps best remembered for his autobiography and his book on games of chance. On his writings see above, ch. 2, n. 10.

division of each section first by the format of the book, folio, quarto, etc. With each work Naudé gives the place and date of publication.

A catalogue of the library of Count Jacques Auguste de Thou, published by Quesnel in Paris in 1679, *Catalogus bibliothecae Thuanae* (476), is rather more extensive and is divided as follows: I theology, canon and civil law, history: II philosophy, i.e. philosophy, mathematics, optics, chronology, cosmography (geography, astrology, arts), medicine (including alchemy) nat. hist; and humanities, i.e. grammar, ancient literature, medieval letters, bibliography, etc. In this catalogue the bibliographical section, following at the very end on histories of academies, is more clearly designated as "Bibliothecae, Catalogi librorum & scriptorum." It is, however, not much more extensive, containing even in the 1704 edition only about 50 items inclusive of variant editions. The indexes to this work are very useful, consisting of indexes of manuscripts, portraits and plans etc., unbound books, and authors, together with an indication of the method by which anonymous works are entered. There are approximately 5,400 authors listed.

Numerous such catalogues were published in the seventeenth and eighteenth centuries and their usefulness as bibliographies is obvious. In their own time they were used, as Naudé indicates, as a basis for selection; the best were viewed as authoritative handbooks and were much sought after. To us they provide, among other things, a means of assessing the relative popularity of individual authors, their degree of influence, and so forth. Some of the best known collections are those of Nicolas Heinsius (1682), Johann Fabricius (1717–24), Otto & Johann B. Mencke(n) (1723), Zacharias Uffenbach (1729–31), Nicolas H. Gundling (1731), Jacob Reimmann (1731), Valentin Loescher (1744–51), Heinrich Brühl (1750–56), Heinrich von Bunau (1750–56), F. O. Mencken (1755). One of the more interesting collections is that of the Mencken family. Father and son built up a large collection and published a catalogue in 1723, the title of which is worth quoting in full (337):

> *Bibliotheca Menckeniana quae autores praecipue veteres graecos et lat. historiae item literariae, eccl. et civilis, antiquitatum ac rei nummariae scriptores, philologicos, oratores, poetas et codices MSS. complectitur, ab Ottone et J. Burchardo Menckeniis, patre et filio, multorum annorum spatio studiose collecta, nunc justo ordine disposita, et in publicos usus aperta*

A second edition was published in 1727 and special catalogues of valuable items were printed in 1729 and 1730 in an effort to attract buyers. The library was eventually disposed of (completely? partly at least to Bunau), and the grandson, F. O. Mencken, set about building an entirely new collection.

The 1723 catalogue contains approximately 9,000 items divided as follows: Historiae litterariae scriptores, Scriptores veteres, Antiquarii, Numarii, Historici, Heraldici (etc.), Politici scriptores, Scriptores Artis grammaticae (etc.), Dictionaria, Scriptores artis rhetoricae, Oratores recentiores, Scriptores artis poeticae, Poetae recentiores (etc.), [Varia], Lexica realia, libri prohibiti vel suspecti, Manuscripta. Within each section the books are even at this late date still divided first by size; place and date are given. The index of authors lists the individual works of each author together with the pages on which they are to be found, e.g. "Leibnitius not. circa vit. & doctr. Cartes, 83. Access. hist. 148. de numm. Grat. 161."

In addition to the publication of catalogues for the convenience of those using the library there was of course the necessity of making a list of books wherever a personal collection was to be sold. Inventory lists were primarily compiled for legal reasons, e.g. when settling an estate; but they were sometimes also used as listings of saleable items. Sale and auction catalogues are not, however, as reliable bibliographical sources as other catalogues. One reason for this is connected with the comment made above about the novel sale practices of the Dutch, in particular with reference to the book auctions introduced into Germany in the early seventeenth century (the first auction in Germany is supposed to have been held in Leipzig in 1609 by Christian Kirchner).[8] The auctioning of a private collection is a legitimate process and one that is still carried on, but the practice existed of including additional, often worthless, works in individual collections, or even of auctioning off a publisher's or bookseller's entire dead stock, an early form of "warehouse sale." The most extreme form of this kind of sales technique was the institution later of the notorious book lotteries,[9] practised even by such a notable figure as Johann Heinrich Zedler.[10] Sale catalogues may therefore *seem* to be the genuine collection of an individual, for example, the *Catalogus plurimorum insignium librorum ex bibliotheca ... D. Antonii Biesii ... quorum auctio fiet Leydae, die xv Decembris & sequentibus apud Joannem Maine Bibliopolam*, 1607 (65), and be sometimes quite substantial as in the case of the *Catalogus bibliothecae Eximiae B. Dn. M. Johannis Langii ... qui auctionis ritu V.D. in aedibus defuncti ... die 7. Februarii & sqq. Anni MDCCI divendendi exponentur ...* (311) which lists well over 8,000 items arranged

---

8 The Dutch first tried (without any success) to introduce auctions in Frankfurt in the 1660s. A license for auctions was issued in 1671 (Pollard/Ehrman). For detailed lists of early auctions in Western Europe see Pollard/Ehrman, also Taylor, *Book Catalogues*, passim. On German auction catalogues, chiefly style and content, see Bernhard Wendt, "Der Versteigerungs- und Antiquariatskatalog im Wandel von vier Jahrhunderten," *AGB*, 9 (1967–69), 1–88.

9 The earliest example I have seen of lotteries in Germany is a catalogue in the collection of the British Museum, dated 1714: *Catalogus verschiedener Juristischer/Historischer und Philosophischer ... Bücher ... welche ... durch eine kleine Lotterey von 701. Lossen ... distrahiret werden sollen.*

10 Felix von Schroeder, *Die Verlegung der Büchermesse von Frankfurt am Main nach Leipzig* (Leipzig, 1904); he also refers to a lottery in Frankfurt in 1710.

solely by size![11] But there is always the possibility that publishers' dead stock and similar extraneous items have been included.

Catalogues of institutional libraries also continued to appear — they are far too numerous to discuss here — and many are later listed in eighteenth century bibliographical works such as Struve's *Introductio* (see below). Two notable examples are Johannes Saubert's catalogue of the Nuremberg Library, 1643 (422) and J. H. Hottinger's *Schola Tigurinorum,* 1664 (249), both of which contain also material pertinent to the history of their respective libraries. Hottinger's list of books, which forms the first appendix to his history of the library (pp. 65–190), is insofar of interest as it gives considerable biographical detail about and comments on the authors, especially where they are of local origin. Another library history, and one which has some interesting sidelights on collecting policy, including statistics, is to be found in Hermann Conring's brief work on the Wolfenbüttel library: *De Bibliotheca Augusta quae est in arce Wolffenbutelensi . . . epistola* 1661 (117).

Obviously enough, bibliographies of various kinds were used by collectors, if only as a basis for organising and cataloguing their collection. Ever since the days of Gessner in fact it had been accepted practice to use such a work as his *Bibliotheca universalis,* checking off, possibly with a catalogue number, those items acquired. By the middle of the seventeenth century there were in fact sufficient bibliographies of various kinds to call for the first bibliography of bibliographies (hereafter referred to as biblio-bibliographies). This was Philipp Labbé's *Bibliotheca bibliothecarum,* which had first appeared in Paris in 1653 under the title *Nova bibliotheca manuscriptorum et librorum* (308). It went through several editions and was extremely influential on subsequent bibliographers. The first edition is comparatively rare and in any case less extensive than the second and subsequent editions; the following comments refer to the second edition of 1664. The most important point apart from the actual selection of authors, listed alphabetically by first name, is the series of indexes. In addition to the index of names which precedes the text, there is a series of indexes at the conclusion of the work, analysing the authors by discipline, nationality, religious affiliation; and listing subjects, hononyms, polygraphs, printers, and libraries — in all eight indexes. The text itself is a comprehensive collection of bibliographies, including, however, also general works of reference and especially biographical collections. Gessner is listed of course and Tritheim; as an example of Labbé's method of citation the following entry appears under the forename Jacobus and is indexed both under Forestus and under Bergomensis:

---

11 A well organised catalogue is that of the valuable collection of Count Schomberg, auctioned in 1643 (433).

Iacobus Philippus Forestus, a Patria Bergomensis vulgo dictus, Eremitarum O. A. Supplementum Chronicorum libris 16. sive opus Historiarum ab initio Mundi usque ad annum 1503. In quo saepe de scriptoribus sacris profanisque multa interserit.

Eiusdem de Claris Mulieribus Christianis liber unus Ferrariae 1497 in folio expensis Laurentij de Rubeis de Valentia.

The title of the second work is cited inaccurately — not, it should be noted, a common failing — "christianis" being a rather inappropriate adjective for many of the women listed.[12]

Labbé's work contains according to Bestermann approximately 1500 items. It was improved and expanded by him and later by others, for example by Teissier in 1686 (472). The appropriate part of the title of the 1705 re-dition of Teissier (*WBB* 3000) indicates sufficiently the wide scope of this work. *Catalogus auctorum qui librorum catologos, indices bibliothecas, virorum litteratorum elogia, vitas, aut orationes funebres, scriptis consignarunt auctuarium ab Antonio Teisserio ... sive eiusdem catalogi pars altera, continens ferme bis mille quingento autores &c.* This title is by no means unexpected, and we have previously referred in passing to the rather different attitude toward bibliography as expressed in, for example, works of the sixteenth century. It should also not be overlooked that, while Labbé's work was the first separately published biblio-bibliography, lists of bibliographies had been included in general bibliographies such as that by Gessner. In the same year, for example, in which the second edition of Labbé's work appeared Hottinger included a lengthy listing of bibliographies as chapter 2 "De bibliothecis" of his *Bibliothecarius quadripartitus* (248). This chapter is not, as might be expected, devoted to libraries but to bibliographies, systematically ordered as universal and particular (by regions, orders, subjects). The bibliographies are followed by a list of library catalogues and histories, alphabetically arranged by library name.

With the publication of the first biblio-bibliography we enter into a period of some terminological confusion, and it is therefore advisable to pause at this point and consider not only what was meant by the various Latin terms employed hitherto, but how these are to be rendered in future in the vernacular. The word *bibliographia* had not been used by the Romans, and the Greeks had used it only in the sense of the act of writing, not of listing or describing, books. Whatever the reason for Gessner's choice of the word *bibliotheca*, his authority was sufficient to ensure the use of this term by succeeding generations of bibliographers. The term *bibliographia* does, however, occur as early as the beginning of the seventeenth century in two works

---

12 The title of this work was given above: *De plurimis claris scelestisque mulieribus.* It contains the biographies of 192 notable women, ranging from Saint Joan to Pope Joan (!) Bibliographical details are lacking even for bona fide authoresses.

by Naudé, namely his *Bibliographia politica* (Venice, 1633, 1642, etc.) and *Bibliographia militaris* (Jena, 1683 originally included in *Syntagma de studio militari* [Rome, 1637]). The same pattern was followed by Scheurl in Germany for his *Bibliographia moralis* (Helmstedt, 1648). These works are not lists of titles, but introductions to specific disciplines on the basis of a chronological survey of their history — which means in effect a critical appreciation of their literature. The word *bibliographia* was also used in this sense by a few later writers in Germany, of whom the most notable was Johannes Fabricius who published his *Bibliographia antiquaria* in Hamburg in 1713; but its use was exceptional.

Although the term *bibliographia* or *bibliographie* (French) was being used, especially in France, but often in differing senses, it did not become accepted in Germany as the designation of "bibliography," largely it would seem, as the result of the influence of Burkhard Struve. He retained the older term and entitled his widely appreciated bibliographies *Bibliotheca philosophica*, etc. The German equivalent *Bibliothek* (*Büchersaal*, etc.) therefore remained in use through the eighteenth and into the nineteenth century in the sense of a list of the literature of a given subject.

The term "literature" still meant of course scholarly writing in any field[13] and the approach to any discipline was through the study of its literature both past and present. The tendency of the period from the middle of the seventeenth century on, was toward the study of knowledge as a whole rather than, or as a preparation for, the study of individual disciplines. The history of literature *(Historia litteraria;* in German *Literärgeschichte* or *Historie der Gelahrtheit)* therefore meant the study of scholarly writing in all fields (past and present) or, put in another way, the study of those scholars who had contributed to the advancement of knowledge by their writings. The study of scholarly writings presupposed a knowledge of books in the sense of knowing *about* books, and this primarily bibliographical approach to literature was termed *notitia librorum*. By this is meant in effect acquaintance with the general bibliographical sources to the history of literature as a whole. In the vernacular this could be translated as *Bücherkunde*, which could lead to some confusion since, although the term originally meant knowledge of the *contents* of books, it could also be used for the study of books *qua* books, that is the history of the book.[14]

---

13 Cf. Henry Hallam, *Introduction to the Literature of Europe* (London, 1827—39), which covers all fields of knowledge.
14 In this connection it might be noted that the Austrian Michel Denis divides his *Einleitung in die Bücherkunde* (Vienna, 1777—78) into: I Bibliographie (by which he means the history of books and libraries), and 2 Literargeschicht (in which bibliographies are included — he calls them Bücherverzeichnisse).

The greater confusion arises in the area of the designation of the numerous types of bibliographical sources. For Germany of the late seventeenth and most of the eighteenth century bibliography as a function meant knowing about books with a view to describing them and evaluating their contents. As an ancillary discipline this was taught at German universities from the end of the seventeenth century on in conjunction with the study of the history of literature. Where this "art of bibliography" fitted in to the system of knowledge was a vexed question, and the complexities of the issue have been described in detail, though not entirely convincingly, by Rudolf Blum (71). The important feature from our point of view is the fact that the terms *Bibliographie, bibliographisch-,* etc., were used in Germany *generally speaking only in a generic sense* in regard to bibliographical sources. Those sources included many things that we would consider extraneous, such as histories of libraries along with library catalogues and classification schemes. But bibliographies as such were not so entitled: they were still known as *bibliothecae* and carefully distinguished from *catalogi* (library and bookdealers' catalogues). Although the location of the various types of bibliography varies in such catalogues as the Cordesiana, Thuana or Bunaviana, the distinctions are usually strictly observed, e.g. "Bibliothecae Generales . . . Catalogi Scriptorum . . . Catalogi librorum manuscriptorum, Catalogi Bibliothecarum . . . Catalogi officinarum Bibliopolarum" *(Thuana).*

There are, not unnaturally, numerous exceptions which depart in different ways from these general rules. The term *bibliotheca,* for example, continued to be applied at the end of the seventeenth century to *general* works of a bibliographical nature that were the outcome of the polyhistorical approach. These are either attempts at universal bibliographies or more general encyclopedic works (few of which attained completion). Georg M. König's *Bibliotheca vetus et nova,* 1678 (291), for example, claims to list all the famous writers in all fields of knowledge and all nations in one alphabetical listing (by surname). There are approximately 15,000 entries in a very concise style. Here, for example, is the article on Tritheim (p. 818b):

> TRITHEMIUS (Joh.) abbas, natus est Anno 1462: obiit Anno 1516. A *Carolo Bovillo, Joh. Wiero & J. Bodino* inter magos numeratur. Reliquit 3 volumina de origine & gestis Francorum: tractatum de viris illustribus: chronicon Hirsaugiense: steganographiam, &c. De Steganographia *Vossius* 1.I. Gramm. Lat. cap. 41. legi poterit. Vid. *Ph. Labbe in B.B. p. 130 & Tom. 1. diss. de S. E. pag. 609. Becman. in Exerc. Theol. pag. 399. Dietericus part 1. Ant. bibl. pag. 205. Ghilinus, vol. 1. pag. 91. Olearius, pag. 268, Naudaeus in B.P. pag. 99.*

The lengthy *Bibliotheca realis universalis,* 1679–85 (318) of Martin Lipenius is more specifically subject-oriented. As he says himself in the preface: "Realem vocamus, ut a Nominibus distinguamus. Hic enim prima nobis cura est de rebus & materiis." The entries are thus ordered purely alphabetically on the basis of the subject content, whereby it becomes clear that the title is the basis rather than the subject of the book, for the author has been misled as, for example, to include the following item under Alphabet (in the vol. "Realis theologica"): "Joh. Fromilii Speise-Kammer; das ist: Schöne Geistl. Lehre-Vermahnungs- ... und trostreiche Gnaden-Sprüche auß H. Schrifft / u. in Ordnung des Alphabeten verfasset" (I, 28b). Under "Amor divini incentiva" we find Kuhlmann's "Himmlische Liebes-Küsse. Jena 8. 1672" (I, 33b).

A good example of his organisation, in the same volume, is the listing: "Funeralia, funebria, c. Exequialia; It. Bibl. Jurid. & Philosoph" (Col. 710bff.). These are divided into "I in genere" (with a cross-reference to "Conciones Funebres") and "II In specie." In part I the entries are alphabetical, e.g., "Andr. Gryphii Leich-Abdanckungen auf alle Fälle gerichtet. Breßlau 8." Sermons for individuals are ordered by country and by class, i.e., beginning with the Emperor, then kings etc. Lutheran theologians are group 5 and these and others in group 6 are listed alphabetically by the name of the person honoured. There is no author index.

A work which is specifically referred to as a *Bibliotheca universalis* was produced by Theophil Spitzel in 1686 (452). However, his universal bibliography is only a sample included with a lengthy list of theological manuscripts. This *specimen nova bibliothecae universalis* has entries from Abacuch to Abzud only, i.e. for Ab. A similar and even more extensive undertaking was the massive *Pandectae Brandenburgicae* of Christopher Hendreich, 1699 (231). According to Bestermann this work lists 15,000 writers and yet it advances from A to the end only of B (Bzovius). As an example the entry for Belial runs to nineteen lines concerning versions of the Processus Belial, at the end of which is a reference: "V. Supra Ayrerus." Under "Ayrer Iac. J.U.D. & Advocatus Norib." numerous Latin works are cited including the reference: "Sub ficto casu diaboli accusantis D.N.J.C. tanquam eversoris inferni sui, modum monstrat processum juris formandi"; and the article concludes "Huius forsan etiam est: Opus Theatricum, seu XLVI Comoediae & Tragoediae varii argumenti German. Norib. 1618.F." Like so many other such large projects it was doomed to failure, being far beyond the scope of any one man.

Not all of course of such general, encyclopedic works were incomplete or as incomplete as Spitzel or Hendreich. Some were completed, and they vary from the relatively useful such as König's above-mentioned *Bibliotheca vetus et nova* and Johann Jacob Hofmann's *Lexikon universale,* 1677 (241) to the purely superficial and unanalytical such as the *Bibliographia historico-politico-philogica curiosa* edited by Samuel Schottel in 1677 and reprinted in 1696 (434). Their references are in any case necessarily brief when compared with those of the bibliographies proper. Compare, for example, the entry for Gessner in Labbé (2 pages) or Hottinger (15 pages) with this entry in Hofmann: "Conradus Gesnerus Medicus et Historiographus insignis, Tigurinus. Bibliothecae auctor, aliorumque operum. Obiit an. 1565 aet. 49."

Despite the polyhistoric trend the number and variety of specialised bibliographies increased rapidly toward the end of the seventeenth century. One of the chief concerns of bibliographers at this time was the elucidation of cryptonyma, that is to say the establishment of the authorship of the large number of works that were published without an author's name, with an incorrect name, or with mysterious initials; or were taken without acknowledgement from earlier works. One of the oldest examples of this kind of research is the establishment by the church of the canon of genuine biblical writings. The primary impetus during the humanistic period was provided by the necessity of distinguishing between different, usually classical, authors of the same name, and later also by the propensity of the humanists for translating their own names into Latin or Greek equivalents.

The study of homonyms (here restricted to the sense of identical names) led to references already in Gessner, but this particular aspect was soon separated from the study of anonyms and pseudonyms (and "initialonyms"), although the major work in the field, namely Johannes Moller's *Homonymoscopia* did not appear until 1697 in Hamburg.[15] A number of early essays in the general field of anonymous and pseudonymous works began to appear about the middle of the seventeenth century, the earliest being perhaps in Heinrich Ernst's *Variarum observationum libri duo* (1636), II, 154–61 (153).[16] However, none of these early works was in any way extensive, the longest list, by Petrus Scavenius, containing no more than a hundred names, and none of them distinguished adequately between the various types and degrees of anonymity. This latter point was first dealt with at length by Adrien Baillet in his *Auteurs deguisez*, 1690 (30). It was left to Vincent Placcius to organise and classify all the existing material and greatly to enlarge upon it.

Placcius' first work, the *De scriptis et scriptoribus anonymis et pseudonymis syntagma* appeared in 1674 (398). In this work he printed lists of authors uncovered by his predecessors, Rhodius and Scavenius, and added a great number of his own, in all 617 anonymous and 909 pseudonymous writings. He viewed this as a beginning only, however, and proceeded to enlist the aid of numerous correspondents and collaborators in the attempt to produce a definitive work. Among the more famous men, with whom he was in contact, were Bayle, Fabricius, Leibniz, and Magliabecchi. Placcius did not live to see his work published, but it appeared in 1708 under the title *Theatrum*

15 For a criticism of Moller see the preface to Reimmann's *Versuch einer Einleitung...* (413).

16 The earliest work in Germany seems to be that by Friedrich Geissler, whose *Disputatio de mutatione nominum* (177) took place on April 29, 1669. His thesis consists of two parts: an analysis of the legal position and an analysis of the reasons for anonymity. The latter part concludes with a list of three "decades" (tens) of discovered anonymous works. The first item in the second decade is Emperor Maximilian's "Thewr-Danck."

anonymorum et pseudonymorum and "exposed" according to Bestermann about 10,000 names. It became a standard authority and with supplements by Heumann in 1711 *(De Libris anonymis)* and Mylius in 1740 *(Bibliotheca anonymorum et pseudonymorum)* remained the authoritative work into the nineteenth century. Although it is from a scholarly point of view sound and bibliographically accurate, for example in matters of citation, neither Placcius nor the supplements, especially Mylius, are conveniently indexed.

Bibliographies of anonymous and pseudonymous works were not the only ones to deal with some aspect of form (in a general sense) rather than with content. In 1688 Almeloveen published a bibliography in a closely related field, namely of works which authors had announced but failed to produce, *Bibliotheca promissa et latens* (10). Among the entries in this fascinating collection we find the following article on Kuhlmann:

> KULMANNUS (Quirinus) juvenis ingenio non destitutus in Prodromo suo quinquenii mirabilis, & in epistolis de arte magna sciendi, seu de combinatoria, magno apparatu promisit artes magnas ut vocat, *artem* nempe *magnam eloquentiae solutae & ligatae: artem magnam sciendi, artem magnam scribendi, linguas discendi,* commentandi, Critices & multa alia: quae ille quasi divino spiritu edoctus proponere hominibus voluit, ut essent prodigiorum ac miraculorum instar. Verum hactenus praeter titulos non vidimus. Morhof. Pol. Liter. L.1. c. 18 p. 233 (p. 27).

Almeloveen's list is organised alphabetically by surname, whereas the *Censura celebriorum authorum* of Thomas Blount (69) is ordered chronologically. This odd bibliographical work (indexed by surnames with dates appended) lists the works written by authors and criticisms of them. Among bibliographers included are Gessner, Labbé, Naudé, and Tritheim. Gessner for example is treated in almost two full pages with quotations ranging from the simplistic, such as " 'decus immortale' Casaub. in Athen. 1.7.C. 18" and " 'erat homo stupendae eruditionis'. König. in Biblioth." to twenty-seven lines from Morhof's *Polyhistor.*

The rapid growth of interest in collecting books and therefore also in the history of printing and publishing per se led inevitably to research on the earliest period of printing. One of the first signs of interest in this field is the publication in Amsterdam in 1688 of van Beughem's *Incunabula typographiae* (48). Cornelius van Beughem was one of the important figures in bibliography at the end of the seventeenth century and more will be said of his work later. In this instance he is of course not the first to be concerned with incunabula since lists had already been made, for example, by Saubert in his history of the Nuremberg library (1643). It is, however, the first work specifically devoted to a systematic listing of incunabula and as such is, despite our vastly greater knowledge of the printing production of the sixteenth century, of considerable historical interest.

The same kind of interest that led to the *Incunabula typographiae* also led to a number of works on "rare books." The term had rather wider application in the eighteenth century and the published lists of rarities include many items that would not be considered nowadays to have been rare. It is, however, an interesting fact that concern with rare books as a class, with the definition of rarity, and with the listing of raria, is an almost exclusively German preoccupation in the eighteenth century. The standard work was Johannes Vogt's *Catalogus librorum rariorum* (491), which was first published in 1732 and reissued several times, in the course of which the number of items listed grew from 860 to 5,000 (by 1793). As an example of how Vogt categorises these rare books, which he defines in detailed premises at the beginning of the work, the following entries are taken from the (2nd) 1738 edition: Under Tritheim are listed the *Steganographia* (Frankfurt 1608 and Darmstadt 1621), the *Polygraphia* (Frankfurt 1550), and the *Liber octo quaestionum,* "Scriptum ob raritatem suam minus cognitum, quod nec inter opera Trithemii junctim edita extat." For Florian Trefler the entry reads: "Trefler: *Methodus ordinandi Bibliothecam.* Augusta 1560. Rarissimus liber, non quidem ob suam prae-stantiam, sed potius ob futilitatem regularum parum congruarum, quas praescribit. V. Wendler dissert. de Libr. rarior. XXVI."

In addition to the general bibliographies which still tend to be markedly biographical there are also many more subject bibliographies. These become increasingly frequent and more comprehensive from about the middle of the seventeenth century on. The majority of them are now of no great significance, although they may yield valuable biographical and bibliographical information about minor and forgotten figures in the various disciplines. As examples from the early and late years of the period under review Pierre Borel's *Bibliotheca chimica,* 1654 (80) and Brückmann's *Bibliotheca animalis,* 1743 (93) may be cited. These two works also serve to illustrate some of the changes which took place over the period of a hundred years. Borel's work is sub-titled *catalogus librorum philosophicorum hermeticorum* etc., reminding us that terminology, especially in titles, may be very misleading. Chemistry is here still largely alchemy and includes also a variety of other more or less philosophical and theoretical works. In the same way the word philosophy in the terminology not only of the seventeenth but also of the early eighteenth century may be used for any one of a number of disciplines or to include a large variety of fields, as was seen above in the case of the *Bibliotheca Thuana.* Brückmann's work on the other hand is symptomatic of changes taking place about the middle of the eighteenth century. Although the title is in Latin, as are also most of the books listed, the sub-title reads *Verzeichniss der meisten Schriften so von Thieren und deren Theilen handeln, was hiervon sowohl, Theologi, J Cti, Medici, Historici, als auch Chymici, Physici und Jäger geschrieben . . .* Although a great deal of the material is therefore traditional, there is an indication that more practical viewpoints have been included. Furthermore, the compiler sometimes adds explanatory or critical comments and these too are in German. For example, Gessner's works are listed with their editions in some detail; of his *Historia*

Animalium Brückmann writes "Ist ein groß weitläuftg [sic] Werck, welches von den thieren viel historische und physicalische Anmerckungen in sich fasset; nachdem es aber eine blosse Collection, so sind auch viel falsche Sachen darin."

Such subject bibliographies and general indexes are merely developments (usually in the direction of specialisation) from existing forms. The new features in bibliography at the end of the seventeenth century, features which become characteristic for the eighteenth century, were the "literary histories" and the scholarly journals.[17] The first genuine learned periodicals date from the latter half of the seventeenth century, the earliest significant one in Germany being the *Acta eruditorum* (1682–).[18] The importance of many of these journals for bibliography lies in the fact that they took over the function that had originally been performed by scholarly correspondence, that is, they provided information about scholarly activities undertaken or recently completed. The extent and depth of coverage as well as the material covered varied very widely, some of the journals concentrating on more personal matters such as degrees, appointments, etc., e.g., the *Novae literariae Germaniae* (1703–09), others on reviewing literary works past and present. Of those journals that concentrated on book reviewing, some did so on an ad hoc basis currently and retrospectively, while others selected works largely retrospectively on an individual and personal basis. An example of the former kind is the *Neuer Bücher-Saal der gelehrten Welt oder ausführliche Nachrichten von allerhand neuen Büchern und andern zur heutigen Historie der Gelehrsamkeit gehörigen Sachen,* 1710– (375). As an exemplification of the latter undertaking reference can be made to Siegmund Baumgarten's *Hallische Bibliothek* (38) which began publication in 1748 and ceased in 1757/58. In this journal the author reviews at length and on the basis of personal selection works primarily from his own library, since, as he points out in the preface, most journals concentrate on reviewing *new* books. The reviews are in many cases quite extensive and attained the very respectable total of 2,774 before the journal ceased publication.

Baumgarten was following a tradition of one-man journal that had been set – at least in this field – as far back as Thomasius and Stolle.[19] One of the weaknesses in fact of these periodicals is the sometimes intensely personal bias of the book selection and criticism. Such journals in all their varied forms are, however, a particularly important facet of early and mid-eighteenth century letters and one which provides important bibliographical information. The

---

17 The basic work on early journals (to 1900) is Joachim Kirchner, *Das deutsche Zeitschriftenwesen, seine Geschichte und seine Probleme* (Wiesbaden, I ²1958, II 1962). See also Robert Prutz, *Geschichte des deutschen Journalismus* (Hannover, 1845).
18 Preceded only by the *Miscellanea curiosa medico-physica* (1670–).
19 Christian Thomasius, *Schertz- und ernsthaffter, vernünfftiger und einfältiger Gedancken . . .* (Halle, 1688–90); Gottlieb Stolle, *Kurtze Nachricht von den Büchern und deren Urhebern in der stollischen Bibliothec* (Jena, 1733–43).

number of journals founded is astonishingly large (according to Kirchner 811 were founded prior to 1750: 58 before 1700, 64 1701–10, 119 1711–20, 134 1721–30, 176 1731–40, 260 1741–50) and, while it is not surprising that few of them lasted more than a year or so, some became very influential as critical organs. One at least, the *Göttingische gelehrte Anzeigen* (originally *Die Göttingischen Zeitungen von gelehrten Sachen*), has had an unbroken tradition since 1739.

One of the problems that periodicals posed for scholars from the outset was that of locating specific items of interest. Few of them ever contained an index and then only of the most rudimentary kind. This need for an index to periodical literature was recognised at a very early stage by one of the keenest bibliographers of the end of the seventeenth century, Cornelius van Beughem. At about the same time that Morhof was working on his massive *Polyhistor* (see below), the Dutch biblographer compiled an index to one of the earliest and best known of journals, namely *La France scavante* (1665–   ); this was published in 1683. Van Beughem then extended his project to include in his *Apparatus ad historiam literariam,* 1689 (47) and subsequent volumes several of the leading European learned periodicals of the day. According to Bestermann the five volumes which Beughem produced cover over 20,000 items. The 1689 volume, for example, excerpts nine journals from Germany, France, and England and lists items alphabetically by the name of the author discussed (there is an appendix of titles of anonymous works). Since the journals excerpted are all review organs, van Beughem's work is essentially an index to, or review of, reviews.

Only one other work appeared in this field at this early date, Christian Juncker's *Schediasma historicum* (278). His work was, however, not an index but a listing of European scholarly journals with information as to their editors, frequency of appearance, etc., and with some comment on the nature and standard of the material published. The *Acta eruditorum,* for example, are discussed in over twenty pages. Although the journals listed (ca. 50) are primarily German, French, and English, journals in other European languages are included. Since the term *Ephemeriden* crops up frequently at this period, it is perhaps worthwhile quoting Juncker's definition:

> Nec perperam fortassis dici potest: Ephemerides eruditorum esse libros, in quibus vel per septimanas, vel per menses annumve editis non libri modò vulgati sed & alia doctorum monumenta, diverso scribendi genere, in usum publicum & promovenda rei literariae causá, vel a singulis Viris vel integris Societatibus recensentur. (A5ᵛ)

These works by van Beughem and Juncker appear to have been ahead of their time, for none received favourable comment, and there were no continuators or imitators. (The 1747 edition of Morhof's *Polyhistor* contains a "Brevis notitia alphabetica ephemeridum literarium" by J. J. Schwabe which lists about 1000 items to that date.) It was to be another century before any serious attempt was again made to cope bibliographically with the flood of material contained in periodicals. By that time the list alone of titles of journals published in the years 1700–1790 was to occupy 360 pages![20]

The other major development of the late seventeenth century, the publication of *Literargeschichten,* becomes equally characteristic of the eighteenth century, but from a bibliographical point of view is rather more problematic. These works have their origin in the polyhistorical approach which derives its authority to some extent ultimately from Bacon's concept of knowledge as expressed in his *Of the proficience and advancement of learning,* 1605 (28). The earliest work in Germany appears to be Peter Lambecius's *Liber primus prodromi historiae literariae,* published in 1659 (309). This was followed by Valentin Heinrich Vogler's *Introductio universalis in notitiam cuiuscunque generis bonorum scriptorum,* 1670 (490), Burkhard Struve's *Introductio ad notitiam rei litterariae,* 1704 (460) and J. F. Reimann's *Versuch einer Einleitung in die Historiam literariam,* 1708 (413). Through the rest of the eighteenth century and in fact until the middle of the nineteenth century there is a steady flow of such works, most of them heavily dependent on their predecessors. The more notable of the works of the eighteenth century are those by Struve, Heumann, and Reimmann.

The basic premise of these works, as reported above, is that all detailed study must be preceded by a general survey of knowledge in the field, and that this can best be achieved by an historical survey of the progress of scholarly literature since its beginnings. This view is frequently expressed in definitions of *historia literaria* preceding these works; the following are just three examples:

> Die historia literaria ist eine Historie, darinnen dasjenige in gebührender Klarheit und Wahrheit vorgetragen wird / was denen curieusen Gemüthern von dem Schicksaal der Gelehrsamkeit und derer Gelehrten insonderheit zu wissen nöthig/ nützlich und vergnüglich ist.
>
> (Reimmann)
>
> Historia literaria est Historia literatum et literatorum, sive narratio de ortu et progressu studiorum literariorum ad nostram usque aetatem.
>
> (Heumann)
>
> Die Geschichte der Gelehrsamkeit ist Darstellung der äussern Bildung und der vornehmsten Schicksale der gelehrten Kenntnisse des menschlichen Geistes.
>
> (Meusel)

To us the attempt to cover the development of scholarship in every field of endeavour and in every part of the world since Adam seems little short of ludicrous. Even allowing for the fact that the quantity of published material (or the record of what had earlier been published) was very much less, it is obvious

---

20   J. H. C. Beutler, *Allgemeines Sachregister* (50), discussed in the following chapter.

that these historical surveys are very incomplete and the bibliographical references very selective. In the majority of these works, however, the greater part of the space is devoted to long lists of works on every conceivable subject and to this extent they may therefore be likened to the earlier universal bibliographies, even though the approach and the organisation are quite different. Their primary value as bibliographies lies in the provision of ordered lists of books which were considered at that time to be authoritative. Since each author built on his predecessor and endeavoured to bring his own work up to date, they also give us insight into the development and contemporary state of scholarship in the various fields. Morhof and Reimmann may serve as examples, the former being of particular interest in that his incomplete work nevertheless covers the area of literature and because he was recognized at least through the first half of the eighteenth century as an authority.

Daniel Georg Morhof (1639–91) was appointed Professor at the newly established University of Kiel in 1665; in 1680 he became also university librarian. Among his numerous publications are the *Unterricht von der teutschen Sprache und Poesie* (1682), but he is best known for his *Polyhistor, sive notitia auctorum et rerum commentarii. Quibus praeterea varia ad omnes disciplines concilia et subsidia proponuntur* (360/61). This was not complete at his death, two parts of the first tome only having appeared at Lübeck in 1688. The remaining part of the first tome was published in 1692 and the first tome republished together with tomes two and three (edited from his notes) in 1707. Other editions followed in 1714 and 1732. For the purpose of this discussion reference is made to the fourth edition: *Polyhistor, literarius, philosophicus et practicus cum accessionibus . . . Ioannis Frickii et Iohannis Molleri* (Lübeck, 1747), since this edition has recently been reprinted.

The first three books are an introduction to general studies, which Morhof justifies with reference to earlier writers, including Bacon. Since knowledge is derived from books, these first "libri" are devoted to "indirect" bibliographical sources, i.e. to those who have written (or write) about books. These sections are in effect a bibliography of bibliographies (of bibliographies) and the later editors have placed before them a list of "ephemeridum literarium" (as noted above). These are in the main reviewing journals.

Of these three books entitled "Liber bibliothecarius," "Liber methodicus," and "Liber parasceuasticos" the first is the most extensive and from the bibliographical point of view most interesting. After chapters devoted to "Polymathia" and "Historia literaria" there are four chapters on libraries before Morhof comes to manuscripts and books. After further chapters on academic societies etc., he returns to writers ". . . ad rem librariam . . ." and covers in this and the following two chapters ("de scriptoribus bibliothecariis, de catalogorum scriptoribus") many bibliographers and library catalogues, including those we have discussed. As an example of his style the following quotation is taken from Chapter 16: "De scriptoribus ad rem librariam."

& quidem primo loco hic ponemus
VALENTINUM HENRICUM VOGLERUM, Professorem Medicum Helm-
stadiensem, cujus extat *universalis in notitiam cujusque generis bonorum Scriptorum Introductio,* Helmstadii An. 1670. in 4. edita. Vir fuit ille doctissimus, &
vastum hoc argumentum ὡς ἐν τύπῳ proposuit. Rudimentum ergo non
spernendum est, & quasi ichnographia magni operis. Generatim agit de modis,
quibus Scriptorum notitia possit acquiri, & omnes inde Autores illos recenset, qui
de Scriptoribus certarum disciplinarum, nationum, summariam recensionem insti-
tuerunt. Sed multa tamen in illo desideres. Nam in generali illa Synopsi non omnia
complexus est, quae dici poterant. Ejus supplementum meditatur VINCENTIUS
PLACCIUS, Gymnasii Hamburgensis Professor, vir clarissimus. Id quoque e Voglero
discimus e cap. 5. istius libri, extare HERMANNI CONRINGII Opus eruditum *de
universa eruditionis a nato Christo propagatione,* ejusdemque *de Scriptoribus*
commentarium privatis lectionibus ab illo conceptum, qui multorum commoda
adjuturus esset, eo judice, si lucem viderit. Verum compendiarius plane libellus ejus
est, quem vidi, *de eruditionis propagatione,* commentariolus Chronologicus, in quo
per singula secula quinque illa capita proponit. I. De Scriptoribus Ecclesiasticis &
Judaicis. 2. De Scriptoribus Philosophicis. 3. De Jurisconsultis. 4. De Medicis. 5. De
Historicis, Oratoribus & Poëtis: quem ego quidem extemporalibus ipsi disser-
tationibus natum suspicor, multis accessionibus augendum, ut est ipse Vogleri liber
longe locupletior. Verum de Scriptoribus commentarium nullum hactenus vidi.

Jakob Friedrich Reimmann (1668–1743), "Superintendent" in Hildesheim, is described in *Meyers Konversations-Lexikon* (1890) as the "Begründer
der Litteraturgeschichte in Deutschland". His *Versuch einer Einleitung in die
Historiam literariam . . .* is divided into six books. 1 introduction to Historia
literaria, 2 the early period, 3 the modern period, 4 "Historia Metaphysicae und
Matheseos," 5 "Historia Politices und Historiae," 6 "Historia Jurisprudentiae
und Medicinae." Since the work is written in question and answer style with
little or no discernible pattern of arrangement other than the chronological
divisions into individual books, the only way to make use of the work now is
through the indexes (by subjects and authors). Taking a couple of random
examples from volume 3, we find "Kuhlmann (Quirinus) 180" discussed in
response to the question: "140 Gib mir doch auch [the previous question was
about Erhard Weigel] von dem Quirinus Kuhlmanno und von seinen neuen
Erfindungen eine kleine Nachricht." About two pages are then devoted to the
works which Kuhlmann had planned and never completed and one page to a
brief account of his travels and fiery end. Looking under Leibniz in the index
we are referred to p. 472 and the question (no. 332): "Wormit hat sich der
Godofredus Guilialmus Leibnizius (a) in rebus Physicis vor andern signali-
siert?"[21] This question gives rise to five pages of discussion of Leibniz's views,
especially with regard to the soul. Here, as elsewhere, Reimann provides

---

21   All the questions are numbered. The index gives page references only.

references in the text and in footnotes to more extensive works. On the whole this is not as useful a work as most of this class, primarily owing to its dialogue form. Such a form was not of course unusual at the time in philosophical and other works, but it was hardly a very practical form for *Literargeschichte.*

A much better organised and successful work was Struve's *Introductio* which ran through many (and varied) editions, including posthumous revisions in 1754 by J. C. Fischer and an expanded version by J. F. Jugler (1754–63) under the title of *Bibliotheca historiae litterariae selecta* (277). Struve also produced some bibliographies, such as the *Bibliotheca philosophica* (459).

Literaturgeschichte as distinct from, although originally a part of, *Literargeschichte,* that is to say, the history of *schöne Literatur,* began to develop on its own after the middle of the eighteenth century and the discursive text of such histories was separated in most cases from comprehensive bibliographies of the same discipline. The strictly bibliographical approach may be said to have culminated in Goedeke's *Grundriß,* while histories of literature have been and still are being written in endless succession. Later developments in the area of *Literargeschichte* will not therefore be considered. Probably the last attempt at a form of *Literargeschichte* – produced under the influence of a different but not entirely unrelated philosophy – was the massive *Handbuch der Literaturwissenschaft,* 1923– (214).

The period from the Thirty Years' War until about the middle of the eighteenth century is characterised by a steady development in subject bibliography and a gradual abandonment of the older concept of universal bibliography. The major new developments, the rise of scholarly periodicals and of *Literargeschichten,* occur almost simultaneously in the latter part of the seventeenth century and both derive a great deal of their impetus from the same polyhistorical approach, the attempt to cover in an organised and related, even if necessarily somewhat perfunctory, fashion the sum of knowledge in all fields since the beginning of time. This was the age of the rationalist and encyclopedist.

In all of this the scholar was the dominant figure, since the important point was the ordering of knowledge not of books. The book trade took a long time to recover from the effects of the Thirty Years' War, but by the beginning of the eighteenth century was flourishing again, and publishing in the vernacular was increasing. The trade contributed little, however, to bibliography during this period – apart that is from the fair catalogues, and the Frankfurt catalogue ceased in 1749.[22]

---

22 One exception is worth noting in passing, namely Simon Paulli, who appears to have been a scholar bookseller. He published an *Historia literaria, sive dispositio librorum omnium facultatum ac artium, secundum materias, in usum philobiblorum* (Strasburg, 1671) and a sales catalogue: *Catalogi librorum in bibliopolo Argentinensi Simonis Paulli venalium* (Strasburg, 1670–71). The former is not, however, properly a *Literarge-*

The rapid advances made in research and above all the enormous increase in publications of all kinds — the "information explosion" in fact of the early eighteenth century — led to frequent lamentations about the impossibility of keeping abreast with new developments. As yet there was no break with the older, historically oriented tradition of scholarship, but the stage had been reached at which it was essential to keep systematic records of what was published *as* it was published, since it was no longer possible for any one individual to survey the whole mass of present and past material or even for a library to acquire more than a very small proportion of this material.

schichte, but an organised list of works suitable for a general course of study such as envisioned in *Historia literaria.* In the edition used (British Library) the printing is on one side only, presumably in order to allow for updating. The catalogue is a not dissimilar listing of titles available through his bookshop.

Chapter 4

From 1750 to the middle of the nineteenth century

It should not be assumed that the year 1750 marks the abrupt beginning of a new era in bibliography, although it is not without significance that the Frankfurt Fair Catalogues cease with 1749 and that Kayser's *Bücher-Lexikon* later covers the period *from* 1750. Older style bibliographies continue to appear through the eighteenth and into the nineteenth century despite the expansion of newer forms developed early in the eighteenth century and despite the rise of further new forms in the latter half of the century. There are two general factors which determine the choice of 1750 as an appropriate point at which to begin a new chapter in bibliography, the one primarily intellectual, the other of a more practical nature.

In the first place it is at about this time that the study of German literature — which is our primary concern — that is to say, the study of the history of literary works in the vernacular and contemporary developments in the same, comes to be recognized as an academic discipline. Symptomatic of the new attitude toward the history of literature is an organisation such as J. B. Mencke's Deutschübende poetische Gesellschaft, which included among its plans the production of a history of German literature. This particular organisation became the Deutsche Gesellschaft under Gottsched and an important factor in the development of literature, even if it did not become the German equivalent of the Académie Française as Gottsched had hoped. In 1732—44 there appeared under the aegis of this society the *Beiträge zur critischen Historie der deutschen Sprache, Poesie und Beredsamkeit* — in some sense a partial realisation of the earlier hopes of the society under Mencke (51). It is probably too much to see a genuine history of German literature in the *Critische Beiträge,* but Kirchner claims at least, "daß in dieser Zeitschrift das nationale Schrifttum zum ersten Male als eigenes wissenschaftliches Fachgebiet behandelt [wird] (I, 64). Nearer the middle of the century there appear the first specialist journals such as the *Beitrage zur Historie und Aufnahme des Theaters* (52),[1] while one of the early nineteenth century bibliographers dates the beginning of German studies from 1752 (below p. 86). Kirchner himself writes: "So machen sich um die Mitte des Jahrhunderts und in der Folgezeit weitere Veränderungen geltend, die eine neuerliche wesentliche Ausweitung des Zeitschriftenwesens bedeuten" (Kirchner, I, 72).

The second major factor in setting the break at around 1750 is the development of the booktrade. Massive developments in publishing — the

---

1 Kirchner notes several journals on the theatre shortly after 1750, but none earlier.

development in fact of a large consumer-oriented publishing industry – were leading to a new attitude toward the book as such. "In der zweiten Hälfte des 18. Jahrhunderts stand die Öffentlichkeit . . . einer Fülle von Phänomenen auf dem Büchermarkt gegenüber, die, zuvor nicht oder nur in weit geringerem Umfang vorhanden, nun mit explosiver Gewalt die tradierten Normen des Schreibens, Lesens und Handelns mit Büchern zu sprengen drohten."[2] The bookseller who could say, "meine Wahren sind von und vor niemand als Gelehrten,"[3] was no longer typical. Typical of the new generation was Philipp Emmanuel Reich with his business instinct, his "Unternehmungsgeist," and above all his desire to see the publishing world join together in a union that would be both protective and productive (discussed below).[4] This period coincides in fact not only with the introduction of the modern system of business in the book world, but also with the early attempts at and eventual success in establishing the association of publishers known as the Börsenverein.

The events in the publishing world as well as the intellectual climate in Germany must be seen against the background of international developments, such as the influence of Enlightenment philosophy, and of national politics. The continuing problems of reprints and copyright, for example, are inextricably bound up with the political developments in the German states. Important as these factors may be, they cannot be discussed here. It can only be emphasized that both the growth of interest in German literature and its past and the growth of a publishing industry are closely connected with the growth of national consciousness in Germany. The net result in the bibliographical field is an increasing emphasis on purely German materials.

Although the middle of the eighteenth century may be viewed as a turning-point it is still not yet the beginning of the truly modern period in bibliography. Rather it ushers in a period of transition which lasts for almost one hundred years. German literature may have been seen as an academic discipline by the middle of the eighteenth century, but bibliography was still seen in much wider terms both in academic circles and in the burgeoning publishing trade. New types of bibliography were created in this period, some of them relevant to the study of German literature; but by and large literature to the academic still meant scholarly writing on any topic, while the publisher or bookseller was primarily interested in developing tools that would include more rather than less of what was published. As a result of the rapid development of a mass market for recreational and informational (non-

---

2 Wittman, col. 619–20 (511).
3 Adrian Beier, *Kurzer Bericht von der nützlichen und fürtrefflichen Buchhandlung* (Bremen, 1690).
4 On Reich and his reform plans see F. Kapp and J. A. Goldfriedrich, *Geschichte des deutschen Buchhandels* (Leipzig, 1886–), especially vol. 3, chap. 1. Cf. the entry in the *ADB*.

scholarly) literature, the interests of scholars and publishers began to diverge. The former began to move toward narrowly discipline-oriented bibliographies, the latter toward lists intended to be unselective and as complete as possible.

Although there were still general bibliographies, journals, and so forth in the middle of the nineteenth century, this process of specialisation was virtually complete by then, but reference will still have to be made in this chapter to general (and scholarly) bibliographies, both national and international. For the most part these do not represent any new departure and may therefore be treated cursorily. At the same time the newer kinds of bibliography become progressively less scholarly as they become more comprehensive. Nevertheless they too must be considered as bibliographical sources − and despite their numerous, all too obvious faults − since academic specialization in the humanities had not reached the point at which disciplinary bibliographies were felt to be an essential part of the discipline and since academic specialization at all periods implies a degree of selection. The general bibliographies are particularly important for the earlier part of this period, since in the early days of mass production much was produced that has been lost from sight, if not lost entirely.

To begin with, *Literargeschichten* continued to be written or reprinted well into the nineteenth century, even though the attempt was rarely now made to cover the whole history of human research from the time of Adam. Typical for the late eighteenth century was perhaps Heinrich Wilhelm Lawätz's massive *Handbuch für Bücherfreunde und Bibliothekare,* 1788–95 (312). At the beginning of the second edition of this work (1793) Lawätz reprinted the notice he had earlier published concerning the aims and arrangements of his work under the title *Bibliographie interessanter und gemeinnütziger Kenntnisse* (1791). According to this his plan was to print "Die möglichst richtigen und möglichst vollständigen Titel derjenigen interessanten und gemeinnützigen einzelnen Abhandlungen, Dissertationen und Bücher aller Zeitalter, Nationen und Sprachen" (p. VII). To each title he adds an indication of the contents of the work, its acceptance (reviews), and its price. The work appeared in separate volumes for the various disciplines; within each volume the order is largely, if not completely, alphabetical by subject. In addition there are fairly detailed indexes. In the index to part I, for example, "Von der Gelehrsamkeit überhaupt," there are 46 entries under "Bibliographie," ranging from "Alterthümer" and "Anatomie" through "Geschichte," "Litteratur," etc., to "Zoologie." The reference under "Allgemeine Litteratur" (i.e., *historia litteraria*) (II, 577) leads to citations of Cornelius à Beughem, Lambecius, Jugler, Reimmann, and Struve.

Johann Gottfried Eichhorn's much shorter *Litterärgeschichte der drey letzten Jahrhunderte,* 1805–11 (146) attempts to cover the period from 1450 and is divided into "Geschichte der Gelehrsamkeit im allgemeinen" and "Im einzelnen" with division in the latter part (the former is only 74 pages) into

"Geschichte der schönen Redekünste in den neuern gebildeten Sprachen" and "Geschichte der Wissenschaften" (philology, history, philosophy, anthropology, natural sciences, medicine, law, and theology). Some idea of the extent of this work may be gained from the fact that German language and literature occupy only 90 pages (339–428). Here as elsewhere throughout the work there are approximately equal amounts of apodictic commentary and lists of relevant critical literature.

The last work on a grand scale in this particular genre is Graesse's six-volume *Lehrbuch einer allgemeinen Literärgeschichte* (202) published between 1837 and 1859 (with its abbreviated versions: *Handbuch der allgemeinen Literaturgeschichte,* 1845–50). Graesse's goal is "eine ganz genau sich über alle Theile der Wissenschaften verbreitende und die Literatur aller bekannten Völker umfassende Literärgeschichte" (p. VIII) and the need for such a work arises, he claims, from the inadequacies of earlier works, chiefly from the uneven treatment of less easily accessible areas. Graesse's own work is divided into four epochs, viz., from the creation to Moses (ca. 1500 B.C.); from 1500 B.C. to 476 A.D. (fall of Rome); from 476 to 1453 (fall of Constantinople); from 1453 to 1836. The text consists of perfunctory historical outlines followed by masses of bibliographical references. The lack of any formal outline of the arrangement and the brevity of the indexes make it difficult to locate specific topics and the reader is virtually forced to leaf through the lengthy sections without even the aid of detailed running heads. Thus in the introduction to volume 2 "Literärgeschichte des Mittelalters" – part one to 1100 – under § 14 (p. 47) the history of Germany in the Middle Ages is reduced to a handful of sententia together with seven pages of references, ranging from histories of literature to broad biographical dictionaries. The list of works on German medieval literature proper is found under B. Poesie, § 28 and is quite comprehensive (pp. 414–20).

This "universalist" approach in bibliography is also evident in the work of what might be supposed to be more practically oriented compilers. The bookseller Georgi, for example, in his *Allgemeines europäisches Bücher-Lexikon,* 1742–58 (179), attempted to put together a list of books in all fields for all the countries of Europe from the sixteenth century on. Using his own experience in the book-trade and familiar reference works (Fair Catalogues, etc.), he claims in the first preface to have included over 120,000 titles. The chief novelty of his work lies in its arrangement, in that each work is ordered by author surname, catchword, or subject entry and everything squeezed into a series of columns. The entry of the central, alphabetically ordered column therefore begins either with the surname or the main word of the title, or with a superimposed subject, while the Christian name or the first words of the title appear in the preceding column. An additional novelty is the inclusion of a statement of the length of the work in signatures and, where possible, the price. The following is a brief excerpt:

120   GED   GEG

Jahr		Titel	Ort	Bog.	thl	gr.
1733	Wohlgegründete	Gedancken Scherz = und ernsthaffte, von der Meynung als einer Mutter aller Irrthümer 8	Cölln.			
1737	Zufällige	Gedancken über eines vornehmen Theologi Betrachtung der Augspurgischen Confeßion, die darinnen gebrauchte Wolffische Philosophie betreffend 4	Dreßden. Heckel.	38	—	8
1738		2ter Theil 4		30	—	8
		Gedanensium Disput. Theol. v. Diss.				
	Christliches	Gedenck = Büchlein zu Beförderung eines Christlichen Lebens 18	Frf. Zunners.	4	—	1
1731		id. Libr. 18	Leipzig. Walther		—	1
1685		nebst 4. andern geistreichen Tractätlein 18	Hamb. Wolff.	12	—	3
1711		id Lib. 12	— Leidenroth	14	—	3
1691		zur Erneurung des inwendigen Menschen, samt Erklärung des 8ten Capitels an die Römer 12	Hamburg.			
1715		Gedenck = Schrifften van de Regieringe van Peter den Grooten, IV. Vol. 8	St. Gravensh.			
1696	1000. Merckw.	Gedenck = Sprüche aus unterschiedenen Autoribus zusammen gezogen, in Versen 8		14	—	3
1611	1632. Simon.	Gedicii Auslegung des 1. Buchs Mosis, 6. Theile f.	Leipzig. Grosse.	631	4	8
1609		Erklärung der Evangelien f.		329	2	16
1615		Calviniana Religio, oder Calvinisteren, so fälschlich die Reformirte Religion genennet wird 8				
1707		Gedichte, auserlesene, Poetische, Hochzeit = Begrädtniß = und Ehren = , 2 Packet.	Quedl. Strunk.	17	—	3
1702	Auferweckte	Gedichte und politische Gedancken S. v. G. 8	Stettin. Plener.	24	—	5
1701	1704	Helden = , Schäfer = und Uberschrifften 8	Hamb. Hertel.	14	—	3
1709		Vorrath allerhand curiöser Ged. oder Etwas für alle Menschen, 10. Parthien 8	Görlitz. Rohrl.	66	—	20
1718		Poetische Ergötzlichkeiten, Sinceri 8	Rostock. Fritsch.	10	—	3
1718		ersten Früchte der grünenden Jugend im Rosenthal 8		9	—	2
1702		die christliche Vesta und irrdische Flora 8		4u.f.	—	10
1729		von H. Versuch einiger Gedichte, Proben Poet. Neben = Stunden 8	Hamburg.	9	—	2
1721		die von den vortrefflichsten teutschen Poeten verfertigten Meister = Stücke, 4. Theile 8	Rostock.			
1723		geistliche und weltliche, J. J. S.S. 3	Basel.		—	5
1721		des Weissenfelsischen Bauer = Hunds Lob = Gedicht 4	Weisenf. Wehrm.	6	—	2
1727		aufgeweckte und Poetische Ubersezungen berühmter Männer 8	Franckfurt.	10	—	3
1713		eines scharffsinnigen Poeten Trauer = und Freuden = Ged. 4	Stettin. Kunck.	69	—	16
1729		Lob = und Trauer = Gedicht auf das Ableben D. Gottl. Werasdorffens 8	Wittenb. Gerdes.	15	—	4
1730		Poesie der Francken, 1ste Sammlung 8	Frf. Monath.	27	—	16
1729		Poetische Seltsamkeit, 1stes Stück 8	Stockholm.			
1717	Lamp.	Sammlung allerhand sinnreicher 8			—	10
		Gedickens Primitiæ veritatis Religionis Christ. oder Grund = Säze der Christl. Religion 8	Berlin. Gedick.	42	—	10
1736		id. Libr. 8		09	—	18
1718		historischer Unterricht von dem Reformations = Wercke 8		20	—	5
1720		Christliche und bescheidene Vertheidigung der Lutherischen Lehre von der Gegenwart Christi Leib und Bluts im Heil. Abendmahl 4		15	—	4
1725		Abfertigung, Schlossers Anmerckungen hierüber 4		8	—	2
1724		Erklärung der Lutherischen Lehre vom Heil. Abendmahl 4		5	—	1
1726		Amica collatio de æstimatione rationis Theologica 4		3	—	1
1732		Evangelische Aufmunterung zum thätigen Christenthum 4		145	1	12
1571	Peter	Gedultigs Biblische Concordanz, 3. Theile f.	Franckfurt.			
1735	Joh. Jac.	Geelhausen de Usu lactis medica 4	Hagæ.			
1679	Petri	Goeslerani de Constantia Christiana 4	Lugd. B.		—	8
1720	Gründlicher	Gegen = Beweiß, daß die Grafschafft Sayn über ihre Reformirte 2c. f.			—	12
1614	kurtzes	Gegen = Bedencken und Bericht von der Chur = Pfältzischen Vicariats = Gerechtigkeit			—	8
1730		Gegen = Information, die Meklenburgische Sache betreffend 4	Hamburg.			

1710

Needless to say Georgi never completed his work. He produced a volume of German material and followed this with one on French (1753). He then added supplements covering new works in Germany for the years 1739–47 (1750), 1747–54 (1755), and 1755–57 (1758), and included in these volumes addenda from earlier times. The idea behind Georgi's *Bücher-Lexikon,* although it is less selective, is the same that underlies the work of Gessner and others like him. But even given a simpler, alphabetical arrangement, it had long since become impossible to collect everything that had ever appeared in print. As an indication of what was then known about earlier literature and as a list of contemporary literature, particularly of ephemera and on account of the prices cited, Georgi's work has its value. There can be no doubt, however, that it too was completely outmoded, if not at the time of publication, then very shortly thereafter.

Although Georgi's work cannot be considered successful in its time, it is significant for two reasons. In the first place it is the work of a bookseller rather than of a scholar or a collector; and in the second place, although selective, its primary criterion – apparently – is availability rather than academic standing. Early universal bibliographies had listed all works that were considered of academic value, and collectors had adopted the same principle in building their libraries. Whatever was said in catalogues of rare books in theory about the "rarity value" of certain non-academic works, collectors for the most part aimed as yet at the acquisition of what were considered to be the "best" books in all fields of human endeavour, and rare book catalogues, which had begun to appear at the beginning of the eighteenth century, were based on the same principle. By the middle of the century, however, booksellers had to cope with a new kind of demand, one that emanated from a new and less predictable reading public. Although rare book catalogues and catalogues of important private collections were still published, they became less frequent and for our purposes less important. The great age of book collectors and book sales was passing and a sign of the times is the kind of list of best books, an instant library, so to speak, put out by Nicolai first in 1780 and again in expanded form in 1787 under the title of *Verzeichniss einer Handbibliothek der nützlichsten deutschen Schriften zum Vergnügen und Unterricht . . . welche um beygesetzte Preise zu haben sind bey Friedrich Nicolai* (377). Catalogues of rare books are now less important than catalogues of books in print and will therefore not be further mentioned (with the exception of Ebert below).

By the middle of the eighteenth century the rapidly expanding publishing industry was firmly centred on Leipzig. This in no way meant that Leipzig became the source of comprehensive and well-organised bibliographical reference works. The Fair catalogues published there were no better for the cessation of those in Frankfurt; they continued to be incomplete and inaccurate. Complaints about the inadequacy of the Fair catalogues are still a commonplace in the latter part of the eighteenth century[5], and the period is in fact characterised by the endeavours of publishers and booksellers alike to create new and more useful bibliographical tools.

Unfortunately there was no concerted effort to produce either of the two main desiderata defined later by Ebert in his introduction to Kayser's *Deutscher Bücherkunde,* namely the systematic listing on the one hand of new works and on the other of the totality of works available. The various more or less comprehensive bibliographies that were produced are not without their value today, even given the existence of later retrospective works, but they were produced by publisher-booksellers whose interests were primarily commercial. They vary widely, but all suffer from the same kind of faults, chiefly a lack of genuine universality and a considerable degree of inadequacy in the provision of bibliographical data.

Although it is not possible rigidly to classify publishers' catalogues in the eighteenth century, certain general types may be distinguished. To begin with, there were still the lists of house publications, a practice almost as old as printing itself. A well known, early example is that of Oporinus, whose alphabetically arranged *Librorum per Ioannem Oporinum partim excusorum hactenus, partim in eiusdem officina venalium, Index . . .* (382) appeared in Basle in 1552. Such catalogues may be expected to be more reliable where they list house publications than if they list the publications of a multiplicity of possibly unknown publishers. Publishers were, however, as a rule also booksellers and listed therefore books *available* from them rather than only their own books. Such catalogues are in effect what would now be called *Sortimentskataloge,*[6] but they will be referred to here as trade lists.

These lists date back to the end of the seventeenth century and were intended to supplant, supplement, or select from the Fair Catalogues. They only came into real prominence in the eighteenth century, when they were in some cases quite substantial, and they were used in their own time as reference works. There are basically two kinds of trade list, namely the *Messesortiments-katalog* which is based on, and usually appeared subsequent to, the Leipzig Fairs; and the *Lagerkatalog* or stock catalogue. The distinction is not of great importance from a bibliographical point of view. Such comprehensive catalogues with their periodic supplements are on the other hand the source from which the later "national" bibliographies were eventually to grow.

---

5 See, for example, Martin Fontius, "Zur literarhistorischen Bedeutung der Messekataloge im 18. Jahrhundert," *WB,* 7 (1961), 607–16, or for a contemporary comment Frömmichen, "Einige Bemerkungen, welche sich über den deutschen Messkatalog machen lassen," *Deutsches Museum,* 7 (1780), 177ff.

6 Nowadays of course the *Sortimenter* is normally strictly a wholesaler, which distinction did not develop until after the establishment of the Leipziger Börse.

The 1731 edition of the catalogue put out by a Berlin bookseller named Haude, for example, is entitled *Catalogus von alt- und neuen Büchern / welche aus der Franckfurter und Leipziger Michaelis-Messe 1731. Mitgebracht und nebst vielen andern zu haben sind . . ."* (222). After a few pages of academic titles and French books about 250 items are listed. Peter Schmid's catalogue in 1736 (430) claims that there are available "Ausser denen in gegenwärtigen Catalogo befindlichen Bücher . . . noch viele andere in besagten Buchladen," and promises a "Continuatio" every quarter. Neither of these achieved anything like the reputation of Schwetschke's or Monath's catalogues. According to Kapp/Goldfriedrich the former circulated in over 6,000 copies (as against 2,000 of the Fair Catalogue), while the latter listed 75,000 titles in the twenty years from 1784 to 1804 (III, 540—42). Monath's catalogue published in 1782 (357) and covering only A—F in 820 pages itself includes the catalogues of other booksellers, e.g., of Haude und Spener (Berlin) and of Heidegger (Zürich). As a final example Montag and Weiss put out a monthly listing of new books (with an annual index) in the early years of the nineteenth century. The issue for 1814 (Zwölfter Jahrgang) is entitled *Monatliche Anzeige ganz neuer Bücher, welche in der Montag- und Weissischen Buchhandlung in Regensburg um die beygesetzten Preise zu haben sind* (359)[7] and lists approximately 120 books per month. The more extensive of these catalogues are listed in works such as Heinsius and were avidly excerpted by bibliographers.

The main objective of all these and similar trade catalogues was to make information conveniently available about books currently on the market. They were not intended to carry out-of-print books, as Monath himself says: "es sind auch meistens solche, die bei denen Verlegern noch zu haben sind; alte und rar gewordene Schriften, zumahl diejenigen, so ich nicht besize, habe ich mit allem Fleis nicht angeführet" (p. *3r). An important aspect was therefore the statement of price — a not inconsiderable problem in those days of varying currencies within Germany, not to mention variations in price due to transport costs — for it was not until 1828 that prices were given in the Fair Catalogues. The comprehensiveness of many such catalogues was, however, also their greatest weakness, for it took time to assimilate new titles, to organise or re-organise the whole and re-publish it. The greater the volume of production, the longer it took to report on it. Consequently a prompter form of advertisement was needed.

Advertisements of new books had appeared already in the late seventeenth century, for example, in the *Monatliche Unterredungen einiger guten Freunde von allerhand Büchern und andern annehmlichen Geschichten,* 1689— (358), but such advertisements were not common. The journals that were developing

---

7 No publisher or printer given.

at that time were intended to provide scholars with items of topical interest and in the case of books this took the form of reviews. With the increasing mass of publications reviews also increased in number and became more and more specialized on the one hand, while on the other the number of purely "entertaining" journals *(Unterhaltungsblätter)* increased by leaps and bounds. By the latter part of the century the number of review organs was considerable, but despite reductions in the length of reviews they were unable to cope with the flood of material, since they now also included notices of popular works that would have earlier been ignored. Probably the best known review journal is Nicolai's *Allgemeine Deutsche Bibliothek,* 1766– (7), which was founded to provide on a quarterly basis "eine allgemeine Nachricht von der ganzen neuen deutschen Literatur." Its first volume contained 26 major reviews and almost one hundred short notices. Ten years later the problem is still not solved and is succinctly defined at the beginning of the "Vorrede" to a new periodical, the *Allgemeines Verzeichniß neuer Bücher mit kurzen Anmerkungen* (9): "Man hat schon lange geklagt, daß man ungeachtet der großen Menge gelehrter Zeitungen und Monathsschriften den ganzen Umfang aller oder doch der meisten und wichtigsten neuen Schriften niemahls übersehen könne, oder, wenn so etwas möglich seyn sollte, daß es doch mit großen Kosten verbunden sey, und man die neuen Schriften nicht anders als sehr spät kennen lerne . . ." And the writer continues: "Gegenwärtige Monathsschrift ist dazu bestimmt, diesen Klagen, wo nicht ganz, doch größtentheils abzuhelfen. Man wird darin alle neuen Schriften . . . ihrem Titel, ihrem Preise und ihrer Bogenzahl nach anzeigen." The first issue lists 181 items on 54 pages, most with a short characterisation. Two pages of French titles are not commented on.

As a final example of this type of journal and of the development that it represents reference can be made to the *Allgemeine Bibliographie für Deutschland* (6) (1836–, the continuation of *Bibliographie von Deutschland, oder wöchentliches vollständiges verzeichnis der in Deutschland erscheinenden, neuen Bücher, Musikalien und Kunstsachen,* 1826–), in which the attempt is no longer made to comment on any of the works listed. There are still the items of information about price reductions, works forthcoming, works censored, etc., but in the main the editor (E. Avenarius) concentrates on straightforward listing of new works. The journal appeared on a weekly basis with quarterly, cumulated alphabetical and systematic indexes, and the first volume listed no less than 7,300 German works and 3,461 works in other European languages.

Another product of the booksellers' desire to provide timely information about new works was the establishment – or attempted establishment, since none was genuinely successful – of journals published by booksellers, the so-called *Buchhändlerzeitungen.* These journals, which have been discussed in detail by Reinhard Wittmann (511), were not organs for the discussion of problems of concern to the profession as such, but rather a means of communication similar to, and indeed presumably influenced by, the *Intelligenzblätter* of the time. Bauer's *Literarisches Wochenblat*, 1769/70 (320), for example, which is classed by Wittmann as a "Vorform," announced that it "Nachrichten verbreiten will, die jeder Gelehrte, jeder Bücherfreund, jeder Neugierige sucht und achtet" (p. A2^r). The intention was not merely to announce books new and forthcoming, but to list books sought or for sale, to report on personalia, to provide a "Notes and Queries" section, and so forth. From a bibliographical standpoint these short-lived journals have only limited value, but they supplement to a certain extent, and in particular for their locality, the information provided by more general bibliographies, review journals, etc.

By the late eighteenth century the number of periodicals of all kinds, whether ephemeral or not, had reached considerable proportions and one effort at least to document and analyse the wealth of periodical literature deserves mention, namely J. H. C. Beutler's *Allgemeines Sachregister über die wichtigsten deutschen Wochenschriften* (50). In the introduction to this work Beutler speaks in eulogistic terms of periodicals in general,[8] although he is also clearly aware of the problems, dangers, and difficulties involved. His subject index covers unfortunately only eight of the major weeklies, but it is fairly comprehensive, omitting only short notices, anecdotes, etc. The entries are organised alphabetically and there are in many cases short comments or notes. For the most part, however, they are quite brief, for example, the reference to Frömmichen (note 5), which appears as: "Meßkatalogus, deutscher, Bemerkungen darüber. D. Ms. J. 80. Aug. S. 176."

Perhaps of greater interest now than the 572 pages of the index are the 360 pages which list in classified form and broken down by decades (after the years 1700–40) all the periodicals that had been founded since 1700 (including also some works that we would consider to be simply collected essays). I would estimate the total at around 2000. To most of the entries are appended some descriptive or critical comments, on average perhaps three lines, many of them quite forthright, for example, comments such as: "Ohne Werth" or "Fand Liebhaber." Finally there is a list of authors that have signed articles in the eight indexed periodicals. This is of greater interest than might at first be expected, since it covers not only those items listed in the index but also those which, for whatever reason, are excluded.

By the end of the eighteenth century the combination of booksellers' catalogues and review or bibliographical journals (with of course the Fair Catalogues as well) no longer satisfied the demand for comprehensive and up to date bibliographies. In the last decade of the century only the foundations were

---

8 "Durch die periodischen Schriften wurde ferner eine so allgemeine Thätigkeit ... des menschlichen Geistes veranlaßt und erzeugt, von der die Geschichte kein Beispiel hat" (p. v).

laid, however, for genuinely comprehensive works, works that were then fully developed in the early part of the nineteenth century. The least successful of the four major figures to be discussed now was Johann Samuel Ersch.[9] He was largely responsible for the *Allgemeines Repertorium der Literatur für die Jahre 1785 bis 1790* (154) which was based on information derived mostly from journals (listed in vol. 3, p. vii–viii). A second quinquennium (1791–95) was covered in a similar publication in 1799. The first two volumes of the first publication are systematically organised (the scheme is outlined p. 1–22) and volume 3 is given up entirely to "sämtliche alphabetische Register." The same systematic approach was taken in Ersch's rather more valuable *Handbuch der deutschen Literatur seit der Mitte des achtzehnten Jahrhunderts bis auf die neueste Zeit...* (155) which was published in two volumes (8 parts in 6), 1812–1814. The systematic plan and "Autoren-Register" follow each part (the word Literatur is still being used in the older, wide sense) while the items are organised within each small unit by date. Each item is numbered within the parts and the final entry for "Literatur der schönen Künste" is numbered 3760, so that there must be in excess of 4,000 items, for several works by the same author may be listed under the same number plus a, b, c, etc. Sophie la Roche, for example, appears under the rubric "Romane ohne historische Grundlage" and has ten entries, 1527 a–k. The classification at this particular juncture is as follows:

Abtheilung VII Schöne Künste
      II Insonderheit
       I) Tonische Künste
       (I) Redekunst
        1 Ohne bes. Rücksicht auf den
         mündlichen Vortrag
        2) Insonderheit
        (2) Dichtkunst
        B Einzelne Dichtungsarten
        (A) Gedichte für d. blössen Vortrag
         d. Declamation
        (DD) Epische u. and. erzählende Gedichte
        b) Romane und prosaische Erzähl. selbst
        aa ohne Rücks. auf deren Bestimm.
         für besond. Leser-Cl.
        (bb) Einzelne Gatt.
        bbb Ohne historische Grundlage

9 Ersch (1766–1818), librarian, professor of geography, and editor or co-editor of numerous, mainly periodical, publications, is called "der Begründer der neuern deutschen Bibliographie" by Meyer's *Konversations-Lexikon,* 4th edition, volume 5 (Leipzig, 1888).

(aaa) ohne besond. Rücksicht
α ernste
β einzelne
(a) Deutsche
N 1523–1636

At the end of the entries for Sopie la Roche is a reference to N. 1326 where four works by the same author are classified under "(aa) ohne Rücks. auf d. besond. Gatt. [cf. (bb) above] – aaa Deutsche – (bbb) Einzelner Vff."

Ersch's work is comprehensive and it had some success in its time. There were re-printings in 1815 and 1819 and a revised edition in 1822–40, while individual parts were reprinted under the title *Bibliographisches Handbuch der philologischen [etc.] Literatur der Deutschen* up to the middle of the century. One must admire the ingenuity of the classification system but at the same time admit that it is a hindrance rather than a help to the mere identification of titles. However, there are author indexes.

The other major bibliographers of the time abandoned the attempt to classify the works they listed and adopted instead the simple alphabetical method. The first of the three leading figures in the next decades was Wilhelm Heinsius, whose life-span coincided approximately with that of Ersch. He developed a comprehensive retrospective bibliography on the basis of his firm's earlier catalogues (1748 [227], 1760) and published it in 1793 under the title of *Allgemeines Bücher Lexikon* (228). Into this work he amalgamated the contents of the earlier catalogues with the publications of 1760 to 1792, omitting on principle only "Piecen und Brochüren welche weniger als drey Groschen kosten" (p. III). Novels, plays, and musical pieces according to the custom of the time are listed separately by title. A supplement by Friedrich Bruder was issued in 1798 and covered the years 1793–97.

In 1812 Heinsius revised and supplemented the earlier volumes and re-published the whole to cover the period from 1700 to 1810 (229). The four volumes of this revision then became the first four in a series that was continued at intervals of approximately five years throughout the nineteenth century.

Heinsius was not, however, the only book dealer anxious to provide the public with comprehensive bibliographies. A second firm entered on the scene in 1798 with a *Verzeichnis neuer Bücher die seit Michaelis 1797 bis Juli 1798 wirklich erschienen sind . . . welche bei [A. L.] Reinicke und [J. C.] Hinrichs . . . zu bekommen sind* (235). This work was intended to provide ". . . ein vollständiges Verzeichniß der jede Messe neu erschienenen Werke . . ." and appeared regularly twice a year. Each volume contained a short subject index by classes.

Finally the work of both Heinsius and Hinrichs was supplemented by C. G. Kayser's comprehensive *Index locupletissimus librorum . . . Vollständiges Bücher-Lexikon enthaltend alle von 1750 bis zu Ende des Jahres 1832 gedruckten Bücher*, 1834–36 (283). Kayser, who had edited volumes 6 and 7 (pub. in 1822 and 1828–29) of Heinsius, and who had previously published a "short-list" of works published between 1750 and 1823 (see below), then continued to publish supplementary volumes through the nineteenth century.

There were thus by the middle of the nineteenth century three parallel "trade" bibliographies, all covering much the same field at varying time intervals. The further development of these bibliographies will be discussed in the following chapter. For the moment it must suffice to point out the main differences in the early part of the century. Heinsius and Hinrichs begin publication at the end of the eighteenth century; Heinsius claims to list works back to 1700, while Hinrichs picks up at 1797. Kayser begins publication early in the nineteenth century and lists works from 1750. During the first half of the nineteenth century Hinrichs appears half-yearly (quarterly from 1846); Heinsius appears quinquennially, while Kayser also develops into a quinquennial form, but continues to include (at least until 1852) works omitted from previous volumes (i.e., from 1750).

All of these works have their faults but all must be consulted in order to verify publications of the period from 1700 to 1850. Heinsius is understandably weak in the earlier period, since he was attempting to list works that were in many cases long since out of print. None is of course anything like complete, despite, for example, Kayser's claim that he would have omitted also some works published after 1750, "läge nicht möglichst absolute Vollständigkeit in dem Plane dieses Werkes" (p. VII, fn.). And even an amalgamation of all of them and Ersch as well would not produce a complete picture of the totality of eighteenth century book production. Reliability and coverage increase of course as the nineteenth century progresses and Kayser is the more extensive. He attempts to collect together all works of any given author, no matter how published, and to enter titles under the "main" word or that word most likely to be thought of, or to provide cross references. In principle he provides entries with author, title, format, place, date, publisher, and price. From 1838 on there is also a "Sachregister."

Turning now to more specific bibliographies mention should first be made of two "selectively" general bibliographies, one of which was produced by Kayser himself. In 1825 he published his *Deutsche Bücherkunde* (282) covering the period 1750 to 1823, a precursor in fact of his later comprehensive works. This one was intended as a concise and simple work, limited to what might be called trade books, omitting pamphlets, cheap books, school texts, and so forth. Entries are limited as far as possible to one line, e.g.,

> v. Goethe, Schriften 8 Bde. Schreibpapier. 8. Lpz. 787–90 8ß
> —   Ebendies, in 4 Bdn auf Druckpapier. 8. Lpz. Göschen 790–91. 3.16.

(in this case Kayser has added dates which he does not normally include); as a result of the condensation Kayser manages to pack in approximately 7500 items (WBB).

An essay on "die Geschichte der literarischen Waarenkunde," i.e. bibliography and bibliographies was contributed to Kayser's *Deutsche Bücherkunde* by Friedrich Adolf Ebert, Librarian at the Royal Library in Dresden, and Ebert himself published on the basis of materials in that library an *Allgemeines bibliographisches Lexikon,* 1821 (142), which stands, as it were, between the old-style universal bibliography or catalogue of rare books and the newer, simpler catalogue of books in print. His aim was to produce a bibliography of European rather than only German books and to satisfy the demands of both scholars and collectors. He included therefore books valued as rare and/or valuable and those viewed as standard and authoritative. The result is a selective but significant bibliography and one that is valuable for the quality of the annotations to individual items. These notes include, for example, in many cases not just the current value but the prices paid for the item at earlier auctions or sales. The 24,280 items are arranged strictly in alphabetical sequence with occasional references, e.g. Trimberg s. Renner. There are no indexes.

Aside from these two relatively comprehensive bibliographies, which may nevertheless be termed in some degree special in view of their limited scope, there were now innumerable individual bibliographies devoted to special topics, for example, to botany, chemistry, or astronomy. A good example of the type of systematic specialised bibliographies now produced is provided by the work of Theodor Enslin and Wilhelm Engelmann. The former set up in business in Berlin in 1817 and soon developed a reputation for his extensive special catalogues. He produced lists of literature on, among many other things, architecture, law, medicine, economics, veterinary science, and commerce. These bibliographies were in many cases continued and expanded by Wilhelm Engelmann, who defends the production of bibliographies by booksellers (in the introduction to the *Bibliothek der schönen Wissenschaften*) on the grounds that academics just do not have the necessary sources at their disposal. The full title of the last named catalogue will be sufficient indication of its scope and usefulness within the general field of literature (previous editions appeared in 1815 and 1823): *Bibliothek der schönen Wissenschaften oder Verzeichnis der vorzüglichsten, in älterer und neuerer Zeit, bis zur Mitte des Jahres 1836 in Deutschland erschienenen Romane, Gedichte, Schauspiele und anderer zur schönen Literatur gehöriger Werke, so wie der besten deutschen Übersetzungen poetischer Werke aus lebenden fremden Sprachen . . . gänzlich umgearbeitet und neu herausgegeben von Wilhelm Engelmann. Zweite Auflage, mit der Inhaltsangabe der Gesammt- und Sammelwerke* (Leipzig, 1837).

Before turning to the situation in German literature proper, there is one field of bibliography which aroused interest at an early date and in which very considerable progress had been made by the beginning of the nineteenth century, namely the field of incunabula. The study of incunabula has always been and still is carried out on an international basis, since the majority of the works published prior to 1500 were in Latin and the scholarship of that day was broadly international. The fruits of the study of incunabula apply, however, equally to German literature as to all other literatures of the day.

Reference was made above to Beughem's first attempt at listing incunabula, an attempt which was only mildly improved upon by M. Maittaire in his *Annales typographici,* 1719 (330), which is a relatively short, chronologically ordered list that does not even list the publishers of the works cited. A so-called supplement to Maittaire was produced by Denis in Vienna in 1789 under the title *Annalium typographicorum* (122). The six thousand items are organised by place and date and are rather more fully described. In addition Denis provides 4 indexes, "Index chronologicus," "Index criticus," "Index bibliographicus," and "Index typographicus."

This was followed by G. W. Panzer's *Annalen der älteren deutschen Litteratur* (387), the first volume of which appeared in 1788 and covered the period to 1520. A supplement was published in 1802, and a second volume covered the years 1521 to 1526 (1805). Unlike the *Annales typographici . . .* (388) in which Panzer lists Latin works by place and date of publication, the *Annalen* are organised chronologically. Finally Hain published in 1826—38 his *Repertorium bibliographicum* (210), a general inventory which has remained to this day a standard reference work on account of the greatly improved level of bibliographical information.

Both the works of Panzer and of Hain have been supplemented of course. A third volume to Panzer was added by E. Weller in 1864—85 under the title *Repertorium typographicum* (500) and this replaces the older work for the period 1520—1526. Hain was supplemented in 1895—1902 by W. A. Copinger's *Supplement to Hain's Repertorium Bibliographicum* (119), in 1902 by K. Burger, *The Printers and Publishers of the Fifteenth Century with lists of their Works* (103), and in 1905—14 by D. Reichling's *Appendices ad Hainii-Copingeri Repertorium bibliographicum* (412). These and other more recent works in the general area of incunabula or on specific publishers, the printing history of individual cities, and so forth, will not be discussed further or referred to in later chapters, since they are too specialised. They may be located through the various bibliographical handbooks which are described in the following chapter.

According to Heinrich Hoffmann (239), "Die deutsche Philologie ist das Studium des geistigen Lebens des deutschen Volkes insofern es sich durch Sprache und Litteratur kundgiebt. Es gehört also in seinen Bereich die ganze deutsche Litteraturgeschichte, Grammatik, Lexicographie, Etymologie, Hermeneutik und Kritik. Aus der wissenschaftlichen Begründung aller dieser einzelnen Theile ist endlich eine Wissenschaft hervorgegangen, deren Werth sehr spät eingesehen worden ist" (p. VI). Hoffmann adds in a footnote that the value of the study of German literature was surprisingly recognised as early as 1752— which coincides approximately with our premise and one of the reasons for the division of this chapter. The question therefore arises as to the existence of bibliographies that are concerned specifically with German literature.

There are in Friedrich Bouterwek's view two possible methods of writing a "Geschichte der schönen Wissenschaften": "Der eine ist der philologisch-bibliographische, der andre der philosophisch-kritische,"[10] and it is certainly true that writers on German literature until about the second quarter of the nineteenth century lean strongly in the one direction or the other. A simple example is provided by the works of Sulzer and Blankenburg. Johann Georg Sulzer produced in 1771–74 *Eine allgemeine theorie der schönen Künste* (462) in encyclopedic form, i.e., with individual entries on specific topics in alphabetical order. The style was discursive, however, without bibliographical references. In 1796–98 there appeared *Friedrichs von Blankenburg literarische Zusätze zu Johann Georg Sulzers allgemeine Theorie* (68), in which Blankenburg provided (aside from minor additions) purely long lists of references. Such general works as Sulzer/Blankenburg naturally have but little space for German literature. However, those works that are devoted to German literature, and there are not many, are, like Sulzer, discursive in nature. They purport to *introduce* the reader to German literature, and their style reflects to some degree the situation from which they developed in most cases, namely from lecture notes. Histories of literature such as those by Schlegel (429), Horn (247), or Vilmar (489) concentrate on providing a connected narrative with illustrations of the authors named, frequently in fact with very lengthy quotations. Background information is largely absent with the exception of often quite extensive biographical information.[11]

The first noteworthy attempt to provide bibliographical details in the course of a literary historical survey was the *Literarischer Grundriss zur Geschichte der deutschen Poesie von der ältesten Zeit bis in das sechzehnte Jahrhundert durch Friedrich Heinrich von der Hagen und Johann Gustav Büsching,* 1812 (209). The authors maintained as far as possible a chronological and thematic order but abandoned any attempt at a "zusammenhängende Darstellung" (p. XIII). Instead they aimed to provide for each work "Der Titel, der Verfasser, die Mundart, die Veranlassung, die Zeit, die Form, der Umfang; die Handschriften und Drucke ... ihre Beschaffenheit und Material. Blätter- oder Seitenzahl, Format, Zeit und Ort, Schreiber oder Drucker und Verleger, und jetziger Besitzer; ... Alles dieses wird mit genauen literarischen Nachweisungen belegt" (p. XIII–XIV).

As a sample of the style, here is the entry for:

---

10 "Vorrede" to *Geschichte der Poesie und Beredsamkeit* (Göttingen, 1801).
11 Bouterwek himself is general and discursive. He states quite openly in the introduction that he, "die Erweiterung und Verbesserung der bis jetzt vorhandenen bibliographischen Werken Anderen überlassen mußte" (p. vi).

Der arme Heinrich, durch Hartmann von der Aue
Handschriftlich, zu Straßburg, in der Johanniter Bibl. A. 94.
(vgl. oben S. 282) Perg., in einem Kodex zusammen mit verschiedenen Erzählungen
mehrerer Dichter. Vergl. Bodmers Vorrede zu Chriemh. R. S. XI Gedruckt,
darnach, in der Müllerischen Sammlung, Bd. 1., hinter dem Parzival, S. 197–208
(1523v.)
Bearbeitungen: Ein Auszug, zu 5 Bildern von Franz Hegi, in dem Taschenbuch Iris,
1810. Übersetzung v. Büsching, eine Probe, in der Zeitschr. Pantheon, Bd. II,
S. 309–28. Das Ganze, besonders, Zürich, 1810, 12., mit den Bildern von Hegi.

There follows one paragraph of comment.

This style was essentially background material for lectures and led in the direction of Goedeke. There was also a more systematic approach to bibliography – although this too is sub-titled *Ein Leitfaden zu Vorlesungen* in Hoffmann's *Die deutsche Philologie im Grundriss,* 1836 (239), the introduction to which was cited above. Hoffmann offered his readers "einen bibliographischen Umriss" that would contain in classified form all the reference and source works necessary for the study of German literature, omitting the primary works themselves. Hoffmann provides a detailed explanation of his procedures in the introduction and is sharply critical of many earlier works, for example, of Lawätz, of which he says: "Schwer dürfte sich ein ähnliches ungenaueres und unzuverlässigeres Machwerk finden lassen" (p. xix). The introduction as a whole provides an interesting survey of the reference works available in the field up to that time. On p. xxii there is some criticism of Hinrichs' bibliography; also of the fair catalogues. The bibliography itself is quite comprehensive and simply classified. The approximately 3,000 items are listed by author, title, place, date, and format with occasional comments, such as: "Wird fortges." Paragraph 41 "Allgemeine deutsche Literaturgeschichte" (Under "II. Litteraturgeschichte") has 33 entries followed by 10 entries in § 42 "Litteraturgeschichte einzelner Zeiträume" and four for "Litteraturgeschichte einzelner Länder" (§ 43). There is an index to authors' names.

It was all too evident at the beginning of the nineteenth century that the extent of knowledge of the history of German literature was not such that a comprehensive and thorough chronological survey could be undertaken. Probably the first such attempt that met with any success was that of Gervinus, whose *Geschichte der poetischen National-Litteratur der Deutschen* (184) first appeared in 1835 and 1836 and was re-worked and re-published over the next decades. It cannot be our concern here to trace the development of the study of "Germanistik," but it is essential to note that the newly developing discipline found outlets primarily in periodical publications. As Hoffmann says, "Mischsammlungen und Zeitschriften für die neuere und neueste Zeit mussten in solcher Ausführlichkeit angegeben werden, schon weil sie für die Geschichte der kritischen Bestrebungen unentbehrlich sind" (p. IX), and he himself lists journal items along with books, programmes, etc. Many periodical items were naturally of minor significance, but the sheer quantity of material published in the numerous journals, some of which were devoted solely to German literature past and/or present, made some form of periodical bibliography inevitable. The first journals of significance for German literature — aside that is from the "literary" journals — appeared already in the 1830s and 1840s, for example, Hoffmann von Fallersleben's *Fundgruben* (1830–37), Haupt's *Altdeutsche Blätter* (1835–40), and von der Hagen's *Germania* (1836–53). The earliest still existing journal is (Haupt's) *Zeitschrift für deutsches Altertum* (1841–). Discussion of periodical bibliographies will be postponed, however, until the following chapter, since these are the special characteristic of the latter half of the century.

There is still one further form of reference source that should receive at least brief mention before moving on to new developments, namely, the biographical dictionary. The bio-bibliographic handbook has been mentioned several times in earlier chapters. In the eighteenth century biographical dictionaries became more and more extensive as the number of "scholars" and "writers" increased enormously. As in the case of literary history the trend is toward specialisation, if only because of the volume involved. The general *Gelehrten-Lexikon* (1715) of J. B. Mencke (338) appeared in a second edition of 1726 and a third in 1733. In 1750/51 Jöcher then put out his own version, the *Allgemeines Gelehrten-Lexicon* (275) in four volumes, the work still of course covering, as he says, all scholars "von Anfange der Welt bis auf iezige Zeit." With his death the next edition ran into problems. It was taken by Adelung up to J (1784–87) and then continued by H. W. Rotermund, who completed only K–R (1810–19).

In the meantime a specifically German work had been produced by Hamberger, namely, *Das gelehrte Teutschland oder Lexikon der jetztlebenden teutschen Schriftsteller*, 1767 (213). This was revised and continued by Meusel (342) who also produced the *Lexikon der vom Jahr 1750 bis 1800 verstorbenen teutschen Schriftsteller* in 1802–16 (344). There is a useful discussion of the problems of collecting biographical information in the introduction to the last-named work, and some additional, useful sources are named. These and related, especially local, works are listed also in Hoffmann (above). If one uses these together with more general reference works, such as encyclopedias, the coverage of writers at least is fairly good during the eighteenth century.

Finally reference must be made, if only briefly, to the slow emergence of a professional organisation in the publishing industry. The lack of any adequate copyright law and the consequent widespread practice of re-printing without consent of either author or publisher had been a problem almost since the first works were run off the press, but it became a much more acute problem in the eighteenth century as the volume, especially of popular literature, increased so rapidly. Many unscrupulous (and often ignorant or incompetent) publishers rushed into the market with cheap reprints. On the other hand it was becoming increasingly evident that writing books was an occupation from which to derive profit. It was primarily then for the purpose of regulating business relations and presenting a united front against the reprint houses that publishers eventually came together. The self-awareness of the new style of publisher is epitomised in Philipp Emmanuel Reich, who turned his back firmly on the Frankfurt Book Fair in 1764 and thus strengthened the movement toward Leipzig. It was under his aegis that the first association of booksellers was formed a year later.

Unfortunately this first attempt did not succeed, primarily, it would seem, as a result of the differences between the north and south German bookdealers, the latter still clinging largely to the old exchange method of payment (and having a much greater share in the reprint business). The common front made by the bookdealers who dealt mainly in Leipzig was sufficiently strong, however, that in 1788 under an agreement known as the "Süddeutsche Schlußnahme" the principle of cash or return was agreed upon as the general basis for trade and Leipzig was accepted as the centre at which payments or returns were to be made (at the Easter Fair). In order to simplify transactions a central place of payment (Börse) was created in 1792 by Paul Gotthelf Kummer, but this was not entirely successful. A more successful bid was then made again in Leipzig in 1797 by Karl Christian Horvath. At the Börse publishers and dealers or their agents met in order to settle accounts.

At various meetings between 1802 and 1817 committees were established with the task of soliciting opinions, on the basis of which a professional association could be established; but nothing came of these. Finally the last appointed group agreed to take over Horvath's Börse, but before they could do so another hastily constituted group under Campe proposed a constitution (April 30, 1825), which gained sufficient support to carry the day. The main concerns of the now duly constituted body were still the same: the establishment of copyright regulations and the prevention of reprinting, the reduction or at least regulation of discount rates, and the establishment of some kind of standards in the training of young people in the book trade. Throughout the nineteenth century the Börsenverein, as it came to be known, was closely involved in the establishment of unified copyright laws throughout the area of the German Reich.

Copyright and similar matters lie outside the scope of this study, and we would not be concerned with the Börsenverein, were it not for the fact that this association became progressively more involved in the field of national bibliography. The first venture was the *Börsenblatt,* which had been started in 1834 by the local Leipziger Verein and which was taken over by the Börsenverein in the following year. In the *Börsenblatt* or a supplement to it publishers announced their newest publications. At first published on a weekly basis, it began to appear twice per week from 1837, thrice per week from 1852, and daily from 1867 on. This publication and its weekly cumulation was an

essential element in the somewhat unsystematic system of "national bibliography" that began to develop around the middle of the century and reached
fruition nearly one hundred years later.

Chapter 5

From 1850 to the Second World War

Numerous factors, among them the work of Enlightenment scholars, the growth of nationalism, and the interest of the Romantics in things medieval (or supposedly medieval), contributed in early nineteenth-century Germany to a great upsurge of interest in literature past and present, an upsurge that found expression increasingly in journals of a more or less specialised nature. There had been specialist journals also in the field of literature as far back as the middle of the eighteenth century, but these had not succeeded. Even in the early decades of the nineteenth century most of the specialist journals, such as Hagen and Büsching's *Museum für altdeutsche Literatur und Kunst,* the *Altdeutsche Wälder* of the brothers Grimm, or Hoffmann's *Fundgruben* were short-lived. It was not until the 1840s that specialist journals in the field of German literature became permanently established.

From the middle of the nineteenth century on the number and variety of periodicals increased rapidly, and with them the problem of recording and indexing the mass of new, primarily critical material they contained. Again, there had been indexes to periodicals earlier, as early indeed as the late seventeenth century, but they had failed to establish themselves, just as also the numerous general bibliographical journals, such as J. C. Adelung's *Allgemeines Verzeichnis neuer Bücher* (9) or J. G. Meusel's *Historisch-litterarisch-bibliographisches Magazin* (238) had failed either to keep up with or satisfy the demand for current information about book production. The need for periodic information was now reinforced by the very existence of so many periodicals and the new periodic bibliographies therefore include both monographs and journal items, while the growing importance of journals and indexes to journals means a shift away from publisher-produced indexes and back to those produced by scholars. The main characteristic of what may be termed the modern period of bibliography is in fact the development of periodic indexes and indexes to periodicals, and since this particular development will be stressed in the following, the dates given for bibliographies will in future normally be for the period covered and not the date of publication.

The second major feature of the modern period is the vast variety of specialized, retrospective bibliographies that are produced, bibliographies that may be general in nature or narrowly specific, but which are often of importance for the study of literary history. It is not possible within the limits of this study even to list a reasonable proportion of these, and it is not in fact necessary, for with the increasing volume of bibliographical materials come also biblio-bibliographies, handbooks on bibliography, and the like. This chapter will therefore be concerned primarily with the general trends in bibliography, with the historical development of what have become in our day the most important *types* of bibliographical sources associated with the study of literature. Consideration of contemporary sources must, however, necessarily be postponed to the following chapter. Both World Wars had a considerable impact on publishing in general and on periodic bibliographies in particular, but whereas bibliographies continued after the First World War along much the same lines as before, this was not entirely the case after the Second World War; and it is the aim of this work in any case to look *critically* at the present range of bibliographies after having completed the survey of their origins and development.

Before examining periodic bibliographies within the field of German literature, it is necessary first to continue the survey begun in the previous chapter of the development of German national bibliography and then to look also briefly at some few comprehensive, retrospective bibliographies. By the middle of the nineteenth century there were in existence three parallel and roughly similar, comprehensive bibliographies of and by the book trade; they are referred to for convenience as Heinsius, Kayser, and Hinrichs. Heinsius had begun retrospectively (1700–) and then continued with volumes covering approximately five years until 1893–4, when the nineteenth and last volume appeared, covering the years 1889–92. Kayser had also begun retrospectively (1750–) and continued to appear in multi-annual volumes until the last (36th) volume of 1911 for the years 1907–10. In the meantime Hinrichs, who had begun on a semi-annual basis in 1797–98, had taken over Kirchoff's quinquennial catalogue for 1851–55 (286). This was continued on a multi-annual basis until 1912.

There was therefore a considerable degree of overlap during the latter part of the century, as can be seen from the following table:

1700–1749	Heinsius
1750–1850	Heinsius and Kayser
1851–1892	Heinsius and Kayser and Hinrichs
1893–1910	Kayser and Hinrichs
1911–1912	Hinrichs[1]

In addition to these Gustav Thelert published in 1893 his *Supplement zu Heinsius', Hinrichs' und Kaysers Bücher-Lexikon ... seit der Mitte des neunzehnten Jahrhunderts* (473). This therefore also covers the period 1850–92. Finally a subject index began to appear in 1889, produced by Carl (or Karl) Georg and (for the first volume only) Leopold Ost. This *Schlagwort-Katalog. Verzeichnis der im deutschen Buchhandel erschienenen Bücher und*

---

1 Details of these works are conveniently, if not always accurately, certainly not identically, listed in Bestermann (below), the Library of Congress Catalogue (discussed in the next chapter), etc.

Landkarten in sachlicher Anordnung (178)[2] also appeared on a multi-annual basis, 1883–87, 1888–92, and so forth. The entries are brief and organized strictly alphabetically but with many sub-arrangements. The entry for Bibliographie, for example, divided into "allgemeine" and "spezielle," has numerous, typographically carefully distinguished sub-entries with some cross-references such as "Bibliographie, spezielle: *Faust s.a. Göthe.*" Entries for authors are divided into works and commentaries, e.g. Heine, where 13 editions and 13 critical works are listed (Vol. 1).

These multi-annual bibliographies were based upon a bewildering variety of shorter-term lists of an official or inofficial nature. The primary source of these lists was the Börsenverein, whose publisher or responsible agent was Hinrichs. There were daily, weekly, monthly, and quarterly lists and/or indexes and cumulations. Not unnaturally booksellers raised objections to this plethora of bibliographies, but it was not until 1912 and the founding of the Deutsche Bücherei (DB) that any serious attempt was made at rationalisation. The DB was set up by a contract between the Börsenverein, the city of Leipzig and the State of Saxony on October 3, 1912.[3] After reaching agreement with Kayser for the cessation of that bibliography (Heinsius had already ceased publication in 1892), the Börsenverein came to terms with Hinrichs on the expiry of the existing contract which ran to 1916. (Also Georg's subject catalogue was to cease as its function would be absorbed into the new bibliography.) At that point the Börsenverein set up its own bibliographical section, but its work and its staff were gradually absorbed into the DB; the process was complete by the end of 1930.

Beginning with 1931, therefore, all the bibliographies were concentrated in the DB, which had taken on the character of a national library and which began to publish from this date the *Deutsche Nationalbibliographie* (132). A rough outline of the development of national bibliography through to the Second World War is thus as follows:

Daily Erschienene Neuigkeiten (Börsenblatt)	1839–1920 Hinr.
	1921–1930 DB
Tägliches Verzeichnis der Neuerscheinungen	1931–1945 DB
Weekly [Allgemeine Bibliographie von/für Deutschland	1826–1835
	1836–1842]
Wöchentliches Verzeichnis	1843–1915 Hinr.
	1916–1930 DB
Deutsche Nationalbibliographie Reihe A	1931–1945 DB

2 Hannover: (1–6); Leipzig: (7), various publishers appear on imprint; also without the words *im deutschen Buchhandel erschienenen* (published by L. Lemmermann).
3 On the founding of the Deutsche Bücherei see (among other works) *Deutsche Bücherei 1912–1962. Festschrift zum fünfzigjährigen Bestehen der deutschen Nationalbibliothek* (Leipzig: 1962)

Fortnightly	
Deutsche Nationalbibliographie Reihe B	1931–1945 DB
[*Monthly* Register from 1843 (Hinrichs)]	
[*Quarterly* from 1846 (Hinrichs)]	
Semi-Annual Halbjahresverzeichnis	1797–1915 Hinr.
	1916–1930 Börs.
	1931–1945 DB
Multi-Annual Heinsius, volumes 1–19	1700–1892
Kayser, volumes 1–36	1750–1910
Kirchoff/Hinrichs, volumes 1–13	1850–1913
Deutsches Bücherverzeichnis 1–22	1911–1940
	(1941–1950 etc)

Under the new system there were monthly, quarterly, and annual indexes to the weekly lists. The main innovation was, however, the institution of a fortnightly list called Reihe B, Reihe A being the continuation of the *Wöchentliches Verzeichnis*. The new list included for the first time much that had hitherto been omitted, namely, such things as dissertations, pamphlets, the productions of private presses, and so forth. Having taken this first step, the DB then proceeded to create new bibliographies or to take over existing ones. Thus, to give only a few examples, it began the *Monatliches Verzeichnis der reichsdeutschen amtlichen Schriften* in 1927 (183); it took over in 1936 the preparation of the *Jahresverzeichnis der deutschen Hochschulschriften* (268) and in 1943 the bibliographies of music known previously as *Hofmeisters musikalisch-literarischer Monatsbericht* (244) and *Hofmeisters Jahresverzeichnis* (243) (new titles: *Deutsche Musikbibliographie* [131] and *Jahresverzeichnis der deutschen Musikalien und Musikschriften* [269]).

More will necessarily be said of the DB later; for the moment it is important to note that the apparently more than adequate bibliographical coverage of eighteenth and nineteenth century book production in Germany is quite illusory.[4] As far as the eighteenth century is concerned, the coverage is very poor. This is demonstrated by even a simple statistical comparison of Heinsius or Kayser with the figures (often complaints) of book production by contemporaries. According to Koppitz (300) Heinsius's coverage for 1700–1750 would be only about 20 %, that of Kayser for 1750–1800 about 34 % (1780–1800 perhaps 50 %). As for the nineteenth century, unless it is a question of determining more precisely the date of publication of a given work, one does not need in practice to use more than the multi-annual volumes – always supposing that the smaller issues have survived. However, although all are in theory committed to providing comprehensive coverage with full and

---

4 A list of *Low* German works up to 1800 was published by Conrad Borchling and Bruno Claussen, *Niederdeutsche Bibliographie. Gesamtverzeichnis der niederdeutschen Drucke bis zum Jahre 1800*, 3 vols. (Neumünster: Wachholtz, 1831–57).

accurate listings, they still leave much to be desired, even though the coverage is for obvious reasons much better than in the eighteenth century. Kayser is the fuller in coverage since Hinrichs was supposed at least to list only the works sent in by publishers. Kayser may therefore list works erroneously, i.e., announced but not published, while Hinrichs may be more accurate in bibliographical detail but less complete. The omissions of all are, however, numerous and this must be borne in mind — they were after all intended primarily as practical reference materials for the trade. Only subsequent to 1910 is the attempt made to satisfy the demands of both booksellers and librarians by providing complete coverage of all printed materials.

The catalogues of individual publishers are perhaps less important though more familiar in the modern period. Mention should be made, however, of one attempt to collate a large number of individual publishers' lists, namely the *Gesammt-Verlags-Verzeichnis des deutschen Buchhandels,* which was published in 1881–94 and attempted to list all publications between 1700 and 1880/93.[5] The sixteen volumes of this work are organised alphabetically first by place name, then by the name of the publisher (separate volumes for Austria and Switzerland). The nature of the entries varies a good deal, depending on the degree to which individual publishers co-operated, and in most cases the list of publications does not extend very far back in time. The lists are useful at least for the nineteenth century and there are some, albeit limited, notes on the origins of some of the major publishing houses. The works too are listed alphabetically except in a few cases where the quantity enforced some sub-division.

While the "national" bibliographies are an essential source for purposes of verification and may usefully be consulted, for example, for discovering or verifying the works of any given author, whether poet or critic, they are not intended to supply direct information on specific fields or topics. For the study of German literature and of the history of German literature (and we are henceforth concerned with *Literaturgeschichte,* not *Litterargeschichte*) there are no such multi-annual bibliographies. As indicated above, the growth of periodical literature gave rise to bibliographies that are periodic in form. However, it was still thought possible in the mid-nineteenth century to compile a comprehensive retrospective bibliography that would be both complete and up-to-date. Such an undertaking was Karl Goedeke's famous *Grundriss zur*

---

5 The title-page has *Buch- und Kunst-Katalog* above the title cited, which continues (vol. 1): *Ein Bild deutscher Geistesarbeit und Cultur. Vollständig bis Ende 1880* (Münster i/W: Adolph Russell, 1881). Before the title page there is a half-title, which reads: *Verlags-Kataloge der Verleger des Deutschen Reiches.* There is no introduction or commentary of any kind, but a brief description of the history of the project is included in volume 0 (sic!), published in 1894.

Geschichte der deutschen Dichtung aus den Quellen,[6] and it is worth considering this in some detail, not merely on account of the complexity of its history, but because it provides a link between past and present and because its fate is symptomatic of the problems besetting bibliography in general.

Goedeke, who records his obligation as a bibliographer to Koch, Gottsched, and Blankenburg, defines the history of literature as "nach der Zeitfolge geordnete Darstellung der im Wort lebendig gewordenen geistigen Entwicklung der Völker" and the task of a history of German literature as "die Entwicklung des deutschen Volkes in der dichterischen Form des Wortes kennen zu lernen" (Einl., p. 1). The basis for such a literary history was to be provided by his *Grundriss,* in which he, like Koch, "strebte . . . nach innerer Vollständigkeit und äußerer Reichhaltigkeit" (Vorw., p. vii). The work was intended to cover the period from the oldest literary remains to the time of Goethe's death (1830), and the first (and in Goedeke's lifetime only) complete edition appeared in 1859–81 in three volumes, containing 8 "Bücher" or chronological divisions.

The link with the past is most clearly seen in the strongly biographical approach. The biography of each author is followed by a list of his works and then a list of critical material, reference sources, and so forth. Individual books, chapters, and paragraphs are prefaced by general comments on the historical development of the period, the genre, etc. There is an enormous number of entries even in the first edition and many of these are of the briefest nature. The following are examples of entries for relatively familiar poets.

> Heinrich von Morunge, aus dem ersten Viertel des 13. Jh.; der Sprache nach ein Norddeutscher, nach Hagens Vermutung aus Moringen bei Göttingen, voll frischer Sinnlichkeit und seine Liebeslieder mit lebhaften Zügen der Wirklichkeit durchflechtend, ohne flach zu werden. HMS. Nr. 31   (p. 39)

There is a two-line quotation on the home of Morungen in the "Nachträge." In the index both references are cited under Heinrich von Morunge; the reference to the "Nachträge" appears also under Morunge.

The following entry is split between "Kirchliche Volksdichtung" and "Gelehrt-höfische Dichtung."

> G. R. Weckherlin. Kurtze Beschreibung deß zu Stuttgarten bey dem fürstl. Kindtauf und Hochzeit jüngst gehaltenen Frewden Fests, verförrtiget durch G. R. Weckherlin. Tübingen 1618. q. Fol.
>
> Georg Rudolf Weckherlin, am 15. Sept. 1584 zu Stuttgart geboren, bezog im 17. Jahre die Universität Tübingen, um die Rechte zu studieren; von 1604 an auf Reisen in Deutschland, Frankreich und England, 1610 Sekretär des Herzogs von

---

6 Publication began in fascicles in 1857 (Hannover: Ehlermann). There have been various editions and re-issues. See Carl Diesch, *Der Goedeke. Werdegang eines wissenschaftlichen Unternehmens* (Dresden: Ehlermann, 1941).

Württemberg, dann der deutschen Canzlei zu London, wo er um 1651 starb. Er war einer der Ersten, welcher die Dichtung an den Dienst fürstlicher Höfe brachten und auf absichtsvolle Nachbildungen des Altertums bedacht waren. Die neue Schule berief sich anfänglich auf ihn wie einen Musterdichter; später wurde er mehr zurückgedrängt und vergeßen. In neueren Zeiten ist er sehr überschätzt. – DD. 1, 234ff.

1) Kurtze Beschreibung [ref. to prev. entry]) 2) Das erste Buch Oden und Gesäng. Stuttg. 1617. 126 S. 8. – 3) Das ander Buch Oden und Gesäng. Stuttg. 1619. 120 S. 8. – 4) Gaistliche und weltliche Gedichte. Amsterd. 1648. 12. (Alle Schriften sind sehr selten.)

In the "Nachträge" there is additional bibliographical information about the *Gaistliche und weltliche Lieder* and a reference to a work on Weckherlin by C. P. Conz.

Although these may be considered typical of entries for the period before the eighteenth century, things are very different in later periods. Especially in book six – "Vom siebenjährigen bis zum Weltkriege. Nationale Dichtung" – the entries for individual poets are expanded until they become in the classical period, in particular for Goethe and Schiller, virtually monographs with lengthy critical comments as well as factual background information. The basic weakness of the first edition was this imbalance between the different periods, something that reflected Goedeke's own prejudices and predilections. He recognised this himself as soon as the first version was in print: "Erst jetzt, da der reinliche Druck die umfangreichen Massen des Materials übersichtlicher hervorhebt, lässt sich erkennen, wo zu beschränken und wo weiter auszugreifen ist" (Vorw., p. x). He therefore set about revising and expanding his work.

As work progressed on the second edition and as more and more material became available, each succeeding chapter increased to a greater degree than the previous one. The first volume became two volumes and the second volume three volumes. Book 3, for example, "Vom Interregnum bis zur Reformation" (§ 68–100), grew from 51 to 281 pages. As the rate of scholarship increased, it became in fact impossible to keep up with new work. At Goedeke's death in 1887 only three volumes of the second edition, that is, up to the end of book 5 (§ 200), ca. 1750, had been completed. The work was then continued by others.

If Goedeke's first edition was unsatisfactory, one can only describe the continuation of the second edition as a monumental error. The exponential growth rate of scholarly publishing, the increasing insistence on absolute completeness of coverage, the problems of "teamwork," all contributed to a slower and slower production of larger and larger volumes. The last thirty years of the original concept (1800–30) required in the end no less than eight volumes, unequally divided between early (2 volumes) and later Romanticism (6 volumes, one of them [11] in two parts). The last of these volumes (15) did not appear until 1964–66, so that the work as a whole has been spread over almost eighty years. In the course of this period an attempt was made to start a third edition of which only § 201–246 were completed, i.e., Book 6, "Nationale Dichtung" up to Goethe (in four volumes: 1910, 1912, 1916, and Nachtrag 1913; a later volume covered bibliography for 1912–50). Also a *Neue Folge* of Goedeke was instituted by the Akademie der Wissenschaften in Berlin for the period 1830–80. Only the general introduction and entries for A (Aar-Ayßlinger) – it was to be arranged alphabetically and to contain as many as 10,000 authors – appeared (1955–62).

The failure of Goedeke's *Grundriss* is a simple matter of logistics. At the time that he began, the boom in scholarly publication was only just beginning. By the end of the century such a comprehensive combination of biography, bibliography, and literary criticism within the confines of one work was no longer possible, just as it had become impossible a century or so earlier to produce universal bibliographies or *Litterargeschichten*. As it now stands, Goedeke as a whole is of only limited use. The lists of original works, particularly those by lesser known authors, are often valuable, but there is little critical literature that is not at least one hundred years old and our knowledge of the life and works of most major authors has advanced considerably. Even the third edition of the Goethe period is already fifty years out-of-date (although a supplementary list of critical literature on Goethe has been added to 1950). For the most part, therefore, only the latest volumes, i.e., those published since the Second World War have any substantial value. An excerpt from Goedeke, *Der Taschengoedeke* by Leopold Hirschberg (236), contains only an alphabetical list of major figures and their works, "Die deutsche Literatur von A–Z ["deutsche Literatur von etwa 1650 an" (p. i)] einschliesslich der Übersetzungen, der Philosophie, der Kunst- und Musikwissenschaft, sowie der gelüfteten Anonyma und Pseudonyma" (p. v.). The Weckherlin entry (cited above) reads, for example, in toto:

> 1641 Gaistliche und Weltliche Gedichte. Amsterdam.
> 1648 Gaistliche und Weltliche Gedichte. Amsterdam.

Only two other attempts at retrospective bibliographies in Germany in the latter part of the nineteenth century need be mentioned. The first of these, Carl Heinrich Herrmann's *Bibliotheca philologica* (232) was not a very significant work. Of the four volumes only one falls into the field of German literature, for the promising title *Bibliotheca philologica. Verzeichnis der . . . erschienenen Zeitschriften, Schriften der Akademien,* etc. covers only the classical languages. Volume 4 of the series is entitled *Bibliotheca germanica* and covers publications on Old and Middle High German etc. in the quarter century 1850–75. It is quite a comprehensive listing in the traditional classified form and is surprisingly full in, among other areas, its listing of contemporary reworkings of older literary works. The bibliographic details provided are quite full, and I estimate the total entries to number approximately 10,000.

The only other person to attempt a comprehensive retrospective bibliography was Karl von Bahder with his *Die deutsche Philologie im Grundriss*, 1883 (29). Unlike Goedeke, whom he does not mention in his preface, Bahder harks back to Hoffmann's "Musterleistung" (discussed above) and cites approvingly also Bartsch's bibliography in *Germania* (below). His is a much more traditional classification than Goedeke's and it is essentially the same as Hoffmann's, although he restricts himself almost exclusively to the older period. He covers New High German language but not literature. Despite limiting himself to "nur die wichtigsten [Arbeiten]" he manages to put together 4110 items in what must be considered as a well balanced bibliography, one that is comprehensive within its given limitations and a considerable achievement for its time.

Mention should also be made at this juncture of two rather less comprehensive, English-language works that attempt to produce a form of bibliography suitable for foreign students of German literature. The first of these, K. Breul's *A handy bibliographical guide to the study of German language and literature* was published in London in 1893 (85) and was intended "to supply students and teachers with the titles of the *most important* periodicals and books" (p. vi). No articles *from* periodicals are cited, however, and there is very little in the way of specific criticism, since no authors (with the exception of Goethe, Schiller, Lessing) are treated individually. The only evidence of advice to the reader is the addition of the letter a, b, p, or c (*a*dvanced, *b*eginners, *p*opular, or *c*aution) to certain works. A more useful but curiously organised work is J. S. Nollen's *A chronology and practical bibliography of modern German literature* (378), which is "to include only what is best, or at least what is good" (p. 5) in the way of bibliographical references. Following on a chronological table (which includes non-German works and historical events), general works, etc., is an alphabetical listing of major authors since the time of Luther. Each entry cites (where appropriate) editions, biographies, and critical works and even includes prices. The following are the entries, for example, for the year 1890 and for Gerhart Hauptmann:

1890 Keller and Cardinal Newman died. Bismarck retired. − Anzengruber, *Der Fleck auf der Ehr.* Ebner-Eschenbach, *Unsühnbar.* Fontane, *Stine.* Isolde Kurz, *Florentiner Novellen.* Hauptmann, *Friedensfest.* Stefan George, *Hymnen.* Bahr, *Zur Kritik der Moderne.* Langbehn, *Rembrandt als Erzieher.* − Loti, *Pêcheur d'Islande.* Zola, *La Bête humaine.* Eugene Field, *Little Book of Western Verse.*
   230 Hauptmann (b. 1862). Works pub. by S. Fischer, B., each v. M.3. to M.4.50. − Biogr. by Paul Schlenther, Fischer, B., 1898, M.5. (the most authoritative); by Ad. Bartels, Felber, Weimar, 1897, M.3.80; by U. C. Woerner, Haushalter, Mn., 2d ed., 1900, M.3; by A. v. Hanstein, Voigtländer, L., 1898, 75Pf. Cf. Nos. 37, 43, 47, 52−54, 59, 72.

Reference was made in the previous chapter to attempts that were made from the end of the eighteenth century on to record and classify on a continuous basis the increasing mass of material published in periodical form. These attempts had been short-lived; they provided at best a limited coverage over a short period of time. In the nineteenth century the publication of popular and general entertainment literature did not at first increase, but the volume of scholarly and especially technical literature did increase and increased quite rapidly. Discipline-oriented periodic bibliographies therefore became essential, but before those in the field of German literature are considered, it is worthwhile looking at one of the few genuinely successful attempts to cover on a periodic basis the whole field of human endeavour rather than just one segment of it, namely, the *Literarisches Centralblatt für Deutschland* (319), which began publication on October 1, 1850 and continued to appear throughout the period covered in this chapter.

The editor of the *Centralblatt (Zentralblatt, LZ)*, Friedrich Zarncke, set himself the task of providing "eine vollständige und schnelle Übersicht über die gesamte literarische Thätigkeit Deutschlands" and to this end he listed all worthwhile books with a summary and sometimes a criticism of their contents and reviewed the contents of journals. The *LZ*, which appeared at first weekly and later fortnightly, maintained the traditional rubrics of theology, medicine, etc., with theology taking pride of place and "Poesie" bringing up the rear (until the NSDAP [Nazi party] insisted that theology be relegated to the rear in favour of ideological works). It is not without interest that Zarncke felt his bibliography would be not merely a source of information on particular subjects, but also a record of cultural development of the nation as a whole; it would remain, he claimed, "auch für den Culturhistoriker ein schätzbares Repertorium."

At first this relatively slender journal (eight pages in double column) coped with one hundred or so works in each issue. As it began its second half century in 1900, its aim was still the same, namely, "der höher gebildeten Welt einen Gesamtüberblick über die wissenschaftliche, nunmehr wieder, wie schon früher, auch über die schöne Literatur . . . zu vermitteln." In addition to the increased size of the journal there was now also a *Beilage* so that in this year alone there was a total of 1100 pages.

The history of the *LZ* in the second quarter of the twentieth century was somewhat more chequered. It was taken over by Wilhelm Frels in 1924 and was published by the Börsenverein from 1925. In its new form the *LZ* provided in Part One a listing of new publications with brief, if any, annotations and in Part Two discursive essays on books, general trends in scholarship, and so forth. In addition there now appeared the *Jahresberichte des literarischen Zentralblattes über die wichtigsten wissenschaftlichen Neuerscheinungen des gesamten deutschen Sprachgebietes* (from vol. 19 on *Das deutsche wissenschaftliche Schrifttum*), the aim of which was, "in kürzester Frist einen Überblick über die deutsche wissenschaftliche Arbeit des letzten Jahres zu bieten. This "reine Titelbibliographie" claims to list (in 1925) over 22,000 items "unter

Ausschaltung unwesentlicher Bücher und Zeitschriftenaufsätze." The items are classified in the usual manner; under "Germanische Sprachen und Literaturen ausschließlich Englisch" there are an estimated 1500 items for the year 1925. In 1927 the *LZ* was taken over by the DB; from 1928 on reference to foreign works was eliminated entirely. Unfortunately the journal dwindled in size over the next few years as subscribers fell away, partly perhaps on account of economic pressures, but partly also probably because of a growing interest in more specialised bibliographies. The journal came under considerable pressure from the NSDAP in 1938 but struggled on for a while before finally ceasing publication with its bibliography for 1942 (vol. 95, 1944).[7]

The *LZ* is not of course specifically concerned with the history of German literature. It includes, however, both literary works in German and scholarly criticism, and does so moreover at times when specialist periodic bibliographies had not yet developed or had suffered a lapse. In addition to this it reflects the interests of the time over a long period and probably to a greater extent than do more complete and differently organised specialist bibliographies. It provides in fact within the limits of its horizon a cross-section of cultural activity that is valuable as sociological background to literary studies as well as a contribution to bibliography in literary history per se.

Presumably because of the early historical, derivative approach to the study of the history of literature, systematic bibliographies developed earlier in the medieval field than in the modern, as witness Hagen and Büsching's *Literarischer Grundriss* (209). The first *periodic* bibliography appeared in the journal *Germania* (181) under the title "Bibliographische Übersicht des Jahres 1862"; subsequent issues were entitled "Bibliographische Übersicht über die Erscheinungen auf dem Gebiet der germanischen Philologie." In the first issue, which contained only 266 items, few journal articles were included. In the second issue the point was stressed that as much as possible would be listed, including items of a general or popular as well as academic nature (both books and articles) — "Vollständigkeit zu erreichen war mein Bestreben." Full bibliographical details are provided and many books are also critically reviewed (or reference is made to reviews). The items are classified in the usual manner, "Grammatik," "Lexicographie," "Mundarten," and so forth, and total in the second issue already 505. This bibliography continued to appear until 1892.

A parallel project to the "Übersicht" was then undertaken by the Gesellschaft für deutsche Philologie in Berlin, which published a "Bibliographie des Jahres 1876" (and 1877, and 1878) in the *Zeitschrift für deutsche Philologie* (517) in 1876 to 1878. After this the bibliography was taken out of the *ZDP* and published as a separate entity under the title *Jahresbericht über die Erscheinungen auf dem Gebiet der germanischen Philologie*, 1879– (263).

---

7   For a short time the NSDAP (Amt Schrifttumspflege) published its own review journal entitled *Bücher Kunde* (1934–); cf. also *Die Bücherei* (1934–).

From 1884 on it covered also the whole of the sixteenth century after agreement had been reached on this question with the instigator of a new bibliography for the modern period, Philip Strauch (see below). The organisation of the *Jahresbericht* is much the same as that of the bibliography in *Germania* or as it had been when it was published in *ZDP*. The intention at least was to cover more than was done elsewhere. Review space is reduced in favour of "meist nur sachlich gehaltene inhaltsangaben," and the coverage extended to books of a general nature, textbooks, and so forth, in addition to scholarly books and articles. Excluded are only newspaper articles and "politically motivated" reviews; "im übrigen strebt der jahresbericht nach vollständigkeit." Presumably it also strove after the accuracy that it found lacking in *Germania*, which is characterised as "noch immer durchaus nicht zuverlässig."

In addition to the "Bibliographische Übersicht" and the *Jahresbericht* there was also the *Anzeiger für deutsches Altertum und deutsche Literatur*, which had been put out as a supplement to the *ZDA*, beginning in 1876. Although this appeared in parts with the *ZDA*, it is paged and often bound separately. Its numbering is of course also different. The *Anzeiger* is a review organ rather than a bibliography and it attempts to examine in some detail all the major publications in the field.

It was then as a supplement to the *Anzeiger* that the first periodical bibliography for the modern period of literature was introduced by Philip Strauch in 1884. This short-lived bibliography (only to 1889) listed both books and articles and covered the period from 1624 to 1830 only: "innerhalb dieser Periode habe ich zwar nach möglichster vollständigkeit getrachtet, bin mir indes sehr wol bewust dass eine absolute nicht erreicht wurde, vielleicht überhaupt nicht erreicht werden kann" (p. 283). The first section lists general works, collections, etc. under a few subheadings; the second section lists writers alphabetically without further sub-division. In all 1129 items are listed; reviews are often included with monographs and not numbered separately.

Strauch's bibliography was superseded by the *Jahresberichte für neuere deutsche Literaturgeschichte* (266) which first appeared in 1892 for the year 1890. The compiler justifies the publication of a comprehensive bibliography by claiming: "schnell wie irgend eine der modernen Naturwissenschaften ist die Beschäftigung mit der neueren deutschen Litteratur zur Wissenschaft geworden" (p. iii). He rejects Strauch's bibliography, however, as too narrow and claims a different and wider intent than other bibliographies, e.g., the *Jahresbericht*. The *Jahresberichte* are to include books, essays, articles, and reviews — those written by and/or for academics. Although the classification system is simple and traditional, the arrangement within sections is quite different. Instead of individual items with specific comments on them there are long discursive essays on the topic of each section with relation to the items that fall within that section. Footnote numbers in the essay refer the reader to the bibliographical details of the item discussed; these are given at the bottom of each page. It is possible, therefore, to work through the listing of items at the foot of the page without reading the commentary or, alternatively, to read the commentary and gain an overall impression of work in the field without referring to individual items.

The number of items covered under the several headings was quite large as a result of the extensive coverage − in excess of 6500 by 1900 − although not every area was covered each year; areas omitted in any one year would be covered for two years in the following year. Consequently it is not surprising that a change in format was introduced after the first ten years. Beginning in 1902 the "Bibliographie und litterarischer Text [sind] besonders bearbeitet," although the divisions remain almost identical. This new format is much more convenient from a strictly bibliographical point of view. It was not to last long, however; as a result of wartime difficulties only the bibliographical portion appeared in 1915 and this was the end of the series. The years of the first World War are covered to a large extent by Alfred Rosenbaum's *Bibliographie der in den Jahren 1914 bis 1918 erschienenen Zeitschriftenaufsätze und Bücher zur deutschen Literaturgeschichte.*[8]

The next major development took place in 1924 when agreement was reached between the editors of the continuing *Jahresbericht* and the now-to-be-revived *Jahresberichte* about a combined operation, albeit at a reduced level. Materials were to be excerpted in common, German items in the DB and foreign ones in the Staatsbibliothek in Berlin. Although everything accessible was to be excerpted, only a list of more important items was actually to be published; the complete handwritten manuscript would remain available in the DB. The division between early and modern literature was laid down as 1700 for the first issue but as 1624 in subsequent issues; the modern *Jahresbericht* was to exclude from consideration authors still living. The first year to be covered under the new system was 1921 and the treatment of items is almost identical in the two volumes. Apart from the bibliographical data there is still a certain amount of at times quite trenchant comment on items listed. Without examining each volume item by item it would be impossible to establish the exact number of entries, since some are sub-divided by a, b, c while others are collective entries for reviews of items listed earlier (reviews are normally listed with the work reviewed). The totals for 1925 are estimated at around 3400 (medieval) and 2100 (modern) of which perhaps 10 % are reviews.

It would also be impossible to determine the precise extent of coverage in these volumes without an exhaustive study of contemporary sources. It was stated in the introduction to the first volume that a degree of selection was necessary, but a study of the list of abbreviations for 1925 suggests that a very

---

8 "Zwölftes Ergänzungsheft" of *Euphorion* 1922; this issue concludes the bibliographies which had been published by *Euphorion* somewhat eratically since its inception.

considerable number of in part quite trivial journals were covered. In all there are about 450 abbreviations cited in the medieval volume and half that number in the modern volume. It must also be borne in mind that the modern volume excludes living authors, for example, Thomas Mann and most of the Expressionists. Where there does seem to be a certain limitation, it is in the number of foreign journals listed. These number only about one tenth of the total, which is a rather small proportion in view of the fact that English language and literature are included in both volumes. The conclusion is therefore that the coverage is quite detailed for German monographs and periodicals, but weak in regard to foreign, primarily English language materials.

Foreign materials were covered to a certain extent elsewhere. A limited number had been cited in the *LZ,* and from 1911 on there existed also a foreign section to a work generally known as Dietrich. This project had begun as a *Bibliographie der deutschen Zeitschriften-Literatur; alphabetisches nach Schlagworten sachlich geordnetes Verzeichnis von ca. 8500 Aufsätzen, die während des Jahres 1896 in ca. 275 zumeist wissenschaftlichen Zeitschriften deutscher Zunge erschienen sind . . .*[9] and the inclusion of popular materials along with scholarly materials is explained in the introduction to the second volume. By 1899 the number of periodicals indexed had risen to 1150 and included newspapers and the previously deliberately excluded medical journals. From this point on the bibliography appeared twice annually (each part with a separate volume number) and included not only periodicals but also "Sammelwerke" such as Festschriften.

In the following years there were several additions and/or changes to this work. A *Bibliographie der Rezensionen und Referate* began in 1900, "ein nach Büchertiteln alphabetisch geordnetes Verzeichnis der in deutschen Zeitschriften während eines Jahres besprochenen deutschen und ausländischen Bücher" (Vorwort to vol. 5, 1899, 2), and in 1908 a supplement was issued (after an earlier unsuccessful *Wöchentliches Verzeichnis* had been proposed in 1902), entitled: *Halbmonatliches Verzeichnis von Aufsätzen aus deutschen Zeitungen in sachlich-alphabetischer Anordnung,* which was to contain "eine Auswahl geeigneter Aufsätze von möglichst dauerndem Wert" ("Zur Einführung," no 1, October 5, 1908).[10]

In 1911 the whole arrangement was changed with the addition of foreign periodical literature and the consequent provision of a new general title: *Internationale Bibliographie der Zeitschriftenliteratur mit Einschluß von Sammelwerken und Zeitungen.* Abteilung A retained the old title; Abteilung B was newly instituted as a *Bibliographie der fremdsprachigen Zeitschriften-*

---

9 Edited originally by Felix Dietrich, published in Leipzig, first by Fr. Andrä's Nachfolger, subsequently by Dietrich; reprinted by Kraus (New York) in 1961.

10 Included in the *Bibliographie der deutschen Zeitschriftenliteratur* 1923–27; weekly 1928–29; monthly 1933–34.

Literatur; Abteilung C continued (from 1913) the *Bibliographie der Rezensionen.* Finally the attempt was made to extend the bibliography backward in time and supplementary volumes were issued for the years 1861–98 (vols. 1–20 in reverse order). The coverage in these volumes is much thinner (and excludes medical literature entirely).

In summary Dietrich covered up to the Second World War:

A	German periodical literature	1861–	(1944)–
B	Foreign periodical literature	1911–	(1943)–
C	Reviews of German and foreign books	1900–1943	
	German newspaper articles (separately 1908–22, thereafter in periodical index)	1908–1944	

Indexes of the subject terms used in A were published for volumes 66–75 and 76–85.

Aside from the grand scale on which it was conceived, the principle novelty of Dietrich's bibliography lay and lies in its strict subject approach. With the exception of the supplements to series A (newspaper articles), which are grouped under discipline headings such as "Sprach- und Literaturwissenschaft," all items are entered once under a single subject which is expressed as precisely as possible within the given limitation of a single word or word-group. The advantages of this system are on the one hand the specificity of subject definition and thus the avoidance of lengthy searches through varied material within a disciplinary category and on the other the conservation of space that can be achieved; having entered an item under a precise topic the title of the item cited may be omitted and the entry thus reduced to author and source. In order to achieve the utmost saving of space, all sources are indicated by number only and a key provided with each volume.

The disadvantages are of the same kind as the advantages. To enter an item under one narrowly specific heading may mean the loss of subsidiary but not negligible aspects of that item, while the entry itself may not be the term under which a user will look. The reduction of the entry to an author and source reference means that the user cannot himself immediately verify from the title the probability or improbability of the item's being useful; and the source must be identified by reference to the key. The disadvantages for the scholar are particularly acute. Precisely because the number and variety of materials covered are so vast, the degree of specificity attained by a single term in any single discipline is low. Thus, while popular periodicals are indicated in the early volumes by an asterisk, this is of little use to a scholar faced with entries under a topic as specific but at the same time as general as Goethe or Thomas Mann. Except where there are gaps in the bibliographical coverage of academic materials, the primary use of Dietrich is therefore for the location of items of general and/or popular interest that would probably not be included in works such as the *Jahresberichte*. It will also provide on occasion "inter-disciplinary" references on general topics. The following is a short example from 1925, 2:

> Barlach, Ernst (H Bachmann) 587aa. 20. J. 180–85. – D. Sintflut. FK 1./9. l –, Träger d. Kleist-Preises (FStrich) KHZ 26./10.

In modern terms these are:

> H. Bachmann in *Gral,* 20 (1925), 180–85
> On the *Sintflut* in the *Frankfurter Kurier,* Sept. 1, 1925
> F. Strich on Barlach's receipt of
> the Kleist prize Königsberg, *Hartung'sche Zeitung,* Oct. 26, 1925

While Dietrich was the only work to attempt a degree of international coverage, there were periodical indexes in existence abroad. However, Poole's *Index to Periodical Literature* (covering 1802–1907 in the USA),[11] Nijhoff's *Index op de Nederlandse periodieken,* 1909– (256), or the British *Subject Index to Periodicals,* 1919–[12] were restricted to national coverage and to works of primarily general interest. The only bibliographies from this period that deal specifically with the study of German literature outside Germany are those published by the Modern Language Association of America and by the Modern Humanities Research Association in the UK. The former began as a bibliographical supplement to the association's journal *PMLA* (383); entitled "American bibliography" (for 1921 etc.), it listed only monographs, articles, and dissertations produced by Americans. It appeared during the first years in essay style with comments in general and on specific items, but without a formal listing of the items cited. In 1926 a more formal and practical style was adopted with alphabetical arrangement of author/title entries under general categories. There were still, however, occasional comments, explanatory rather than critical, on individual items. In the bibliography for 1930 a total of 35 abbreviations of journals, i.e., for all fields, is listed; there are 160 items in Germanic studies.

The British equivalent, entitled *The Year's Work in Modern Language Studies,*[13] began in 1930 after an unsuccessful attempt had been made by Gilbert Waterhouse to establish a series in 1920 with his *Year Book of Modern Languages* (495). The editor states in the preface to the first volume: "This volume aims at providing a concise, even laconic, and discriminating summary of the chief results and tendencies of research." Its style is discursive, as was

---

11 Originally covering 1802–81; rev. ed. Boston: Houghton Mifflin, 1891; supplements 1882–1906.
12 Published in London for/by the Library Association for the period from 1915, lacking 1923–25.
13 Published by the Modern Humanities Research Association.

that of the MLA bibliography at the outset, but, although it is intended to be more consciously selective, coverage is not restricted as in the case of the MLA to work by nationals, in this case British authors. On the other hand the bibliography is not intended for the specialist but for the general reader, librarians, and so forth.

Like the MLA bibliography the *YWMLS* covers all (major) language areas, not just German, and it is more comprehensive than the preface would lead one to believe. In 1935, for example, the style is still that of individual essays with the bibliographical details of the works cited included in footnotes. Germanic studies are covered in this year in fifty pages within the following categories: philology, medieval literature, literature 1500–1740, Classical period, Romanticism and after, 1880 to the present. In all there are approximately 1000 items as compared with only 150 items in the MLA bibliography for the same year.

Although the establishment of periodicals and consequently of periodic bibliographies is by far the most important feature of the period under discussion, more traditional forms of bibliography continued to develop also in new directions. The method and in most cases also the procedures remain, however, much the same, no matter how many different forms these bibliographies take – and the number and variety is truly vast. For convenience these continuing types of bibliography will be roughly categorised as bio-bibliographies, subject bibliographies and form bibliographies.

The biographical dictionary is virtually the oldest established bibliographical source in Germany, but the first genuinely comprehensive national biography did not begin to appear until the end of the nineteenth century. The first volume of the *Allgemeine deutsche Biographie* (8) dates from 1875 and the work was completed in 56 volumes (instead of 20, as originally planned) by 1912. Such a work cannot of course include minor figures in literature, since all fields must be covered: "Aufgenommen werden sollen . . . alle bedeutenderen Persönlichkeiten . . . in Geschichte, Wissenschaft, Kunst, Handel und Gewerbe" (preface, p. v–vi). Also space restrictions do not permit complete bibliographical references in the case of writers. The value of such a work is therefore severely restricted as regards information on writers and *their works;* it does provide, however, reference to existing bibliographical sources and is of course invaluable as a source of background information.

In the field of literature proper the variety of biographical sources is bewildering; there are for example, lists of authors by area, by sex, and by religion. The following examples from the end of the century must suffice. An *Allgemeines sächsisches Schriftsteller-Lexikon* was published by Wilhelm Haan in 1875 (208); Franz Brümmer published a *Lexikon der deutschen Dichter und Prosaisten* to 1800 in 1884 and a similar work for the nineteenth century in 1885 (94/5); Sophie Pataky produced in 1898 her *Lexikon deutscher Frauen der Feder* (390). The scope and approach of these and numerous other (also earlier), similar works varies widely, but for the most part they are intended to be as complete as possible, i.e. consciously *un*selective. Pataky's work, for example, includes — as her title is intended to indicate — not merely authoresses in the strictly literary sense, but also essayists, newspaper columnists, journal editors, and so forth. Brümmer in his preface to the *Lexikon . . . des neunzehnten Jahrhunderts* states quite emphatically: "Meine Aufgabe bestand lediglich darin, zu sammeln und zu registrieren" (cited from the fourth edition, p. 3).

Perhaps the best known, however, of the general literary bio-bibliographies is that by Wilhelm Kosch, the *Deutsches Literatur-Lexikon,* first published in 1927–30 (301). Kosch's work is based on Hermann Krüger's similarly titled one volume lexicon of 1914 (303), which in turn goes back to Adolf Stern's *Lexikon der Nationalliteratur* (455). The degree of indebtedness of one work to another is less important than the modifications and improvements that are made. Krüger's entry for Jung-Stilling, for example, has 20 lines of biographical and critical summary that are almost identical with the 18 lines in Kosch.[14] The entries under "Behandlungen" are also similar, but Kosch has 9 lines of "Literatur" to Krüger's 2. The procedures are also very similar and both works include not only persons in fields related to literature (critics, philosophers, etc.), but also topics (genres, technical terms), places associated with literature, and so forth. Kosch is therefore encyclopedic in scope rather than a bio-bibliography.

All such comprehensive, retrospective works — some, such as the *ADB,* deliberately exclude even living authors — suffer with the passage of time, although they may, as in the case of Kosch, be brought up to date in subsequent editions. There is only one comprehensive work in the area of literature which attempts to remain current by the publication of annual issues and that is Kürschner's *Literatur-Kalender.* This actually began (under the title *Allgemeiner Deutscher Literaturkalender*) in 1879 in the form of a diary (305), to which was appended useful information for writers, new works published, the names of those who had died, etc. In succeeding years (the diary part was soon dropped) the work listed separately, and still does list, authors living and those that have died in the past year. Since the works of each author are given in each volume, one can see at a glance who was writing what at any given time and, if the death date is known, one can check rapidly on an author's works, since these are listed fully at the time of death. The necrology part of this work became in fact such a useful feature that the necrologies for a 35-year period (1901–35) were gathered together and published separately in 1936 under the title of *Nekrolog zu Kürschners Literatur-Kalender* (373), "ein nach Vollständigkeit strebendes Werk" (p. vi). There are indexes both by birth-date and death-date.

---

14 Stern has 29 lines of biography and 25 lines listing works (the lines are shorter); there is no critical literature.

A distinct off-shoot of the bio-bibliographical approach is the personal bibliography, that is the bibliography devoted to a single author (or work). There are basically two forms in the case of a person, namely a listing of the author's works or a listing of criticism of his works. The two forms may of course also be combined or restricted to a single work or a group of works by a single author. The listing and description of an author's work with the various editions and impressions, etc. is one area where analytical and enumerative bibliography are closely connected, and research of this kind is often related to the production, and/or forms part, of what are known as historical-critical editions. Here the editors of medieval texts were again – for obvious reasons – early in the field, while the publication of enumerative bibliographies of critical literature on later writers is an interesting criterion for the measurement of contemporary interest in any given author or work. The main distinction between the two is that the bibliography of an author's works may be superseded and replaced by a later more definitive work as knowledge increases, whereas improvements to an enumerative bibliography are normally in the form of additions only. Goedeke's work is an interesting attempt to combine both "subjective" and "objective" literature (i.e. original works and criticism) – and biography! – and many of the authors he lists have never subsequently become the subject of individual bibliographies. A few early examples in this area are the following: Friedrich Panzer, *Bibliographie zu Wolfram von Eschenbach*, 1897 (386); Theodor Abeling, *Das Nibelungenlied und seine Literatur*, 1907, 1909 (2); Friedrich Meyer, *Maler-Müller-Bibliographie*, 1912 (346); Otto Mallon, *Brentano-Bibliographie*, 1926 (334). The major weakness of such bibliographies is that they are usually organised solely on a chronological basis, but more will be said of this in the following chapter.

A special type of subjective personal bibliography is Wilhelm Frel's bibliography of autographical materials in the field of German literature: *Deutsche Dichterhandschriften von 1400 bis 1900 . . . in den Bibliotheken und Archiven Deutschlands, Österreichs der Schweiz und der ČSR*, 1934 (165). The scope of this work is evident from the title (there are only very few references, for example, to private collections), whereas the scope of Max Armin's *Internationale Personalbibliographie* is much less easy to define (18). This work originally appeared in 1936 and covered the period 1850–1935. It is devoted strictly to subjective personal bibliography, recording as succinctly as possible those places where a listing of works may be found published by any notable person throughout the world, "diejenigen Verzeichnisse, die das literarische Lebenswerk eines Gelehrten oder Schriftstellers in vollständiger oder annähernd vollständiger Form . . . enthalten" (ca. 25,000 entries). The balance is weighted perhaps toward the German scene, but even there the selective process means that only major figures can be included. The following example, the entry for Heine, is from the 1936 edition; a second edition appeared in 1944 (cf. Bestermann, below).

Fdr. Meyer: Verzeichn. einer Heinr.-Heine-Bibliothek 1905 (Nebst) Register 1910. – E. Elster: Die Heine-Sammlung Strauss. 1929. – H. G. Atkins: Heine, 1929 S. 270–275 (eng. Übers.). – A. Gottschalk: H. Heine, 1934.

Although a list of critical writings on a given author may be considered an (objective) personal bibliography, it is also in effect a subject bibliography, the subject being the person, work, or works in question. Moreover each author has his or her place in the study of the history of literature as a "subject." It is therefore appropriate at this stage to discuss developments in these comprehensive works.

Increased knowledge of the literature of the past coupled with an increasing volume of detailed research made it virtually impossible by the end of the nineteenth century for a single scholar to cope with the whole of the history of German literature. Increasingly works were limited to specific periods or authors. Increasingly also scholarly histories of literature included relatively detailed bibliographies rather than the excerpts from author's works which had been a feature of early histories and were still to be found in such works as Robert König's *Deutsche Litteraturgeschichte,* first published in 1878 (292). The phrase "relatively detailed" is used advisedly, since it is evident that the bibliographical details could not be permitted to outweigh the text, while the shorter the period covered, the greater *could be* the degree of bibliographical detail provided.

The only worthwhile attempt to cover the whole period of German literature was made by Josef Körner in 1928, when he contributed a selective bibliography to Walzel's new, expanded edition of Scherer's *Geschichte der deutschen Literatur* (426), a work which originally (1880) had had only few bibliographical references. Although this bibliography is not slavishly restricted to supporting the text, it is directly linked to and organised on the basis of it. Thus the only way to find the bibliographical references is by locating in the index the pages on which a given author is discussed and then consulting those page references in the bibliography. Such a bibliography is evidently highly selective, covering as it does the entire period of German (literary) history in only 160 pages (excluding the brief list [10 pages] of general works, collections, etc.). There is room, however, for selective bibliographies when the available material exceeds a certain limit, and the demand for them not unnaturally increases with time.

In the area of more specialised literary histories reference may be made to Richard M. Meyer's *Deutsche Literatur des 19. Jahrhunderts,* 1900 (347), to which was added in 1902 a *Grundriß der neueren deutschen Literaturgeschichte* (348), which took the form of a much more extensive but nevertheless still selective bibliography for the same period. As a separate publication this work has its own organisation, even though it is indebted to the companion text to the extent of adopting the same chapter divisions. The expanded 1907 version is divided into "Allgemeiner Teil" and "Spezieller Teil" (63 and

238 pages) and within each of the 24 chapters of the latter part each numbered paragraph is devoted to an author or topic, the individual items being identified by a, b, c, etc. I estimate the total entries (exclusive of reviews) to be between 35,000 and 40,000. Although "keineswegs eine vollständige Bibliographie" (p. 64), this is nevertheless a substantial quantity. As an example the entry for C. F. Meyer is found in chapt. 11, "Die Wiedereroberung der Geschichte," sub-heading "Die historische Novelle" — "462 C. F. Meyer (1825–98)." There are 19 items (a–t, the first two biographical) followed by 9 (u–bb) under "Biographisches" and 8 (cc–kk) under "Literaturhistorisches."

As contrasts to this work the bibliographies by Hans Pyritz and Gustav Ehrismann may be cited. The former is a much more consciously selective work, "die indessen alles Wichtige zu umfassen sich bemüht" (p. 478), appended to Paul Hankamer's *Deutsche Gegenreformation und deutsches Barock* (215). The latter includes copious bibliographical references both in the text and in the footnotes to his extensive *Geschichte der deutschen Literatur bis zum Ausgang des Mittelalters* (145). Quite another type of — similarly selective — bibliography is offered by Schottenloher's *Bibliographie zur deutschen Geschichte im Zeitalter der Glaubensspaltung 1517–1785* (436). Based on bibliographical sources for lectures in the field of history, it has been useful for work in literature in the absence of a satisfactory literary bibliography for the period.

While Körner's work is excellent within its specific and intended limitations, it is not really typical for its time. Typical for the early part of the twentieth century is rather the necessity of focussing more closely on narrower areas, on authors, on works — at most on definable periods of literature. The volume of published research is such in fact that already so-called *Forschungsberichte* begin to appear regularly, compendious reviews of recent research in a given field or on a given topic.[15] Who could be expected — to take only one example — to cope with the Goethe literature of the twentieth century? The only part of Goedeke to appear in a third edition comprised a Goethe bibliography in three parts, totalling nearly 1700 pages while a later list of works on Goethe between 1912 and 1950 ran to 877 pages.[16]

The ultimate then in subject bibliography at this time is the collection of bibliographical references not to a single author or to a single work, but to a single, sometimes restricted, sometimes more general, topic. This development was not entirely new and owed much to motif research in medieval literature, where there was a common stock of often used material, and to research in "folk lore," fairy tales, and the like. One might include in this category Emil Weller's pioneer work *Annalen der poetischen National-Literatur der Deutschen*

---

15 See, for example, the series "Wissenschaftliche Forschungsberichte," edited by Karl Hönn.
16 Goedeke's *Grundriss* Bd. IV, Abt. V, Ergänzung zur 3. Aufl. (ed. Herbert Jacob).

im 16. und 17. Jahrhundert, 1862–64 (499),[17] which is an early attempt to apply strict bibliographical principles to a heterogeneous and inchoate body of material, namely "folk-songs." The vast quantity of material and its organisation, bibliographical detail, etc. render it even today a necessary source of reference.

The study of individual legends, themes, etc. in the Middle Ages led on the other hand to innumerable studies of individual types (the peasant, the burger, the teacher, the priest, the blind) and individual themes (friendship, youth, imperialism), which, though not primarily bibliographically oriented, nevertheless often contain extensive bibliographical material. This development brought about the bibliography of "Stoffe" and "Motive," in which such studies (and bibliographies) were collected together. The first major work in this field – in effect a form of biblio-bibliography – is K. Bauerhorst's *Bibliographie der Stoff- und Motivgeschichte der deutschen Literatur,* 1932 (37).[18] A related kind of work in a specific field is Arthur Luther's *Deutsches Land in deutscher Erzählung,* 1936 (325/6) in which, under an alphabetical listing of villages, cities, areas etc., prose works are listed (ca. 13,000) that have particular places as their mise en scene. There is a systematic index of places and an alphabetical index of authors. A later work by Luther covered German history on a similar basis (324/6).

A similar kind of work, although on more general lines, and one which contains also a good deal of bibliographical reference material is the *Reallexikon der deutschen Literaturgeschichte,* 1925–31 (141). This work excludes the personal (biographical) element and is thus complementary to Kosch.

The term "form bibliography" is used in this chapter rather loosely to include lists of works that have something in common other than their content, authorship, etc., but it does not refer to format – at least not primarily – although such oddities as bibliographies of miniature books, books bound in human skin, and so forth, do exist. Included are rather such things as bibliographies of cryptonyma, of dissertations, and the like.

Reference works on cryptonyma were discussed in detail in chapter 3, and the tradition is continued in this period by M. Holzmann and H. Bohatta, *Deutsches Anonymen-Lexikon,* 1902–8 (245), the seven volumes of which contain a total of 12,000 entries. The same authors were responsible also for the *Deutsches Pseudonymen-Lexikon,* 1906 (246), in which only the names of authors are listed without any indication of their works. The preface to the latter work contains a brief discussion of the problems of defining anonymity,

---

17 This work is the source of the quotation on p. 6.
18 One of a series entitled "Stoff- und Motivgeschichte der deutschen Literatur," ed. Paul Merker & G. Lüdtke (Berlin: de Gruyter, 1929–); even Stern (above) has a special index in his lexicon of "Artikel über dichterisch behandelte(n) Stoffe und Motive."

pseudonymity, etc., and the term has been widely interpreted to include, among other things, the names adopted by members of the Sprachgesellschaften. To this particular field of cryptonyma may also be added appropriately perhaps the *Bibliotheca Germanorum erotica et curiosa* by Hugo Hayn and A. N. Gotendorf.[19] This extensive collection, which includes many popular works that would today hardly be considered erotic or even curious, was first published pseudonymously by Hayn in 1875; the later, considerably extended edition of 1912– was reprinted in 1968. The listing, which is based on the holdings of the Bavarian State Library, provides comprehensive bibliographical details and some commentary.

The listing of incunabula is continued with the *Gesamtkatalog der Wiegendrucke*, 1925– (297). The Kommission für den Gesamtkatalog had compiled its census of works in German libraries by 1911 (over 145,000 items) and first published a supplement to Hain (298) and then a bibliography of *Einblattdrucke des 15. Jahrhunderts*, 1914 (296).[20] Unfortunately publication of the *Gesamtkatalog* with its attempted coverage also of non-German libraries was very slow. By 1938 publication had gone no further than from A to Eigenschaften, at which time the estimate of the total production of incunabula had risen from 30,000 to 40,000. Further reference to incunabula is made below.

Somewhat similar to the bibliography of broadsheets (Einblattdrucke) is the work of Paul Heitz and F. Ritter, *Versuch einer Zusammenstellung der deutschen Volksbucher des 15. und 16. Jahrhundert*, 1924 (230), which lists 735 items, a regrettably small proportion of a kind of literature that must surely have existed in many more hundreds of editions. Two other more restricted kinds of bibliography are Lothar Brieger's *Ein Jahrhundert deutscher Erstausgaben* [1750–1880] (86) and E. Schulte-Strathaus's *Bibliographie der Originalausgaben deutscher Dichtungen im Zeitalter Goethes* (439). The latter work, which contains numerous illustrations, is a good example of fairly full bibliographical description. The notes are limited but the descriptions are lengthy and include attempts to reproduce original type-faces, etc. Only separate publications, i.e., no journal articles and the like, are included.

Other "form" bibliographies of greater general interest are those that list journals, dissertations, and programmes – to mention the three perhaps most significant examples. A list of German journals of interest to scholars in

19 Leipzig: n.p., 1875 (N. Hay!); Leipzig: Unflad, 1885 (Hayn); München: G. Müller, 1912–29 (= vols. 1–8 plus suppl. 9). Cf. also Hayn's *Bibliotheca erotica et curiosa monacensis. Verzeichniss französischer, italienischer* [etc] *Erotica und curiosa, von welchen keine deutschen Übersetzungen bekannt sind* (Berlin: Harrwitz, 1889).

20 *Einblattdrucke des XV Jahrhunderts; ein bibliographisches Verzeichnis* (Halle: Karras, 1914); not to be confused with the series of *Einblattdrucke* put out by Paul Heitz (Strassburg, 1901–).

literature was published by Carl Diesch in 1927, *Bibliographie der germanistischen Zeitschriften* and contains ca. 4,700 items (135). The coverage is broad but far from complete as is evident from the numbers cited elsewhere in this work. The Staatsbibliothek in Berlin produced lists of dissertations from 1885 on, also an annual list of works published by schools, *Jahresverzeichnis der an den deutschen Schulanstalten erschienenen Abhandlungen* (267), which includes what are known as *Programme* or *Programmschriften,* an elusive, but for the German literary scholar, important type of publication.

As a final example of a more esoteric kind there is the private press bibliography put out by the Deutsche Bücherei in 1931: *Deutsche Bibliophilie in drei Jahrzehnten* (128). This lists the productions of 27 bibliophile organisations from 1898 (there was little private press activity in Germany before this date) to 1930. All kinds of literary work are included, from a facsimile edition of the *Wessobrunner Gebet* to contemporary original works.

Some of the more important "form" bibliographies, such as those of incunabula, are based on the holdings of particular libraries, and the importance of library catalogues in the modern period can not be overestimated. Reference has been made much earlier to the existence of catalogues of institutional libraries, but these were highly selective, academic collections at a time when the volume of manuscript and/or printed material was relatively small. Later, primarily in the eighteenth century, many valuable and extensive personal collections were established and catalogues of them made public.[21] By the end of the nineteenth century some of the larger institutions had published comprehensive catalogues, such as that of the Bodleian library, 1843 (72); but a few libraries had built up large general collections – often by a process of amalgamation and accretion – to the point that they became virtually national institutions. Librarians had also become aware by this time of the necessity of publishing catalogues in order to make the holdings of any given library available to a wider public, and it is at this stage that the publication of the huge catalogues of national or quasi-national institutions begins.

The British Museum led the way with its *Catalogue of the printed books,* 1881 (88), revised and reprinted under the title *British Museum. General catalogue of printed books* from 1931 on (87). One of the useful features of the British Museum catalogue is the system of cross-referencing and the inclusion of critical works on an author as an appendix to the author entries. In addition to the general catalogue there were special catalogues of incunabula and *An index of German books 1501–1520.*[22] The subject index begun for the

21 Personal libraries are still a factor of course, though a minor one in the twentieth century. See, for example, Edward Grisebach, *Katalog der Bücher eines deutschen Bibliophilen* (Leipzig: Drugulin, 1894).

22 By Robert G. C. Proctor (1903) = *An index to the early printed books in the British Museum,* part II, section 1.

period 1881—1900 (1902) and continued on a multi-annual basis is of rather less value for the scholar in a limited field (89/90).

The *Catalogue général des imprimés de la bibliothèque nationale* (389) followed in 1897 but proceeded unfortunately at a very slow pace. By the outbreak of the second World War only A-Rukser had been completed. Even less complete at that time was the *Deutscher Gesamtkatalog* (133) which had been intended to comprise the holdings of the Prussian state Library and of fifteen other libraries in Prussia, but to include also from the holdings of the Bavarian State Library and the Austrian National Library those works held there and not in the Prussian system. The eight volumes published between 1931 and 1939 did not even complete the letter B.

We must return at this point to a consideration of two bibliographies in the field of German literature, which might have been discussed above as successors to Hoffmann and Bahder. They deserve, however, to be considered towards the end of this chapter as representing something of a new direction in bibliography, one that brings them closer to biblio-bibliographies. The first of these two works is Robert Arnold's *Allgemeine Bücherkunde zur neueren deutschen Literaturgeschichte,* 1910 (20). What is new in this work is not the comprehensiveness, or the careful organisation, or the copious annotation, but the deliberate attempt to instruct the reader in bibliographic *method* as well as to inform him; for by this time the number and variety of bibliographies had become such that a literature search required recourse to many and different kinds of resources. Accordingly, both the organisation of Arnold's work and his general comments are intended to instruct and assist the reader in methodically constructing a list of works on whatever topic is desired.

Arnold's work is therefore not purely a bibliography or even a *bibliographie raisonnée* but rather a bibliographic handbook — he himself reverts to the older *Bücherkunde* for his title. There had been of course reference in earlier works, even in such a simplistic work as Breul, to the method of collecting citations, and in a sense Arnold only picks up where the eighteenth century *Literargeschichten* had left off. But his is the first work which is specifically designed to enable the student or scholar to know in detail both how and where to look for information and how also to take at least the first steps in doing the same thing in related disciplines.

A detailed analysis of Arnold's book is hardly necessary. The volume of material and its detailed organisation are impressive. The scope, nature, reliability, etc. of many works are succinctly circumscribed. A second, revised edition appeared in 1919 and a third revision was completed (still by Arnold himself) in 1931. Over fifty years after the date of the first edition his work was still valuable enough to reprint ([4]1966).

Less successful is Fritz Loewenthal's *Bibliographisches Handbuch zur deutschen Philologie,* 1932 (321), in which the author attempted, "das Gesamtgebiet der deutschen Philologie ... in seinen wesentlichen Teilen systematisch [zu] erfassen" (p. iii). The major divisions "Allgemeines," "Frühgeschichte/Mythologie/Volkskunde," "Sprachwissenschaft," and "Literatur- und Geistesgeschichte" are further divided and sub-divided into a multitude of sections, but the resultant entries are often disappointing and not unnaturally provide many examples of overlapping. In general the information offered is meagre, for example, the personal bibliographies of major authors, where there is rarely more than a single entry and explanatory comments are few and far between. The items total only 2079 in all, excluding ten pages of "Nachträge und Berichtigungen."

There is one other type of bibliography which becomes essential in the twentieth century and which has not yet been mentioned in this chapter, namely the bibliography of bibliographies. Admittedly, the biblio-bibliography is also not new, though of much later date than, for example, the bio-bibliography. Reference has been made above to Labbé and others. There were some important examples of this kind of bibliography in the nineteenth century, but they were universal in scope and, perhaps not unnaturally, inadequate through their superficiality and/or inaccuracy, incompleteness, and so forth. The most important German work in this field is probably Julius Petzholdt's *Bibliotheca bibliographica. Kritisches Verzeichniss der das Gesamtgebiet der Bibliographie betreffenden Literatur des In- und Auslandes,* 1866 (397). This work is in effect a world-wide bibliography of bibliographies, heavily weighted toward works in the German language. For its time it is a remarkable piece of work, containing as it does not only full bibliographical details of each work listed, but in many cases also trenchant and/or lengthy comments. One of the more notable features of the work is the considerable number of personal and dealer's catalogues it lists in all fields. The following is Petzholdt's comment on Kayser's *Bücherkunde:*

> Ein mit vielem Fleisse zusammengestelltes und für bibliopolische Zwecke zum schnellen Nachschlagen ganz nützliches, aber für bibliographische Studien durchaus entbehrliches und unzureichendes Werk. Der Anhang, der ein "alphabetisches Verzeichniss der Romane und Schauspiele, welche von 1750 bis Ende 1823 in Deutschland erschienen sind", enthält, ist 1827 auch apart ausgegeben worden. (p. 292)

Even more narrowly restricted to the interests of librarians/bibliographers are such books as Georg Schneider's *Handbuch der Bibliographie,* 1923 (432), which lists almost exclusively works of a general bibliographical nature,[23] not discipline-oriented bibliographies as is the case with Petzholdt (at least in part). It was left in fact for Theodore Bestermann to create the first biblio-

---

23 "Er [the author] hat es nur mit allgemeinen internationalen und nationalen Verzeichnissen, nicht mit fachwissenschaftlichen, zu tun" (p. iv).

bibliography that is both comprehensive (world-wide in scope) and yet detailed enough to be of use to scholars working within the bounds of a discipline.

There are two major features that set Bestermann's *A World bibliography of bibliographies,* 1939–40 (46) apart from its predecessors. In the first place he applies the term bibliography strictly; and secondly he adopts a purely subject approach. Earlier bibliographies had been generous in their interpretation of the term bibliography and had included not merely biographical dictionaries and encyclopedias, but also general compendia of many kinds and bibliographies included within non-bibliographical works. They had also adopted one or other of the general classifications of knowledge that had persisted, however modified, since the Middle Ages and still persist today. In this they differed only little from their older counterparts, the writers of *historia literaria,* or from their contemporaries, the discipline-oriented scholars who sought to sub-categorize their own discipline. Bestermann abandoned all this and entered every bibliography under as specific a single heading as possible within a single alphabetical sequence. It therefore matters not at all where the Middle Ages are divided from the Renaissance, or whether a particular author belongs to this or that period. Each author is to be found under his or her name alone and each topic under its appropriate heading.

A work of so broad a scope as this, vast as the number of entries may be, cannot be as particular as a scholar in a narrow discipline such as German literary history would like. There are nevertheless many relevant entries to be found here, both wide topics such as German national bibliographies and specific topics such as individual authors or themes. What entries there are, are complete, succinct and accurate to a degree not hitherto attained. Notwithstanding the limitations inherent in a work of this breadth, Bestermann's bibliography is a very useful work and one unlikely to be surpassed in this form in the future. The following example is from the first edition and may be compared with the same entry in the latest edition:

> Heine, Heinrich
> Friedrich Meyer, Verzeichnis einer Heinrich Heine-Bibliothek. Leipzig 1905. pp. [v]. 175. [1000]
> Bernhard Wachstein, Bibliographisches zu Heinrich Heines fünfundsiebzigstem todestag. Wien 1937. pp. 7. [173.]

In the brief but refreshingly sensible and pointed introduction to his bibliography Bestermann points himself to the weakness of all bibliographies, namely that they are out of date from the time they are published. In the case of biblio-bibliographies the time lag is greater, since it includes the time delay of both the original bibliography and of itself. It is therefore hardly surprising that the same solution was sought for bibliographies as for journal articles, namely, the creation of periodic indexes, or, more accurately, periodic bibliographies of bibliographies. Such periodicals became essential not merely on account of the volume of individual bibliographies, but because so many of these bibliographies appeared in obscure places and were not easily accessible, even to the initiated. The first periodic lists of bibliographies are in fact intended for librarians rather than for what one might call primary users.

One of the first such bibliographies began as part of the *Zentralblatt für Bibliothekswesen* and appeared separately in annual form as the *Bibliographie des Bibliotheks- und Buchwesen* (1904–12; 1922–25), subsequently as the *Internationale Bibliographie des Buch- und Bibliothekswesens mit besonderer Berücksichtigung der Bibliographie* (258). This bibliography was not, as might appear from the title, restricted to works on library science and book history, but lists works of use to librarians and includes among its subject divisions also "Fachbibliographien." Under this heading are found, for example, in the 1905 volume in the sub-category "Sprachen und Literaturen — Germanische Sprachen — Deutsch," 6 works, ranging from the most recently issued part of Goedeke to a bibliography of *Skrifter i tysktalande länder för aller mot dryckesseden 1501–1602*. There is, however, no subject index to this work.

From the 1930s date also the *Internationaler Jahresbericht der Bibliographie*, 1931–,[24] the *Bulletin de documentation bibliographique*, 1934– (101), and the *Bibliographic Index*, 1938– (53). The last-named is a comprehensive work, covering ca. 1000 periodicals and organised purely alphabetically by subject headings; it has the advantage of being cumulated from quarterly issues into multi-annual volumes, the first of which was for the six-year period 1937–43. In this volume there are approximately 50,000 entries, including, for example, three under "Grail" and five under Thomas Mann. However, many of the "bibliographies" cited here are merely brief lists appended to articles, dissertations, and critical works.

Rather than examine at this point what might be considered as the first bibliography of bibliographies of bibliographies, namely Aksel G. S. Josephson's *Bibliographies of bibliographies*, 1901 (276), we shall conclude this chapter — fittingly perhaps — with one of the few examples of international co-operation in the field of bibliography, with the *Index bibliographicus*,[25] first

---

24 Ed. J. Vorstius (Leipzig: Harrasowitz, 1930–). The first issue had appeared in volume 3 (1931) of the *Archiv für Bibliographie, Buch- und Bibliothekswesen*, and in the introduction Vorstius refers to other unsuccessful attempts to produce periodic bibliographies. This one ceased in 1940 (vol. 11).

25 Not always an easy work to track down, the *Index bibliographicus* appears in English as: 1925 — League of Nations, Committee on Intellectual Co-operation, *Index Bibliographicus. International Catalogue of sources of current bibliographical information (Periodicals and Institutions)* (Geneva); 1931 — League of Nations, International Institute of Intellectual Co-operation, *Index bibliographicus. World list of current bibliographical periodicals* (Berlin/Leipzig: de Gruyter); 1952 — UNESCO (or IFD), *Index bibliographicus. Directory of current periodical abstracts and bibliographies*, 2 vols. (UNESCO, Paris; IFD/FID, The Hague) = UNESCO pub. no. 863, IFD pub. no. 247;

published by the League of Nations (Committee on Intellectual Co-operation) in 1925. In contrast to the preceding works (and to Bestermann) the *Index* was intended from the outset to be a list only of *current periodic* bibliographies, for, as the editor suggests: "Une bibliographie des bibliographies courantes est comme la clef de la production scientifique et littéraire quotidienne" (p. ix—x). With these sentiments one can only agree, but, having said that, it must also be said that one thousand or so periodical works spread around the entire scientific and literary world cannot mean anything but either superficiality or, at most, very uneven coverage.

In the second edition (1931) things improved somewhat with almost double the number of titles (1900) from 37 countries. The organisation, as in the first edition, is still by Dewey decimal classification; the indexes (previously by country, title, etc.) are reduced to one general index, which does not of course include subjects. As is to be expected, the entries — divided as a result of the Dewey classification between 42—46 (philology) and 83 (literature) are only of the most general kind. Under "83 Deutsche Literatur" there are only 7 items, viz., *Jahresbericht,* "Kürschner," *Die Literatur, Die neue Literatur, Revue germanique,* and the *Jahrbuch der Goethe Gesellschaft.*

In surveying the bibliographical situation in the early decades of the twentieth century, three salient features emerge. In the first place bibliographical development seems to reach an endpoint, a culmination, however far from perfection it might be. National bibliographies list the sum total of the production of the innumerable presses, while comprehensive and detailed scholarly bibliographies, both periodic and retrospective, list the products of academic research. Bibliography itself, enumerative, descriptive, etc., has become an accepted academic pursuit and individual bibliographies are produced on every conceivable aspect of literature.

This leads to the second point which is the fact that bibliographical work has become a major concern of all those to whom books are the substance of life, to book producers (publishers), booksellers, librarians and academics. It is not simply that the public at large has become more book conscious; rather that the book producers at the one extreme, the book users at the other extreme, and the book "handlers" (retailers and librarians) in the middle have become aware of the necessity of interchange and co-operation. The symbol and practical outcome of this attitude is the Deutsche Bücherei in Leipzig.

Thirdly — and this is the factor that points to the future — it also becomes clear by the 1930s at the latest that existing bibliographical procedures must inevitably break down under the burden of an ever increasing volume of material. The essential quality of bibliography is completeness; at the same

1959 — Brussels, Institut international de bibliographie (Institut international de documentation) *Index bibliographicus,* 4th edition, Fédération internationale de documentation (The Hague, Willem Witseplein 6).

time it must also provide *timely* information in order to be of use in the trade and in research. It becomes increasingly evident as the century progresses that currency cannot be maintained in the face of increasing volume without unacceptable financial commitments. Production slips behind or coverage is limited and cumulation becomes impossible. Precisely the latter point is of particular concern to those in the field of literature, for critical literature itself does not greatly lose currency with time, so that, as each annual bibliography appears, one more volume is added to that long row that by the 1930s already stretches back seventy or eighty years into the nineteenth century.

The bibliographical sources available in the field of German (language and) literature had therefore fairly clearly entered a cul de sac by the 1930s. The utmost that could be done, had been done through the refinement of procedures, through co-operative ventures, etc. Things would have to change in the future.

Chapter 6:

The contemporary scene

There is no point in a work such as this in attempting to describe in detail the bibliographies that have been or have become available in the field of German literary studies since the second World War. Although the war temporarily or permanently put a stop to the publication of some periodic bibliographies and although the division of post-war Germany has produced many problems for bibliography, in general those works that have recently been published differ only very little from those published prior to the war. Moreover, further works have appeared whose main purpose is to provide systematic access to the sum total of bibliographical sources in the field, sources both old and new. This survey of contemporary sources will therefore be limited to an indication of the extent to which there have been significant changes in various broad areas of bibliography and of the extent to which there has been a distinct break in publication history on account of the war. Reference will also henceforth be in the main to the most recent editions available. The more important point to be considered subsequently is no longer what kinds of bibliographies exist and how they are arranged (or how they come to be what they are), but rather how well do the current major bibliographies do what they are supposed to do after such a long period of development and refinement?

Broadly speaking, the current bibliographical scene is characterized on the one hand by an avid desire to create more and completer bibliographies and on the other by an almost total lack of initiative in developing new procedures or employing newly developed technological aids. At the national level the bibliographical tradition has continued almost unchanged, although divided between the Deutsche Bücherei in the German Democratic Republic (Leipzig) and the Deutsche Bibliothek[1] in the Federal Republic of Germany (Frankfurt). The former continues the *Deutsches Bücherverzeichnis* (134), which is based on the *Deutsche Nationalbibliographie* – Reihe A (weekly, *Neuerscheinungen des Buchhandels*), Reihe B (fortnightly, . . . *außerhalb des Buchhandels*), and Reihe C (monthly, dissertations, etc.); the latter has instituted the *Deutsche Bibliographie* (125) with much the same format *(Wöchentliches* and *Halbjahres-Verzeichnis)*. Similar national bibliographies are now available also in Austria and Switzerland, although these are covered for the most part also by

---

1 On the Deutsche Bücherei see above; on the background of the Deutsche Bibliothek see *Bibliographie und Buchhandel: Festschrift zur Einweihung des Neubaus der Deutschen Bibliothek* (Frankfurt: Börsenverein des deutschen Buchhandels, 1959) and *Die deutsche Bibliothek 1945–65; Festgabe für Hanns Wilhelm Eppelsheimer zum 75. Geburtstag* (Frankfurt: Klostermann, 1966).

the German works. The latest product of the Deutsche Bibliothek is the weekly *Neuerscheinungen Sofortdienst (CIP)* and its companion *Monatsverzeichnis* (1975–). Each item is listed in catalogue-entry form in accordance with the principles of CIP (Cataloguing in publication). The entry – which is also printed in the work when published – appears under the appropriate *classification* in the weekly issue, while the monthly and quarterly issues are arranged alphabetically. The annual list of dissertations is continued by the Deutsche Bücherei; a new series has been instituted by the Deutsche Bibliothek and is of particular interest for its use of a single-sequence index with authors, titles and KWIC title entries (on KWIC, see below) – the title differs slightly (126).[1a]

The only genuinely new development at the national level has been the creation (in the FRG) of a comprehensive annual listing of books in print, the *Verzeichnis lieferbarer Bücher,* 1971/72 – (487). This publication, which listed 220,000 items in the 1973/74 edition, is intended primarily for, and is indeed produced by, the booktrade and is a counterpart to similar publications which have been in existence in other countries in some cases for a considerable time. In the most recent issue the author and title entries, previously separated, have been united in a single alphabetical sequence (1975/76). A similar, much smaller publication in the GDR is entitled *Bücher aus der DDR*, a continuation of the *Leipziger Bücher-Katalog* (97).

Regrettably little has been done on the other hand – partly no doubt as a result of the division of Germany and the often parlous state of individual libraries – in the area of library catalogues. During the second World War the Library of Congress in the USA published *A Catalog of books represented by Library of Congress printed cards issued to July 13, 1942,* 1943– (316), and this was followed by periodic issues and annual cumulations, eventually also by *The National union catalog, pre- 1956 imprints* (366), a listing of the holdings of numerous major American libraries as reported to the Library of Congress. In the wake of these publications came the book-form catalogues of the holdings of many libraries, a particularly relevant recent example being that of Harvard University, as the catalogue is divided into subject areas, e.g., *German Literature,* Widener Library Shelflist 49, 50, 1974 (221). Unfortunately the impetus provided by such publications did not extend to Germany. Only a few catalogues became available, such as the *Bibliothek des Instituts für Weltwirtschaft, Kiel,* 1967 (63) and the *Bibliothek des Instituts für Zeitgeschichte, München,* 1967 (64).

1a After this work had gone to press the first volumes were received of a new work which cumulates all the major national bibliographies for the first part of the twentieth century: *Gesamtverzeichnis des deutschsprachigen Schrifttums (GV) 1911–1965,* ed. Reinhard Oberschelp (München: Verlag Dokumentation, 1976–). Entries from the dozen or so bibliographies used have been cut out, pasted up in alphabetical order, and photographically reproduced.

At the international and biblio-bibliographical level Bestermann's *A World bibliography of bibliographies* has been revised (4th edition 1965—66). The Heine entry, for example, has been expanded to three quarters of a column comprising works by Meyer (1905), Wachstein (1931), Tschörtner (1956), Handrick/Klingenberg (1957), Lang et alia (1957), Levinton (in Russian — 1958), Arnold (1959), and Wilhelm/Galley (1960) (cf. above). Arnim's *Internationale Personalbibliographie* has also been revised, first by Arnim himself (1943—) and subsequently by Bock/Hodes. In volume III, which covers the period from 1944 to 1959 with additions to the entries in earlier editions, the following is the Heine entry for comparison with Bestermann:

> Heine, Heinrich [Dichter] 1797—1856
> Goedeke: Grdr. dt. Dicht. 8, 1905, S. 549f., 714f.; 15, 1955, S. 295—297. — Meyer, Fr.: Verzeichnis einer H. H.-Bibliothek. (Nebst) Register. Leipzig 1905—1910. — Ester, E.: Die H.-Sammlung Strauss. 1929 — Atkins, H. G.: H. 1929, S. 270—275. — Gottschalk, A.: H. H. 1934. — H., H.: Works of Prose. New York 1943, S. 345f. — H. H. Berlin 1947, S. 467—471. — Spaeth, Albert: La Pensée de H. Paris 1947, S. 177—179. — Tabak, Israel: Judaic Lore in H. Baltimore 1947, S. 315—320.

The *Index bibliographicus* has been revised too, but of the latest edition ([4]1959) so far only the volume on science and technology has appeared (see above, ch. 5, n. 25). Greater efforts have also been made in Germany to keep track of the increasing number of specialist bibliographies contained in non-bibliographical publications ("versteckte Bibliographien"). The Deutsche Bücherei published in 1956 a *Bibliographie der versteckten Bibliographien aus deutschsprachigen Büchern und Zeitschriften 1930—53* (56) and continued this for the period from 1954 to 1966 with the *Bibliographie der deutschen Bibliographien, Jahresverzeichnis der selbständig erschienenen und . . . versteckten Bibliographien* (55). This is now superseded by the monthly *Bibliographie der Bibliographien.*

Handbooks of bibliography have increased in number without there being, however, any appreciable change in format. One of the best in this area is W Totok and R. Weitzel, *Handbuch der bibliographischen Nachschlagewerke,* (1954), now in its fourth edition (477). In the narrower field of German studies a number of new bibliographical handbooks replace Arnold and Loewenthal, chief among them being at present Johannes Hansel's *Bücherkunde für Germanisten* (217), first published in 1959 and republished many times since then, especially in the *Studienausgabe.* This work is currently the most comprehensive guide to *how* and *where* to look for information in the whole field of "Germanistik."

A comprehensive listing of periodicals has been begun by Joachim Kirchner, *Bibliographie der Zeitschriften des deutschen Sprachgebiets bis 1900,* 1969 (287), and this is supplemented by specialised lists, such as Fritz

Schlawe's *Literarische Zeitschriften 1910–1933,* 1962 (428). The only comprehensive *index* to general periodical literature remains Dietrich's *Internationale Bibliographie,* which, however, underwent a sea-change in 1965 to re-emerge as the *Internationale Bibliographie der Zeitschriftenliteratur aus allen Gebieten des Wissens* (ed. Otto Zeller). Volumes are still semi-annual, but the previous division into Reihe A and Reihe B has been abandoned. The same editor is responsible also for the *Internationale Bibliographie der Rezensionen wissenschaftlicher Literatur,* 1971– (257).

At this juncture reference must be made to what is in effect a form of "period" bibliography, namely Paul Raabe's *Index Expressionismus,* 1972 (255). Period bibliographies become in fact much rarer in the twentieth century and this is certainly not a true bibliography for its period (1910–25), since it is restricted to literary journals. Its importance, aside from its focus on literary rather than on critical periodicals, lies in its innovative indexing method: "Der 'Index Expressionismus' will . . . als Modellversuch verstanden werden, als 'pilot project', das die Möglichkeiten der bibliographischen Erschliessung literarischer Zeitschriften mit Hilfe eines neuen Verfahrens erprobt und zur Diskussion stellt" (p. ix). The new process referred to is the employment of computer technology to produce various systematically arranged printouts of the index entries. Each of the more than 37,000 articles registered (from over 100 periodicals) appears in all or most of five separate series of indexes: alphabetical, systematic, by journal, by title, by genre (Gattung). For example, the following entry:

> Kerr, Alfred
> Robert Musil
> [Aufsatz]
> in: Die Aktion 1
> (1911), Sp. 1229–1233
> 9147

appears in the alphabetical part under Kerr; in the systematic part (Dewey decimal) under the superimposed headings "830–4: Kerr, Alfred: 05" and "830–4: Musil, Robert: 45" (05 = Essay, 45 = Abhandlung); in the "Zeitschriften" part under *Die Aktion;* and under the title in the abbreviated form:

> Robert Musil
> Kerr, Alfred

Finally it is listed in the index by "Gattungen" under Aufsatz:

> Aufsatz
> Kerr, Alfred
> Robert Musil.

While the value of this system may be disputed,[2] it is at least a step in the direction toward transferring the laborious task of bibliographical organisation to the computer, which is a more reliable and much faster worker – if properly used.

In the field of German literary studies very little has changed from a bibliographical standpoint, very little, that is, beyond the refinement of existing forms. The biographical tradition continues with Kürschner,[3] and a new edition of Kosch (1966) now omits the entries on *topics* included in earlier editions and is devoted exclusively to persons. A single volume abbreviated edition was published in 1963. At the national level the *Allgemeine deutsche Biographie* is being replaced by the *Neue deutsche Biographie, 1953*– (vol. 10 Hufeland-Kaffsack, 1974 [374]). The encyclopedic tradition also continues with a new edition of Merker/Stammler's *Reallexikon, 1955*– (411) and a "Nachtrag" to Stammler's *Verfasserlexikon, 1955* (130). A comprehensive retrospective bibliography in German literature is of course virtually a thing of the past, and the only near representative of this genre is Körner's select bibliography, which was republished in 1949 separated from its original companion text, the *Literaturgeschichte* of Scherer/Walzel. The number of literary histories that have been produced – or at least begun, for the majority are not complete and seem likely to remain so – since the second World War is prodigious. For the most part they also include what might be termed "generously selective" bibliographies, for example, the individual bibliographies (OHG, MHG, etc.) of the *Handbuch der deutschen Literaturgeschichte: Abteilung II, Bibliographien,* edited by Paul Stapf (453). One of the most extensive bibliographies is that associated with the *Geschichte der deutschen Literatur* ... produced by a Kollektiv für Literaturgeschichte in the GDR (185). The bibliographical supplement, entitled *Internationale Bibliographie zur Geschichte der deutschen Literatur von den Anfängen bis zur Gegenwart,* 1969–72 (4), contains over three thousand pages of small print in its three volumes! One minor trend is that towards what might be termed interdisciplinary rather than period bibliographies. Examples are the *Stoff- und Motivgeschichte der deutschen Literatur* continued by Franz Anselm Schmitt (431), the *Bulletin bibliographique de la société internationale Arthurienne,* 1948– (100), and the bibliographies on medieval studies (e.g. *Medieval Music* [1974] by Andrew Hughes), published by the University of Toronto Press (250).

Personal bibliographies have become such a feature of the twentieth century that biblio-bibliographies have already become necessary. There is, for

---

2   It had a mixed reception. See, for instance, *Germanistik,* 14 (1973), 689–91 and *Times Literary Supplement,* 23 March 1973, p. 332.
3   56th edition of the *Literatur-Kalender* and *Nekrolog 1936–70* ([both] Berlin: de Gruyter, 1973).

example, E. Friedrichs' *Literarische Lokalgrößen 1700–1900,* 1967 (166), a listing of bibliographical sources for around 8000 names and 2000 pseudonyms. A similarly extensive list for the twentieth century is the *Bibliographie der Personalbibliographien zur deutschen Gegenwartsliteratur,* 1970 by Wiesner/Živsa/Stoll (506) a "Verzeichnis von Monobibliographien und Forschungsberichten, mit dem der Versuch unternommen wird, eine annähernd vollständige Übersicht über die bisher geleistete personalbibliographische Arbeit zu rund 500 deutschsprachigen Autoren des 20. Jahrhunderts zu geben" (p. 10). In both cases the names of authors are listed alphabetically; in Friedrichs there is in addition a valuable bibliography of biographical sources, both general and by region. The only other significant work in this field is Hansel's *Personalbibliographie zur deutschen Literaturgeschichte* (218), but this proved, when it finally appeared in 1967, to be somewhat limited in scope (only 300 entries). Such bibliographies as these are important precisely because there are already so many individual personal bibliographies (subjective and objective), even several for one single author, e.g. for Thomas Mann and for Hesse. In addition there are societies devoted to the interests of a single author and these put out in some cases periodic bibliographies, such as that for Eichendorff in *Aurora* (Jahresgabe der Eichendorff-Stiftung e.V. Eichendorff-Bund).

The situation then at the present time in the field of bibliography of German literature is hardly to be brought within the compass of a single study. There is already a vast number of retrospective bibliographies on every conceivable kind of topic (and of every degree of quality, needless to say). In addition countless periodic bibliographies are published either separately or as part of a periodical of more general or specific nature. Finally there are bibliographies of bibliographies, both retrospective and periodic. The only way for the newcomer to cope with this situation is to follow the Ariadne thread through the labyrinth of one of the bibliographical guides such as Hansel, and, having located the major sources in the field, to keep abreast of research by maintaining close contact with the periodic bibliographies and with periodical literature.

It would clearly be quite out of the question to discuss, describe, or even simply list a fraction of the large number of retrospective bibliographies currently available, but at least something must be said, if only briefly, about some of the principles upon which such bibliographies are or should be based. The following examples have not been chosen for any other reason than that they were to hand and that they attempt to cope with two quite different situations. As it happens, one is a (relatively) good example, the other a bad example, but both show weaknesses which are of principle concern to the users of all kinds of bibliographies.

Older bibliographies of a single author or single work such as those cited in the previous chapter adhered in the main to a strictly chronological arrangement of entries, an arrangement that documented and reflected interest in the development of the field of research being covered. Such a principle has a long tradition, for example, in *historia literaria,* and was favoured by Leibniz even as a basis for a library catalogue. Heinz Küpper's *Bibliographie zur Tristansage,* 1941 (304) adheres to this practice, while Hans-Hugo Steinhoff's recent *Bibliographie zu Gottfried von Straßburg* (454) applies it only to a limited extent within the framework of an arrangement which is fairly typical of many bibliographies that deal with a relatively restricted topic and not merely typical of the series of which it is a part (Bibliographien zur deutschen Literatur des Mittelalters). Steinhoff's bibliography is restricted to literature on Gottfried's *Tristan,* i.e., effectively to a single work, and within this limitation and the time set he claims to be virtually complete. It is not our concern to examine this claim but rather to consider the usefulness of the work, assuming it to be (and it certainly seems to be) complete and accurate within its terms.

Steinhoff enters all works chronologically under the following subject divisions:

Bibliographien
Forschungsberichte
Überlieferung – 1. Handschriften, 2. Untersuchungen
Ausgaben
Wörterbücher
Übersetzungen
Darstellungen in Handbüchern
Gesamtwürdigungen und Urteile
Biographie und Chronologie
Literarische Beziehungen – 1. Zeitgenossen (außer Wolfram), 2. Wolfram von Eschenbach, 3. Nachfolger
Weltanschauung – 1. Allgemeines, 2. Minneauffassung, 3. Tragik und Humor, 4. Verhältnis zur Antike
Sprache und Form – 1. Wortschatz und Wortbedeutung, 2. Grammatik und Syntax, 3. Stil, 4. Bauformen, 5. Raum und Zeit, 6. Verskunst
Einzelprobleme – 1. Prolog und Akrostichon, 2. *edelez herze,* 3. Literaturexkurs, 4. Gottesurteil, 5. Minnegrotte, 6. Musik und Kunst, 7. Einzelne Stellen
Realien
Stoffgeschichte – 1. Gesamtdarstellungen, 2. Einzelne Motive, 3. Thomas und Gottfried, 4. Eilhart und Gottfried, 5. Nachwirkung in der Neuzeit, 6. Bildende Kunst

The question is, is this an effective method?

This kind of subject division raises many problems. In the first place a work may belong to more than one subject division and Steinhoff recognizes this himself by including some, but not many, cross references. Secondly, the inclusion of any given work at a particular place in the division may not correspond to the user's expectation. Supposing, for example, that one were looking for anything to do with aspects of medieval law. There is no indication in the list of contents of where this might be found; the nearest possibility seems to be the section devoted specifically to the "Gottesurteil." There one must read through all entries, since they are listed chronologically, and there is in fact a cross reference to "Realien," items 638 and 633. Reading through the "Realien" section, it becomes clear that "Realien" is a catch-all title for many varied aspects of Gottfried's work, but, since it too is arranged chronologically, items on related topics are not listed together. Relevant items to a search for legal problems might be, for example, 585 (Zinsknechtschaft), 595 (Blutrache), 615 (Schwertleite), in addition to 633, 634, and 638 which only come close together because of their publication dates.

The greater difficulty is encountered, however, in locating items on specific parts of the poem (e.g. the Gandin-episode), individual characters such as Brangaene, or topics such as Leid. The section "Einzelprobleme" deals only with larger and more frequently discussed portions of the poem; "Einzelne Stellen" covers words or lines; "Einzelne Motive" is within the "Stoffge-schichte" division and therefore includes only work on parts of the poem from that particular aspect. In fact these three sections really need to be closely related; the occasional cross-references are inadequate. Looking for Brangaene, for example, one finds a reference under "Einzelne Motive" to the "unter-schobene Braut" but no cross reference to an article on Brangaene (243) which is listed under "Weltanschauung – Allgemeines." In this same section there are many items that have general application, but which also have particular significance, such as Maurer's work on Leid (cross-referenced only from word-studies), character analyses, blood mystique, and so forth. Only rarely is there a cross reference to these from other sections, as in the case of 255 and 301, to which there are references from "Musik und Kunst."

What is lacking therefore is a subject *index* as opposed to a simplified subject *arrangement,* one that would bring together the various aspects for which a user may be searching. That this is necessary, is recognized to a limited extent already by the use of cross-references, although it can be argued that the volume of material is limited enough for every user to be expected to read through a whole section for individual items. Such an approach is time-consuming, however, and it assumes, furthermore, that the user is reading through the section to which the bibliographer has assigned the work.

Of its type Steinhoff's bibliography is a good example in that the divisions are meaningful (but see below) and the entries themselves full, accurate and complete. It is quite a different story with Everett's bibliography on Günter Grass (158). Even the title of this work raises a question, for it reads: *A select bibliography of Günter Grass (From 1956 to 1973), including the works, editions, translations, and critical literature.* Whatever may be said by the purists about the term "select bibliography," it must nevertheless be expected that any bibliography that claims to be select(ive) must contain some justification for or explanation of the principles of selection. In this case there is no such justification; on the contrary, it is implied that the bibliography aims at comprehensiveness, since it is called: "the fullest attempt to date." The word "editions" in the title suggests a list of the various editions of Grass's works. In fact the bibliography is simply divided into works, translations, and critical literature with only one edition of each (original) work being listed. The editions, if anything was meant by the term at all, have fallen by the wayside.

If chronological arrangement has any place in a bibliography, then it is surely in a listing of an author's work and in particular of the work of an author still living. And yet in Everett's bibliography Grass's works are listed alphabetically by title, thus allowing no possibility of following the author's development. The titles are moreover alphabetized in an odd manner, definite articles being ignored (*Die Ballerina* under B), indefinite articles being treated as part of the title, so that "Eingemauert" appears between "Eine Stimme . . ." and "Ein glücklicher Mensch."

The critical works, which include large quantities of trivia ("select"?), are ordered alphabetically by the author and are not remarkable except for the frequency of typographical/spelling errors, which lead one to suppose that the work has not been proofread by anyone with a knowledge of German. The critical works are, however, divided into "Books" and "Journal and newspaper articles." No reason is given for this arbitrary division which results in articles in scholarly journals being separated from articles in collective works such as Festschriften. Under "unpublished material" (a sub-division that is nowhere listed) are included published dissertation abstracts.

Everett does, however, have a subject index – and what an index! It consists simply of seven categories: poetry, prose, drama, biography, literary technique, world outlook/political and social thought, and general. Each item, with the exception of four which apparently were added at a late stage and therefore not included in the index, has been assigned to only one of these broad categories. To call this an index is of course absurd; it is far less of an index than Steinhoff's subject divisions and could just as well have been accomplished by printing the items in sections. One can only assume that it was done in this way in order to avoid having to make an alphabetical author index. There is consequently absolutely no way in which to find work on any given novel(le), for example, on *Katz und Maus,* except by checking every one of the 259 items listed as dealing with prose or reading through the entire 801 entries under critical literature looking for the abbreviation KuM (such abbreviations are appended to the titles of individual entries to indicate the work discussed).

As was indicated above, these two bibliographies were not chosen to exemplify any particular points. Both the good and the bad indicate, however, certain basic requirements in bibliographies. It should, for example, be self-evident – but clearly is not always understood – that in any bibliography the purpose, scope, chronological and other limitations (including the cutoff date), etc., must be precisely defined. Beyond that the arrangement will depend on the one hand on the purpose of the bibliography and on the other on the nature of the material treated. But whatever arrangement is selected, it should allow the user access to whatever material might be desired. In the case of Everett the arrangement is virtually pointless. Steinhoff on the other hand has adopted a subject arrangement and married this to a chronological order. It is true that within the subject divisions the chronological arrangement is more useful than the alphabetical, since an alphabetical index is also supplied, but this is still a form of capitulation and admitted as such by the addition of cross references. The main danger which this work exposes is that of basing a subject arrangement on research interests of the past rather than encouraging current and future research by organising the material on a more objective, "un-committed" basis, one that allows the user equal access to every possible topic.

Whatever may be said about retrospective bibliographies in general, or even in particular, there can be no doubt but that the main emphasis in the bibliography of German literary studies is currently on periodic publication and international coverage. Since the *Jahresbericht* ceased with 1939 and supple-mentary volumes were subsequently issued only for 1940–45 (1960) and 1946–50 (1966), there are now the following serial publications:

1. *Bibliographie der deutschen Sprache und Literaturwissenschaft* (151) – cited as *Eppelsheimer (EPP)*.
2. *International Bibliography* of the Modern Language Association [of America] (328) – cited as *MLA*
3. *Germanistik* (182) – cited as *GER*
4. *The Year's Work in Modern Language Studies* (514) – cited as *YW*.

A fifth work, the *Zeitschriftenaufsatzkatalog (ZAK)*, represents an entirely new form of publication and will therefore be considered separately.

Of these four works only *YW* has remained true to its pre-war format. *MLA* changed radically in 1956, when it began to list for the first time works other than those by scholars from the USA. Only from this point on is there therefore broad coverage of scholarly work in German studies (previously it was called *American Bibliography*) – something that is often overlooked or not made clear in bibliographical reference works, such as Hansel. *EPP* and *GER* are entirely new. The former has been appearing annually since 1969 after multi-annual "catch-up" volumes for the period 1945–68;[4] and a cumulation (referred to subsequently as Köttelwelsch [295]) for the 15 years 1945–69 is in progress (1973–). *GER* has appeared on a quarterly basis since 1960 and has only a cumulated annual index. There are therefore two comprehensive annual bibliographies *(EPP and MLA)*, one selective annual *(YW)*, and one quarterly bibliography *(GER)*.

---

4 1 1945–53; 2 1954–56; 3–8 every two years

Since there are therefore even without the *ZAK* 4 current bibliographies in the field of German (language and) literature, the question naturally arises as to their relative merits. Users will of course not necessarily agree on the relative value to be placed on specific features of any bibliography, but the major areas of concern must surely include at least the following:

1. scope (extent and depth of coverage)
2. arrangement
3. extent and accuracy of information
4. timeliness.

None of these factors is easy to gauge, but at least some idea of the degree of similarity or disparity between these periodic bibliographies can be gained by a comparison of entries within a given period of time. It should be emphasized, however, that the evaluation is only relative, since it is not within the scope of this study (even if possible) to establish an absolute against which to measure them all.

The limitations on such a comparison are not negligible. In the first place publication schedules vary widely, as do also the elapsed times between the publication and reception by individuals of any issue. In the same way the bibliographies themselves are subject to the publication and mailing delays of the works they list. In absolute terms (i.e., with application to all biblio-graphical works) it must be borne in mind that the year of publication as printed in a book or journal not only applies to the whole period between January and December, but may even be incorrect by the actual date of publication. In the following discussion no attempt has been made to verify the actual date of publication of any item listed in bibliographies other than to establish in cases of ambiguity the nominal year of publication. From the content point of view it must be noted that the subject boundaries (especially the narrower ones) are never precisely defined and that the interpretation of these may vary not only from work to work, but from editor to editor or from year to year.

1. Scope

With the exception of *YW* all works discussed here claim to be comprehensive and to list, if not all, then all significant contributions to the subject. The difficulty not unnaturally lies in the lack of definition of the term significant, which is applied — objectively or subjectively — by the individual bibliographer in each area. In all of these bibliographies the scope is international and includes books and journals in a dozen and more languages. The major variation even within a given work is in the treatment of dissertations and reviews. The former used to be included, for example, in *GER* but are now omitted. Reviews are listed only in *EPP*. If not explicitly stated, it is implied that with the

possible exception of dissertations — which are entered as such — all items have
been published. Some general indication of the coverage can be obtained from
the following simple statistics. The total items enumerated over a four-year
period in the three comprehensive bibliographies (i.e. excluding *YW*, the items
in *YW* are not numbered, but probably do not exceed 1000) was as follows:

	EPP	GER	MLA (incl. linguistics)
1970	5130	5314	2655 (3616)
1971	5675	5380	2482 (3385)
1972	5923	4947	2873 (3695)
1973	6169	4946	2941 (3716)

Some reviews are included in *EPP*. The totals given for *MLA* are made up of the
sections entitled "German Language and Literature" (all); "Netherlandic
literature to 1500"; "Scandinavian literature to 1500"; "Icelandic." Festschriften and other general collections are not included. It should be noted in
addition that articles on linguistics are in a separate volume and are not
included with the literature section. In the linguistics bibliography the
Germanic section (exclusive of English) numbers 961, 903, 822, and 775 items
in the years 1970–73. The figures in parentheses include these figures.

From these general statistics it would seem that there is a fairly close
relationship in level of coverage between *EPP* and *GER,* while *MLA* lags
behind. These statistics are, however, found to be misleading, when individual
entries are examined. If we take the items entered under Rilke, for example, in
the year 1970 (including cross references) the totals are:

EPP	GER	MLA
29	36	27

The number for *EPP* excludes one review; the number for *GER* is the average
of 35 (1970) and 37 (1971), since it appears on a quarterly basis and therefore
includes items from 1970 in issues for 1970 and 1971. This would appear at
first to substantiate the relationship between the total entries as cited above.
However, the surprising thing about the actual items listed is the fact that only
7 are common to all three works and only a further 8 are common to 2 of the 3
works. In other words approximately 50 % of all entries appeared in only one
of the three bibliographies. It should further be noted that only 1 of the total
of 5 (!) entries in the selective bibliography *YW* was common to the other
three. Similar results can be obtained with a quite different figure, for example,
with Grabbe. The totals in 1970 for this author are 5 in *EPP* (excluding one
review), 7 and 2 in *GER,* and 5 in *MLA.* Here there is a greater similarity in
number, but *none* of the entries occurs in all three works; 6 items occur in two

of them. While the total figures *may* therefore be indicative of the relative degree of coverage, an equal number of entries cannot be assumed to mean the *same* entries.

Although the publication of each annual volume is delayed until such time as it may be reasonably assumed that all items for the completed year have been received — usually the late autumn of the year following — it is nevertheless likely that some items will still be received too late for inclusion in the appropriate volume. It is therefore assumed, if not actually stated, that items may be included from the year previous to that which is nominally covered. The *MLA*, for example, does state: "Items received too late (after 15 January) any year will be entered in the next, so that reasonable completeness may be achieved in two issues." The implication is that everything will have been included not later than in the second year, i.e. there will be no items listed in the third year. That this is not the case will be seen below. *GER* too lists items from earlier years although the original intent was not to list items that had been missed in the year of publication and in the succeeding year.[5] The statement in *MLA* then continues: "Over ninety percent of the important scholarship is thus made available annually on schedule." Our statistics must therefore be extended over a two-year period in order to establish whether or not complete coverage is achieved for the one year.

The total Rilke entries for *EPP* and *MLA* in 1970/71 and for *GER* in 1970/71/72 number: *GER* 94, *EPP* 62, *MLA* 54 (excluding reviews in *EPP* of works listed in earlier volumes, and one correction in *MLA* to an item previously listed and one item repeated in 71 from 70); 6 items in *EPP* are entered as one, since they are so listed in *GER*).

Of the 210 entries 22 are common to all three bibliographies and 31 to two of them. There are therefore 135 different items. Only 46 of these items derive from the year 1970, and of these 13 are listed in all three and 7 in two of the three.

A search in either *GER* or *EPP* or *MLA* would in other words produce only between 52 % and 67 % of those items listed collectively by all three for 1970 (*GER* 31/46, *EPP* 24/46, *MLA* 24/46), even though the search is extended over two and in the case of *GER* over three years. Clearly there is not the degree of coverage suggested (for example, by the *MLA's* "ninety percent"), unless there is a greater degree of selection than is implied. Equally clearly on the other hand any omissions are not based on comparable criteria, since the number of unique items is roughly comparable: 13 in *GER*, 7 in *EPP*, 6 in *MLA*. The question as to what items, if any, might be listed in *none* of the

---

5 The editor of *Germanistik*, Herr Krömer, writes in this connection: "Der optische Eindruck ist sicher besser, wenn man ältere Titel einfach wegläßt; ich finde es aber fairer, sie dem Benutzer doch zu bieten, auch wenn es für die Statistik der Aktualität unserer Berichterstattung ungünstig ist."

three must be left unanswered; but at least it can be established whether or not there are evident special reasons for the unique items.

Not unexpectedly both *GER* and *EPP* have unique items from Germany (3 each), while *MLA* has unique items from the USA. The remaining items are spread widely but evenly with a noticeably greater number in *GER* from far afield. Looking at the unique items from all issues (i.e. including those listed from years other than 1970), there is an even heavier preponderance in *GER* and *EPP* of German items (16 each), heavier in fact than the preponderance of items in *MLA* from the USA (4). The pattern is otherwise the same with *GER* providing the greatest spread from a dozen different countries (totals are: *GER* 49, *EPP* 21, *MLA* 12).

These figures suggest one (or both) of two possibilities. Local coverage may be fuller and/or local coverage may be less critical. In reverse terms foreign materials may be less accessible and/or may be more critically scrutinized. At all events it can hardly be said, even without looking outside the material available here, that any one of these three journals is genuinely comprehensive within its own stated limits. The full statistics are given in the following, including a breakdown of unique items. The entries under "type" are not necessarily accurate inasmuch as some dissertations appear as books where no indication is provided that they are dissertations. Editions and reprints (with dates) have been noted in parentheses.

Rilke Items Summary
GER (1970/71/72), *EPP* (1970/71), *MLA* (1970/71)

No.	Name	Journals	Date	Type	Source	Date
1	Alemparte	G	71	book (ed)	Spain	68
2	Alemparte	G	71	book (ed)	Spain	68
3	Allemann	E	70	article	Germ	67
4	Andreas-Salomé	G	70	book	Germ	68
5	Anderle	G	71	article	USA	71
6	Apitz	G	71	diss	Germ	71
7	Azadovskij	M	70	article	Russ	69
8	Balakian	G	71	article	Can	69
9	Balota	GEM	71/70/71	article	Germ	70
10	Bartlett	M	70	diss	USA	70
11	Bauer	GEM	70/70/70	book	Germ	70
12	Bauer, M	E	71	book (repr.)	Liecht.	70(31)
13	Behrens	G	70	article	Germ	68
14	Berger	G	70	article	Germ	68
15	Berger, K	G	70	book (repr.)	USA	68(31)
16	Binion	G	70	book	USA	68

17	Bjorneboe	E	71	article	Germ	71
18	Blanchot	G	70	book (repr.)	France	68(55)
19	Blume	G	70	article	USA	70
20	Bosisio	M	70	article	Italy	68
21	Boventer	GM	70/70	book	Germ	69
22	Brown	E	71	book	Germ	71
23	Chun, Gegens.	G	71	article	Korea	70
24	Chun, Widerst.	G	71	article	Korea	70
25	Cohen	M	71	diss	USA	71
26	Demetz	E	70	article	Germ	67
27	Dettmering	GM	70/70	book	Germ	69
28	Eifler	G	71	article	USA	72
29	Fagg	EM	71/71	diss	USA	71
30	Fingerhut	GE	71/70	book	Germ	70
31	Franyo	M	70	article	Ruman.	70
32	Franz	EM	71/71	article	Germ	71
33	Gabetti	GE	71/71	article	Germ	71
34	Garber	EM	70/70	article	USA	70
35	Gasser	E	71	book (repr.)	Liecht.	70(25)
36	Gaulupeau	GEM	70/70/70	article	France	70
37	Good	EM	71/71	article	Italy	71
38	Günther	G	70	article	Germ	68
39	Hähnel	E	71	diss	Germ	70
40	Hamasaki	M	71	article	Japan	70
41	Hamburger	M	70	article	Germ	70
42	Hamburger	GM	72/71	article	USA	71
43	Hausmann	G	70	article	Germ	70
44	Heck	GE	71/71	diss	Germ	69
45	Herzog	E	71	art. (repr.)	Germ	71
46	Himmel	GEM	71/70/71	article	Austria	70
47	Hoshino	GE	70/70	article	Japan	69
48	Grýnczuk	GEM	71/71/71	article	Poland	71
49	Jaccottet	E	70	book	France	70
50	Jaeger	G	70	article	USA	69
51	Jaeger	G	72	book	Switz.	71
52	Jonas, Begegn.	GM	70/70	article	USA	69
53	Jonas, HSS	GE	71/71	article	Germ	71
54	Jonas, Krit.	E	70	article	Germ	67
55	Kasamatsu	G	72	article	Japan	71
56	Kaufmann	E	70	article	Germ	69
57	Kayser	G	70	article	Germ	67
58	Kirchgraber	GM	71/71	book	Germ	71
59	Kitao	G	72	article	Japan	72
60	Kobayashi	GE	72/71	article	Japan	71
61	Kohlschmidt, Ch.	G	70	article	Denmark	70
62	Kohlschmidt, Sak.	E	71	article	Germ	71
63	Komatsubara	G	72	article	Japan	71

64	Kramer-Lauff	G	71	book	Germ	69
65	Kronegger	G	70	article	France	69
66	Kuh	G	71	diss	Germ	67
67	Kunz	GEM	72/70/71	book	Germ	70
68	Lang	GEM	72/71/71	article	USA	71
69	Loock	E	71	book	Germ	71
70	Mayer	G	72	book	USA	72
71	Memming	EM	71/71	diss	USA	71
72	Miyasaka	G	71	article	Japan	70
73	Mohandessi	GEM	71/71/71	article	USA	71
74	Müller	EM	71/71	book	Germ	71
75	Nostitz	G	70	article	Germ	67
76	Paul	E	70	article	Germ	67
77	Peterkiewicz	G	71	book	UK	70
78	Peters	G	70	book	Germ	68
79	Pickle, diss	EM	70/70	diss	USA	70
80	Pickle	GEM	72/71/71	article	USA	71
81	Pierard	M	71	article	France	71
82	Rehm	G	70	article	Germ	69
83	Revzin	GE	71/71	article	Germ	71
84	Rilke, Aspects	E	70	book (repr.)	USA	70(38)
85	Rilke, Gedichte	E	70	book (ed.)	Germ	70
86	Rilke, Sicht	GE	72/71	book	Germ	71
87	Rilke, Stunden	G	72	book (ed)	Germ	72
88	Rolleston	GEM	71/70/70	book	USA	70
89	Rosteutscher	GEM	71/70/71	article	S.A.	69
90	Ryan, J	GE	72/71	article	Germ	71
91	Ryan, L	GM	70/70	article	Germ	69
92	Saalmann	EM	71/71	diss	USA	71
93	Sabouk	G	70	article	Czech	68
94	Sandbank	GM	71/71	article	Palest	71
95	Schadewaldt	GE	71/70	article	Germ	70
96	Schleiner	M	70	article	Germ	69
97	Schmitz	GEM	70/70/70	article	Germ	70
98	Schoolfield	GEM	72/71/70	article	USA	70
99	Schnack	E	70	book	Germ	70
100	Schultz	GM	71/70	book	Germ	70
101	Seifert	GM	71/70	book	Germ	69
102	Sheets	GEM	72/71/71	article	USA	71
103	Simoens, Briefe	GEM	71/70/70	article	Belgium	70
104	Simoens, Auto	G	72	article	France	72
105	Simoens, Verw.	M	71	article	Holl	71
106	Sokel	GEM	72/71/71	article	Germ	71
107	Spitzer	G	70	article	Germ	69
108	Stahl	GEM	71/70/71	article	Germ	70
109	Starobinski	G	70	article	Switz	70
110	Steffensen	G	70	article	Swed	68

111	Steffensen	E	71	article	Germ	71
112	Steiner, Gegenw.	E	70	article	Germ	67
113	Steiner, Stimmen	E	70	article	Germ	67
114	Stephens, Puppe	GEM	70/70/70	article	Can	70
115	Stephens, Probl	GM	70/70	article	UK	69
116	Stern	GEM	72/71/71	article	USA	71
117	Strauss	E	71	article	USA	71
118	Strzalko	G	71	article	France	70
119	Strzaklowa	G	70	article	Poland	70
120	Szell	GM	71/71	book	Hung	70
121	Tatsuta	G	70	article	Japan	67
122	Thiekötter	GEM	72/71/71	book (diss)	Germ	71
123	Torres	G	71	article	Argentina	71
124	Uewada	G	72	article	Japan	71
125	Usinger, Grab	G	71	article	Germ	70
126	Usinger, Dicht.	G	71	article	Germ	70
127	Waidson	G	71	article	UK	71
128	Webb, Buch	EM	70/70	diss	USA	69
129	Webb, Themes	GEM	70/70/70	article	USA	70
130	Weissenberger	G	70	book	Switz	69
131	Willard	M	70	book	USA	70
132	Wilson	M	70	article	USA	70
133	Wolf, Coll.	GM	71/70	article	UK	70
134	Wolf, Surf	G	70	article	Can	69
135	Wolff	GEM	71/71/71	article	UK	70

Total items: 135
Total items 1970: 46
of which —   13 common to all three
              7 common to two
              26 unique

Unique items

GER	1970	1970–72		*EPP*	1970	1970+71		*MLA*	1970	1970–71
Germ.	3	(16)		Germ.	3	(16)		USA	3	(4)
Korea	2	(2)		Liecht.	2	(2)		Germ.	1	(2)
Argentina	1	(1)		USA	1	(2)		Japan	1	(1)
Denmark	1	(1)		France	1	1		Ruman.	1	(1)
France	1	(4)			—	—			—	
Japan	1	(6)			7	21			6	
Poland	1	(1)			—	—			—	
Switz.	1	(3)						France		(1)
UK	1	(2)						Holl.		(1)
USA	1	(7)						Italy		(1)
	—							Russ.		(1)
	13								—	
	—								13	
									—	

Spain	(2)
Can	(2)
Czech	(1)
Swed	(1)

49

The scope of YW is not comparable with that of the other three, being supposedly "selective." It is worth noting, however, that there is no evidence of any principle behind the selection; on the contrary there appears to be every indication that items are included haphazardly, presumably because they were to hand. In 1970/71/72 there is a total of 14 Rilke items, the majority of them from the UK and Germany; three are from the USA and one each from Canada, Denmark and Italy. Six books are listed and eight articles from six journals.

2. Arrangement

All of the bibliographies referred to here maintain the traditional classification system by subject area, period, and so forth. Nothing in fact more clearly demonstrates the tenacity of older academic attitudes to bibliographical organisation than a juxtaposition of classification schemes past and present. In the following the schemes used by major periodical bibliographies discussed in the preceding and current chapters are matched as far as possible with one another. Needless to say, it is not possible to include all the, in some cases numerous, sub-divisions.

1878/79-Jahresbericht (medieval)

1 Lexicographie
2 Namenforschung
3 Allg. Grammatik
4 Dialecte
5 Literaturgeschichte
6 Altertumskunde
7 Kulturgeschichte
8 Recht
9 Mythologie und Sagen
10 Gotisch
11 Scandinavische Sprachen
12 Althochdeutsch
13 Mittelhochdeutsch
14 Englisch
15 Altsächsisch
16 Niederdeutsch
17 Friesisch
18 Niederländisch

1925-Jahresberichte (combined)

Ia. Geschichte der germanischen philologie
Ib. Enzyklopädie und bibliographie
II. Indogermanische sprachwissenschaft und germanische sprachen
III. Gotisch
IV. Nordische sprachen
V. Deutsch in seiner gesamtentwicklung
VI. Althochdeutsche sprache
VII. Mittelhochdeutsche sprache
VIII. Neuhochdeutsche sprache
IX. Hochdeutsche mundarten
X. Niederdeutsche mundarten
XI. Niederländische sprache
XII. Friesische sprache
XIII. Englische sprache
XIV. Frühgeschichte

19 Latein
20 Geschichte der germanischen Philologie

1902-Jahresberichte (modern)

Litteraturgeschichte
Geschichte der deutschen Philologie
Poetik und ihre Geschichte
Volkskunde
Die Litteratur in der Schule
Gesch. d. Erziehungs- u. Unterrichtswesens
Gesch. d. nhd. Schriftsprache
Metrik
Stoffgeschichte
Kunstgeschichte
Mitte des 15. bis z. Anf. d. 17. Jhs.
Allgemeines
Lyrik
Epos
Drama
Didaktik
Luther und die Reformation
Humanisten und Neulateiner
Anfang d. 17. bis zur Mitte des 18. Jhs.
Allgemeines
Lyrik
Epos
Drama
Didaktik
Von der Mitte des 18. Jhs. bis zur Gegenw.
Allgemeines
Lyrik
Epos
Drama und Theatergeschichte
Geschichte der Oper
Didaktik
Lessing
Herder
Goethe
Schiller
Romantik
Das junge Deutschland

XV. Religionsgeschichte, sagenkunde, märchen
XVI. Runenkunde
XVII. Volksdichtung
XVIII. Altnordische literatur
XIX. Deutsche literaturgeschichte bis 1624
XX. Althochdeutsche literatur
XXI. Mittelhochdeutsche literatur
XXII. Neuhochdeutsche literatur
XXIII. Niederdeutsche literatur
XXIV. Niederländische literatur
XXV. Friesische literatur
XXVI. Englische literatur
XXVII. Latein
XXVIII. Metrik

1. Allgemeines
   a) Grundsätzliches
   b) Bibliographie
2. Formprobleme
   I. a) Poetik und Stilistik b) Metrik
   II. Poetische Gattungen a) Drama
   b) Epos c) Lyrik
3. Geistige Strömungen
4. Stoffgeschichte und vergleichende Literaturgeschichte
5. Neuere Literaturgeschichte
6. 17. Jahrhundert (1624–1700)
7. Anfänge der Aufklärung (1700–1750)
8. Vorklassische Zeit und Lessing
9. Klassische Zeit
   a) Goethe und Schiller
   b) Zeitgenossen Goethes und Schillers
10. Zeit der Romantik
11. 1830–1848
12. 1848–1871
13. Neueste Zeit
    A. 1870–1890
    B. Von 1890 bis zur Gegenwart
14. Theaterwissenschaft
15. Mundartliches
16. Auslandsdeutschtum

1973-Germanistik

    I. Verzeichnis der ausgewerteten
       Periodika und Sammelwerke
    II. Allgemeines
    III. Germanische Altertumskunde
    IV. Allgemeine und indogermanische
       Sprachwissenschaft
    V. Germanische Sprache
    VI. Ostgermanische Sprache
    VII. Nordgermanische Sprachen
    VIII. Westgermanische Sprachen
    IX. Deutsch in seiner Gesamtwicklung
    X. Althochdeutsche und altnieder-
       deutsche Sprache
    XI. Mittelhochdeutsche und mittel-
       niederdeutsche Sprache
    XII. Frühneuhochdeutsche Sprache
    XIII. Neuhochdeutsche Sprache
    XIV. Alt- und mittelniederländische
       Sprache
    XV. Hochdeutsche und niederdeutsche
       Mundarten
    XVI. Wort- und Namenforschung
    XVII. Allgemeines zur Literaturwissen-
       schaft
    XVIII. Vergleichende Literaturwissen-
       schaft
    XIX. Nordische Altertumskunde
    XX. Altnordische Literaturgeschichte
    XXI. Deutsche Literaturgeschichte
       Allgemeines
    XXII. Von den Anfängen bis zum Beginn
       der höfischen Dichtung (660–1170)
    XXIII. Hochmittelalter (1170–1250)
    XXIV. Spätmittelalter (1250–1450)
    XXV. Vom deutschen Frühhumanismus
       bis zum Einsetzen der Reformation
       (1450–1520)
    XXVI. Das Zeitalter der Reformation
       (1520–1580)
    XXVII. Barock (1580–1700)
    XXVIII. Aufklärung, Empfindsamkeit und
       Vorklassik (1700–1770)
    XXIX. Goethezeit (1770–1830)
    XXX. Von der Spätromantik bis zum
       Realismus (1830–1880)

1973-Eppelsheimer

    I. Allgemeine Linguistik
    II. Allgemeine Literaturwissenschaft
    III. Allgemeine Literaturgeschichte
    IV. Germanistik
    V. Deutsche Sprachgeschichte
    VI. Deutsche Mundarten
    VII. Deutsche Gegenwartssprache
    VIII. Deutsche Literaturgeschichte
    IX. Mittelalter
    X. 16. Jahrhundert
    XI. 17. Jahrhundert
    XII. 18. Jahrhundert
    XIII. Goethezeit
    XIV. Goethes Zeitgenossen
    XV. Romantik
    XVI. 19. Jahrhundert. 1830–1880
    XVII. 19. Jahrhundert. 1880–1914
    XVIII. 20. Jahrhundert. 1914–1945
    XIX. 20. Jahrhundert. Nach 1945

Examples of sub-divisions in EPP

Deutsche Literaturgeschichte (VIII)

Allgemein
Literaturgeschichte einzelner deutscher und
deutschsprachiger Länder und Städte
Formen und Gattungen (Theorie und Ge-
schichte)
Lyrik
Drama (Schauspiel/Tragödie)
Epik (Erzählkunst/Roman)
Die kleineren Formen
Stoff- und Motivgeschichten/Themen

18. Jahrhundert (XII)

Zum Ganzen
Gattungen
Aufklärung
Irrationale Strömungen
Rokoko
Sturm und Drang
Klassik
Herder
Lessing
Wieland
Zu weiteren Autoren

XXXI. Vom Naturalismus bis zur Gegen-
      wart
XXXII. Volksdichtung
XXXIII. Theaterwissenschaft
XXXIV. Verschiedenes

1973-MLA

General Germanic Literature
Bibliography
Miscellaneous
Yiddish Literature

German literature

  I. General
  II. Themes, Types, Special Topics
  III. Literature to 1500
  IV. Sixteenth and Seventeenth centuries
  V. Eighteenth and early nineteenth
      centuries
  VI. Nineteenth and early twentieth
      centuries
  VII. Recent literature
  VIII. American Germanica

Netherlandic literature

  I.   General
  II. Frisian literature
  III. Netherlandic literature to 1500
  IV. Sixteenth and seventeenth centuries
  V. . . . etc.

Scandinavian literatures

  I.   General Scandinavian literatures
  II. The Scandinavian literatures to 1500
  III. Danish (and Faroese) literature
  IV. Icelandic literature
  V. Norwegian literature
  VI. Swedish literature

1973-YWMLS

  I. German Studies
      Language
      Medieval literature
      The sixteenth century
      The seventeenth century
      The Classical Era
      The Romantic Era
      Literature, 1830–1880
      Literature, 1880 to the Present Day
  II. Dutch Studies
  III. Danish Studies
      Language
      Literature
  IV. Norwegian Studies
      Language and Early literature
      Literature since the Reformation
  V. Swedish Studies
      Language
      Literature

From these tables it will be seen that the vast bulk of entries is contained within fairly rigid time periods and that the only change has been a slight shift in emphasis from sub-classification by genre to a general acceptance of the principle of categorisation primarily by authors within literary-historical rather than historical periods. It is to be assumed that this shift reflects in part at least a trend in scholarship. The figures for the 1970 volumes of *GER, EPP,* and *MLA* are as follows:

General	Periods	These figures do not include the general items that
GER 2349 (I–XXI)	2905	precede each period; the categories in GER and EPP
EPP 1860 (I–VIII)	3270	include specific language sections; the figure for MLA
MLA 197 (1148)	2458	in parentheses includes all items on Germanic linguistics

The present system may therefore fairly be described as one in which works of a heterogeneous or general nature are assigned to relatively unspecific categories of "generalia" preceding the series of period sections or, if they relate at least to a specific period, to a category of generalia at the head of that period section. Within each period section the arrangement is primarily alphabetical by the main author discussed (cross-references are few), and items are entered under each author alphabetically by the name of the critic with only some attempts at sub-categorisation.

Thus, for example, the 1970(4) issue of GER offers 20 items (excluding cross-references) under Thomas Mann, first those by Mann himself and then those by critics in strictly alphabetical order. The same procedure applies to Goethe where there is one initial entry by Goethe, followed by twenty-nine critical items. The MLA volume for 1970 has under the section entitled "Recent" 53 entries for Brecht (and ten cross-references); in the preceding section ("Nineteenth and early twentieth centuries") there are 59 entries for Kafka and 9 cross-references. All these entries are in strictly alphabetical order.

Within the general sections an attempt is made in GER to overcome the problem of "unassignable" works by providing a) sub-headings and b) cross-references. In the same issue of GER, for example, the section "Allgemeines zur Literaturwissenschaft" is sub-divided into [1] "Allgemeines – Bibliographien – Handbücher," [2] "Edition und Technik," and so forth. Similarly the section "Vergleichende Literaturwissenschaft" is divided into numerous parts of which the first is entitled "Allgemeines – Bibliographien – Methoden – literarische Übersetzungsprobleme – Weltliteratur." Within this and the other sub-divisions entries are again in alphabetical order so that one is sometimes at a loss to know whether an item is included because it is about translation problems, or about world literature. Included in these sub-divisions are, however, many cross-references which create in effect a primitive form of subject index. The sub-division just referred to, for example, ends with 32 references by item number and subject, ranging from "Kongress" and "Terminologie" to "Wegerlebnis" and "Zufall" (these references are in numerical order by item, not in alphabetical order).

Compared with those in GER the general categories in MLA are lean and even less organised. "German Literature: I General" is sub-divided only into "Bibliography" and "General and Miscellaneous" while the other general category, "Themes, Types, Special Topics," has such curious sub-divisions as "Drama and Theater," "Folklore," and "Themes" (sic). Each period division is also preceded by one such general category with similar sub-divisions. In GER such general "period" groups are organised purely alphabetically.

The arrangement in *EPP* differs from that in *GER* and *MLA* to the extent that, in addition to similar but much clearer and more detailed sub-divisions in the general sections (e.g. the organisation of "Stoff- und Motivgeschichte/ Themen" alphabetically by subject), the longer author entries are also sub-divided. Thus there are separate sub-sections and sub-divisions for Goethe and sub-divisions also for many authors where the volume of material is far less. Even where there are no formal sub-divisions, works are entered in a logical order, viz. editions, letters, etc. preceding general and specific critical literature. The alphabetical principle is in fact largely abandoned at this level in favour of a subject-oriented approach. A simple example is the entry for Hauptmann which is sub-divided as follows:

> Dokumente
> Ausgabe
> Leben und Werk
> Zu einzelnen Werken (ordered by work title)
> Studien
> Beziehungen, Vergleiche
> Wirkungsgeschichte.

Given the variation in organisation, it is not unnatural that there should be differences in the place at which individual works are entered in bibliographies. To attempt a detailed comparison of the discrepancies in the assignment of given works to given categories would be pointless, since arguments would of necessity have to be based on a critical assessment of the most significant aspect of every item. The following examples from *GER* 1970 (4) must therefore suffice.

Das Epitaph des Misanthropen. Metamorphosen einer Gruppe von griechischen Epigrammen
GER   Vergleichende Literaturwissenschaft: Allgemeines
(4445)   (ref. *from* Deutsche Literatur und griechische und lateinische Literatur)
MLA   General II: Drama and theater

Hölderlin et Camus
GER   Vergleichende Literaturwissenschaft: Deutsche Literatur und romanische
(4468)   Literaturen
               (ref. *from* Hölderlin)
MLA   Hölderlin (ref. *from* Camus in French bibliography)

Victor Hugo. The Baron von Eckstein and the 'profondeur des allemands'
GER   same as above
(4469)
MLA   not in German; only in French bibliography under Hugo

Calderons 'Dame Kobold' aus dem Stegreif. Ein Szenarium der 'Baadnerischen Gesellschaft' deutscher Schauspieler
GER   same as above
(4467)

| MLA | Not in German; only under Calderon in Spanish. |

Mozarts und Cervantes' Spiel mit einer Geschichte aus dem Volksmund

GER	Vergleichende Literaturwissenschaft; Deutsche Literatur und romanische
(4465)	Literaturen.
EPP	Deutsche Literaturgeschichte: Die kleineren Formen: Märchen

Tragödie ohne Sühnetod. Kleists Prinz Friedrich von Homburg und Rotrous Vencelas

GER	same as above
(4466)	
EPP	Under Kleist

Problem der Rezeption amerikanischer Literatur in der DDR

GER	Vergleichende Literaturwissenschaft: Deutsche Literatur und angelsächsische
(4472)	Literaturen
EPP	20. Jahrhundert – nach 1945: Allgemeines: Einzelne Länder: DDR

Literaturgeschichtliche Strömungen in der deutschen und angelsächsischen Literatur im Übergang vom 20. zum 21. Jahrhundert. Insbesondere die Bedeutung utopischer wissenschaftlicher Romane

GER	Vergleichende Literaturwissenschaft: Deutsche Literatur und angelsächsische
(4473)	Literaturen.
EPP	20. Jahrhundert – post 1945: Allgemeines: Darstellung und Diskussion
MLA	Recent: General and Miscellaneous.

Whatever the similarities or dissimilarities between *GER, EPP,* and *MLA,* the *system* remains essentially the same, namely the assignment of every item to that point in the detailed classification scheme deemed most appropriate, with some, but not many, cross references. The underlying assumption is that the user will search for material primarily through the classification scheme. For example recent literature on Kleist's *Michael Kohlhaas* will be sought under the appropriate literary/chronological period:

GER	=	Goethezeit
EPP	=	Goethes Zeitgenossen
MLA	=	Eighteenth and early nineteenth centuries.

The major distinction between the three bibliographies lies in the degree to which general and author entries are sub-divided. *Michael Kohlhaas* is found

in *GER* under Kleist in an undivided alphabetical list of critical works following primary works

in *EPP* under "Kleist: Zu einzelnen Werken" in a list of Kleist's works ordered by title

in *MLA* under Kleist in an undivided alphabetical list containing all works by or on Kleist.

The use of classification schemes, no matter how specific these may be, suggests that entry into the bibliography by subject terms is not considered essential. This assumption is borne out by the indexing of these bibliographies. To begin at the bottom, so to speak, the *MLA* has no index other than an alphabetical list of authors (i.e. critical authors), so that every writer and any subject can only be located, if at all, through the classification scheme (in 1970, for example, Gottfried Keller does not appear in the index even though his works in translation are listed under his name within the alphabetical series [8589]). In *GER* there is an index of authors and writers or titles for anonymous works (and also a list of reviewers). There is no subject index. However, the index appears only at the end of each fourth issue, so that recourse must be had to the classification scheme for issues 1–3. *EPP* has an author index and a "Sachregister," which latter includes writers as subjects along with all subjects that have been used as entries; for example, individual words on which items have been written are entered under "Wörter, Wortfamilien und Sinnbereiche" in the section headed "Deutsche Sprachgeschichte." Not included are subject terms that occur in items entered by author, title, and so forth. *GER* and *EPP* include in the index cross-references both under the item *from* and the item *to* which reference is made.

The group entries in *YW* are arranged alphabetically by the writer's name within the subject periods. Thereafter there is no visible arrangement other than the placing of works by the writer (editions, letters, etc.) before works about him, the latter being segregated solely by monographs being treated before articles. There is, however, an attempt to provide some kind of subject index which is separate from the index of names (writers and authors). Sampling suggests that this is as haphazard as the selection of material. Only one reference could be found to the Rilke entries 1970/71/72. namely, under "animals" in reference to Fingerhut's *Das Kreatürliche im Werke RMR.s.* There was no index entry for narcissism for Kunz's *Narziss. Untersuchungen zum Werk RMR.s* in the same issue. Nor were there entries for the motifs mentioned in reference to Rolleston's book (1971) or in the title of Wolff's article (1971). In 1972 there is an entry for Rodin in the index of names for an article entitled "Rilke, Rodin and Jugendstil" but none in the subject index for Jugendstil.

3. Extent and accuracy of information

The bibliographical information provided by these bibliographies may be roughly divided into technical data and supplementary explanation. Under the former category one should expect to find author, title, place, publisher and date of publication, series title, page numbers, and so forth. All three works provide most if not all of these details, although they vary of course in style. The major variation in treatment is of essay collections. In some cases these are cited bibliographically at the point where an essay is cited, in others they are listed as collections and reference is made back to them from individual essays.

The major difference between *GER, EPP,* and *MLA* lies in the fuller details provided by the first two works, both of which give (besides the date, which is omitted in *MLA* [and *YW*] when it is that of the year nominally treated) page numbers of monographs, while *GER* adds to this the format and the price. In the style of entry there is little variation. *EPP* uses many abbreviations in titles and places the item number flush right, rather than left, which can sometimes be confusing, as can also the natural instead of inverted order of author names. There is the occasional omission in *MLA* of a sub-title. *GER* is more reliable in the provision of series titles. The following may be considered typical entries (from the Rilke list discussed above):

> *GER* 5174 Bauer, Arnold: Rainer Maria Rilke. − Berlin: Colloquium Vgl (1970). 95 S. 8° = Köpfe des 20. Jh. Bd. 59 Pp. DM 5.80
> *EPP* Arnold Bauer, R.M.R'. Bln: Colloquium Verl. '70. 94 S. [3951]
> *MLA* 8809. Bauer, Arnold. *Rainer Maria Rilke.* Berlin: Colloquium.

The accuracy of the information provided is not in dispute, and an exhaustive analysis from this point of view would have no value. In the course of this study only very few minor errors were noted, such as are only to be expected in works as complex and voluminous as these. There are, however, more important considerations than misprints, namely the provision of supplementary information to elucidate otherwise misleading or incomprehensible entries. There are many reasons why a straightforward bibliographical entry, full and accurate though it may be, is valueless, and these vary from the use of an "exotic" language to the fact that many items are identical with items published earlier, something which does not always emerge from the entry and may in fact not be mentioned even in the work itself.

In *GER* many books are reviewed so that there is less necessity for annotations. There are, however, annotations to some unreviewed works, brief comments on articles with vague titles, translations of titles in exotic languages, and an indication, where relevant, of the existence of abstracts in less exotic languages. Some simple examples of these practices are found on p. 694 of issue 1970(4): a three line annotation explains the nature of a group of three preceding monographic works; an explanatory comment "[Zum hist. Roman]" aids understanding of an article entitled, "Das Erbe Münsters"; an explanation of the changes in the second edition of a work listed includes a reference back to the entry of the first edition; two items from Jugoslavia have parenthetical German translations.

Similar practices obtain in *EPP* where, however, exotic titles − which are far fewer − are not translated. The comments are perhaps briefer. *MLA* also provides brief comments, though rarely; sometimes, but by no means always, it describes the content of items in exotic languages.

YW is in theory a *bibliographie raisonnée.* In practice there is rarely any commentary except on the major monographic publications; general and theoretical works are usually commented on at greater length. Monographs are listed with adequate bibliographic details (author, title, place, publisher, pages), but without date unless the date is other than that of the year being covered. Periodical items are cited in the usual manner but also without date in the same way. The value of the commentary is in many cases debatable, at least where it goes beyond factual summary. Such a summary of content is undeniably of interest to the user, since many titles are vague or misleading. But "critical" comments must of necessity be themselves too vague to be of value, given the fact that there is not space in which to justify criticism. Consequently one finds for the most part equivocal statements such as "an interesting study" (1970, p. 623), "a reasonable attempt" (1970, p. 625), "interesting and often stimulating reading" (1971, p. 650), "a polished, even bland, survey" (1971, p. 652). This space would perhaps be better used for elucidation of the contents of works not otherwise analysed.

On the whole there is little to choose between the three major bibliographies on the score of bibliographical and supplementary information except that *MLA* lacks the paging of monographs and that *GER* provides more in the way of technical details for monographs. In all three one would often wish for additional information in order to be able to ascertain without having recourse to the article itself whether it is relevant to one's search. All too often titles are vague or misleading and the classification systems are so simplistic that the narrower relevance of an item cannot be estimated.

4. Timeliness

The date at which information about published materials is made available to those who are looking for it is determined primarily by two factors, namely the time required to collect the relevant material and the time required to organise and publish it. The first factor is the more complex of the two since it involves locating and collecting sources from all around the world, and the difficulties that may arise vary from personal relationships to fluctuating international exchange rates. The second factor is essentially an economic problem. Given that the material is made available, how much can a publisher afford to spend on a) organising and b) publishing it? The organisation of material should not greatly delay publication, provided that a sufficient number of staff is available – and there is a strict limit to the number that can usefully be employed – since material will presumably be handled as it arrives, that is, on a continuous basis. Publication too ought not to be subject to delay, since the work may be planned in advance and copy may even be set as it becomes available and later material inserted wherever necessary. However, the publisher is not necessarily in strict control of the mechanical processes of publication, which may be affected by labour problems or material shortages, to mention only the most obvious sources of delay.

What then are the time delays experienced in the publication of *GER, EPP,* and *MLA* (and *YW*)? If we return to the Rilke survey, we find that of the 22 articles which appeared in all three bibliographies in volumes for 1970 and

1971 one derived from 1969, 13 from 1970, and 8 from 1971. Recalling also the fact that only about half of the Rilke articles appeared in more than one bibliography in 1970/71, it seems evident that there must be a far greater time spread than indicated here. The dates for *all* Rilke items in *GER* for example, in the 1970 issues are as follows: 1967 : 3, 1968 : 10, 1969 : 12, 1970 : 10. Even in the following year 1971 there is still one item from 1967; 2 are from 1968 and 5 from 1969. Recalling also that each volume of *EPP* and *MLA* is published up to two years from the beginning of the volume-year, then it becomes clear that several years can elapse before an article is listed in one or other of these three bibliographies.

The least time delay should be expected in *GER* since there are not normally more than three months between publication dates. If, for example, an item published in January of one year is received that same month, it should be possible to list it in the April issue (no. 2; from 1971 on month of publication is not indicated). A certain delay must be expected, however, for books that are sent out for review. The Rilke items *published in 1970* and listed in *GER* in 1970–72 appeared in the various issues as follows (with a breakdown by articles/books):

	total	articles	books
1970,1	0		
2	1	1	
3	2	2	
4	7	6	1
1971,1	6	4	2
2	4	2	2
3	5	3	2
4	6	4 (6)*	(1)*
1972,1–3	0		
4	1		1
	32	22 (24)	8 (9)

* 2 articles listed from one book reviewed as a whole.

All but one of the 1970 items therefore appeared not later than the end of the year following the year of publication. 31.25 % appeared in 1970 and 65.6 % in 1971. Books appeared on the average later than articles.

That items cannot appear in *EPP* and *MLA* as soon as in *GER* is self-evident, for these works continue to collect material until after the end of the bibliographical year – according to their own statements 15 January for *MLA* and 31 March for *EPP*. They do not appear until at the earliest at the end of the year following the year covered. The 1970 volumes for *EPP* and *MLA*, for example, were published in October 1971 and June 1972 respectively. By 31 December of 1975 neither *EPP* nor *MLA* (nor *YW*) for 1974 had been received.[6] Rilke items published in 1970 were therefore spread in *EPP* and *MLA* rather more widely than in *GER*, namely as follows:

	1970	1971	1972
EPP	19	10	2
MLA	19	6	2

The actual *dates* on which items appeared in *GER*, *EPP*, *MLA* and *YW* are as follows:

			GER	EPP	MLA	YW
1970	Mar	(1)				
	Jun	(2)	1			
	Aug	(3)	2			
	Dec	(4)	7			
1971	Mar	(1)	6			
	Jul	(2)	4			
	Oct			19 (1970)		
	Dec	(3)	5			5 (1970)
1972	May	(4)	6			
	Jun				19 (1970)	
	Jul	(1)	0			
	Sep	(2)	0			
	Oct			10 (1971)		
	Dec	(3)	0			

6 *EPP* had in fact been published on 30 September 1975; *MLA* for 1974 was not received until after the completion of this manuscript, namely on 27 July 1976. Publication dates in the following discussion were provided by the respective publishers and I should like to thank them at this point for their co-operation.

		GER	EPP	MLA	YW
1973	Jan				1 (1971)
	Feb (4)	1			
	May			6 (1971)	
	Oct		2 (1972)		
1974	May			2 (1972)	

While it may seem that the obvious is being unnecessarily belaboured, it should be noted that those items listed latest are the ones that come from furthest afield, just as those first listed are closest to home (the first 1970 Rilke item in *GER* is in a work put out by the publisher of *GER*). Of the six items from 1970 listed in *GER* 1971 (4), that is to say, listed late, one comes from the UK and one from Argentina, while two come from Japan; 2 articles are listed from a German book reviewed in the same issue and may therefore have been delayed for that reason. The two items from 1970 listed in *EPP* 1972 and *MLA* 1972 are identical: one derives from Italy and the other from South Africa. The main reason for making this rather obvious point is to stress the fact that late listing of an item is not likely to be connected in any way with its intrinsic intellectual value.

The Rilke items in *YW* were hardly an adequate basis for comparison. Only one discrepancy was noted. The Rolleston book listed in *GER* 71, *EPP* 70, *MLA* 70, appeared in *YW* in 1971. A survey of Thomas Mann items in the 1970 volume of *YW* turned up 1 book from 1969 and 2 articles from the same journal of 1968 out of a total of 22 items. The Brecht entry included one book from 1964 (? !) and another from 1969.

In summary, then, it seems that the time delay for the listing of an item in *GER* can be from three months to about two years. For *EPP* and *MLA*, however, it is from a minimum of nine/ten months *(EPP)* to a maximum of 45 months *(EPP)* or 53 months *(MLA)*. It is, to say the least, questionable whether the end-product justifies the effort expended.

The Zeitschriftenaufsatzkatalog (519).
The *ZAK* is a totally different form of bibliography, in fact not a true bibliography at all but an index. It is based on two major premises, the first being Bradford's law that the greater part of significant research is published in a small proportion of the total number of *periodicals*[7] in the field (not in

---

7 See chap. 9 of S. C. Bradford, *Documentation* (Washington, 1950): "The whole range of periodicals thus acts as a family of successive generations of diminishing kinship, each generation being greater in number than the preceding, and each constituent of a generation producing inversely according to its degree of remoteness."

books) and the second that it is more important to be informed *quickly* about *most* new work than to wait a long time for "complete" information. A third premise behind the production of the *ZAK*, but one which is not fully followed through, is that the index user is looking primarily for information about a subject and that arrangement by specific subject must therefore be the main principle. The concept of the *ZAK* dates from 1962; material in the area of Germanic studies became available from 1969 on. The whole project, which covers the sciences as well as the humanities, is under the aegis of the Deutsche Forschungsgemeinschaft.[8]

The mechanical process by which the material is supplied is the following. The entries are typed eight to a page, in a pre-determined order and the pages are then duplicated onto card material. These cards are cut and fed into a collator which sorts them into the correct numerical and alphabetical order. For purely mechanical reasons each packet of cards mailed out contains 88 cards (1 delivery number card and 87 cards for filing). Packets may be mailed individually or in bundles. For example, the last delivery received before completion of this study (postmarked December 23) contained three packets, numbers 27–29; the last cards for 1975 were not mailed until 12 March 1976. The last packet was numbered 33, so that there were for the year 1975 2871 cards in all (including index cards).

The type of index determines also its format. Since it appears as fast as material becomes available, i.e., in a continuous flow, it must be cumulable. The format is therefore that of standard library catalogue cards and these cards are, moreover, unit cards, that is to say, the full bibliographical details are printed on each one. The number code and subject term are super-imposed and permit the individual cards to be assigned to the appropriate location. The entire index can be cumulated immediately and indefinitely.

The basic arrangement of the index is a very much modified form of the traditional classification schemes discussed above. Germanic is divided into "A Allgemeines," "B Altgermanistik" "C Deutsch," "D Niederländisch," and so forth. B and C (as well as D etc.) are sub-divided by numerically designated subjects, and sub-sub-divided by decimals. Section 3 is organised alphabetically by the surname of the writer (or by anonymous title). In this case the writer's name is of course the subject and the arrangement is a mechanical one (alphabetical) rather than the subject-hierarchical system employed in sections 1 and 2. An example of hierarchical order is the following entry (a complete outline is given below):

> Germ C 2,43 Epos
> Jacobs, Juergen
> Das Verstummen der Muse . . .

8 See M. S. Batts, "The International current awareness service of the German Research Council," *RQ*, 12 (1973), 19–22

Hierarchical order:

(Germanistik)
    C Deutsch
        2,4 Gattungen und Formen
        2,43 Epik.

Within each lowest level of classification group the order is alphabetical by author, but sub-classification is also possible by terminological differentiation, e.g. in Germ A — "Germanistik: England" or in Germ C 1,1 "Terminologie: Fachgebiet" (sub-divisions are indicated by a colon). In section C, 3 which is by far the largest, the sub-classification is by subject, using numerals and words. Broad categories 1—5 define the area of research, e.g. 1 = biography, etc., 5 = works, after which terms may further limit the range, e.g., by naming individual works under 5:

    Germ C 3 Goethe, Joh. Wolfg. von 5
    Ueber Kunst und Alterthum

The hierarchical order is therefore:

    Writer
       number
          sub-heading
             alphabetical author of item.

Depending on the nature of the item indexed, there can be up to five entries, each of which contains the full data and for each of which a card is supplied. An example from 1975 is the following:

    Frye, Lawrence O
    The language of high feeling. A case of dialogue technique: Hoffmann's Kater Murr
    and Novalis' Heinrich von Ofterdingen etc.

This is entered under:

    Germ C 2,2 (= Literaturgeschichte)
        Romantik
    Germ C 2,43 (= Gattungen und Formen: Epik)
        Dialog
    Germ C 3 (= authors)
        Hoffmann, E.T.A.: 5
            Kater Murr
    Germ C 3
       Novalis: 5
          Heinrich von Ofterdingen

An article by Wisniewski on "Werdekeit und Hierarchie. Zur soziologischen Interpretation des Minnesangs" appears under:

Germ C 1,61 (= Wort- und Bedeutungsforschung: Einzelne Wörter)
  werdekeit [mhd]
Germ C 2,2 (= Literaturgeschichte)
  Mittelalter:
      Minnesang
Germ C 2,2
  Ritter:
      Tugendsystem
Germ C 2,41 (= Gattungen und Formen: Lyrik)
  Minnesang.

The main technical objection to an index of this sort is the employment of single concepts or descriptions that may not be the terms under which the user is looking. One means of solving this problem is of course the classification system, which enables the user to browse through, for example, all entries in the section "Stilistik" or "Namenforschung." And it is presumably this browsing function which justifies the classification system as such. Were this function not desired, then there would presumably be no reason not to list every entry on a strictly alphabetical basis by descriptor. Another aid for the user is the "index," or dictionary of terms, which lists every term employed in alphabetical order. The user is referred to the (lowest) level(s) of classification where the term is employed. As new terms are added these are supplied with the index cards and the index thus kept up to date. As an example there are the following entries in the dictionary for Arbeiter and its composites:

Arbeiter C 2,5
Arbeiterbewegung C 2,2
Arbeiterbewegung: Wortschatz C 1,7 (Wortschatz has no entry itself).
Arbeiterdichtung C 2,1
            C 2,41
Arbeiterklasse C 2,5
Arbeiterroman C 2,44
Arbeitertheater   A
            C 2,42

There are occasional see-references as in the following:

Ausgaben [einzelne Autoren]
s. Germ C 3 [einzelner Autor]: 1 Edition.

The complete outline is as follows:

A. *Allgemeines* (einschl. Geschichte, philosophische Grundlegung und Methodik der Germanistik)
B. *Altgermanische Sprache und Literatur*
  1. *Altgermanische Sprache*
    1,1 Allgemeines (einschl. Grammatik)
      1,11 Geschichte der Sprache

1,2 Lautlehre
1,3 Wort- und Formenlehre
1,4 Satzlehre
1,5 Stilistik
1,6 Wort- und Bedeutungsforschung
    1,61 Einzelne Wörter und Wortgruppen
    1,65 Namenforschung
Weitere Untergliederung, wenn erforderlich, nach der Systematik der Deutschen Sprache
  2. *Altgermanische Literatur*
    2,1 Allgemeines (einschl. Methodik)
    2,2 Literaturgeschichte
    2,3 Poetik, Ästhetik, Stilistik
      2,35 Metrik
    2,4 Gattungen und Formen
    2,5 Stoffe und Motive
Weitere Untergliederung, wenn erforderlich, nach der Systematik der Deutschen Literatur
  3. *Autoren und anonyme Texte der altgermanischen Literatur (alphabetisch)*
C. *Deutsche Sprache und Literatur*
  1. *Deutsche Sprache*
    1,1 Allgemeines (einschl. Grammatik)
      1,11 Geschichte der Sprache
    1,2 Lautlehre
    1,3 Wort- und Formenlehre
    1,4 Satzlehre
    1,5 Stilistik
    1,6 Wort- und Bedeutungsforschung
      1,61 Einzelne Wörter und Wortgruppen
      1,65 Namenforschung
    1,7 Sondersprachen (z.B. Berufssprachen), auch jiddisch
    1,8 Mundarten (auch niederdeutsch)
      1,81 Einzelne Mundarten
    1,9 Rechtschreibung
  2. *Deutsche Literatur*
    2,1 Allgemeines (einschl. Methodik)
    2,2 Literaturgeschichte
    2,3 Poetik, Ästhetik, Stilistik
      2,35 Metrik
    2,4 Gattungen und Formen
      2,41 Lyrik
      2,42 Drama
      2,43 Epik
      2,44 Roman
      2,45 Novelle
      2,49 Sonstiges
    2,5 Stoffe und Motive
    2,6 Literaturgeschichte einzelner Regionen und Mundartdichtung
  3. *Autoren und anonyme Texte der deutschen Literatur (alphabetisch)*

In comparing *ZAK* with the bibliographies previous considered, it is essential to bear in mind the different nature of *ZAK* which is a subject index rather than a bibliography. Its chief function is not to be complete but to provide a strictly defined proportion of the total material with the minimum of delay. The scope is an important factor, but in a rather different way. The question is not, how much does the index cover, for this is exactly defined, but rather, what effective proportion does this coverage represent? The question is a particularly important one, because the listing of a periodical in other bibliographies does not necessarily mean that all or even any items from that periodical have been included. The *MLA* volumes for 1970 and 1971 for example, both list *Doitsu bungaku* among the periodicals excerpted, but there is no sign of any of the articles from no. 44 (spring 1970) of that journal in either volume.

One way to approach this question is, however, to compare the lists of excerpted journals. In the list issued by the Deutsche Forschungsgemeinschaft in January of 1973 there are 115 journals, from which *all* items are to be listed in *ZAK*.[9] These derive from 17 different countries (counting the FRG and the GDR as two). The number of journals listed by *GER* for the same year is 200 and for *EPP* 484; it is not possible to include *MLA* (or *YW*) where the lists are general ones for all foreign languages. The *ZAK* list includes titles that do not appear in all cases in the other bibliographies. Thus, 34 of them are not in *GER*, 19 not in *EPP*, and 6 not in *MLA*. This means, then, that *GER* has 119 and *EPP* nearly 400 periodicals not covered by *ZAK*. However, it must be noted that a periodical not listed in *GER* or *EPP* in any one year may nevertheless be included in other years. It is possible, particularly with annuals, that no issues became available in that one year.

The only satisfactory way to compare coverage in *ZAK* with that of the other bibliographies is to examine the articles listed in *GER,* etc., in order to establish to what extent they come from journals excerpted by *ZAK*. The following analysis is restricted to literary topics, not, or not solely, because of our greater interest in literature, but because of the degree to which items on linguistics, especially in *MLA,* are separated from the literature in the same language.

If we turn once again to our Rilke survey, we find that the articles listed in *GER, EPP,* and *MLA* in 1970/71/(72) appeared in 43 different journals, 25 of which are covered by *ZAK.* The remaining 18 are from the following countries: Japan 6, Germany 2, USA 2, and one each form Argentina, Canada, France, Holland, Italy, Korea, Israel, and Rumania.

While 25 out of 43 may not seem a large proportion (58 %), it is not necessarily a true reflection of the extent to which these are the real sources of

---

9 Subsequent to the completion of this manuscript a number of *linguistic* journals were dropped from the list as a result of the inception of a new index to linguistic periodicals.

material. The Rilke articles published in periodicals and listed in *all three* of the bibliographies in 1970/71/(72) occur in only 15 journals, of which 14 are on the *ZAK* list. *ZAK* would therefore list 14 out of a total of 16 items (2 articles in one journal), i.e. 87 % of items *common to all three*.

Taking as additional examples the 1972 volumes of *GER, EPP,* and *MLA,* there are 12 journal articles listed there on the *Nibelungenlied;* 8 are in journals covered by the *ZAK.* A similar tally for Bobrowski literature gives a coverage of 6 out of 9. Several of the articles included in the bibliographies are in journals which are obscure and/or in fields not directly related to German, e.g., *Costerus, Explicator,* and *Conradiana* (English studies). It would seem then that, while the number of journals covered by *ZAK* may represent only a small proportion of journals "in the field" (collectively at least 500 are covered by the other bibliographies), it nevertheless produces about two thirds of the items listed by all the others in any given year.

The accuracy of the information provided by *ZAK* seems to be on a par with that of the other works considered, and the question of supplementary information does not arise, since its form is that of an index and therefore analytical per se. It is worth noting, however, that *ZAK* has the possibility of correcting errors and does this by supplying corrected cards with which to replace incorrect ones.

Of greater significance is the question of timeliness, for immediacy of reporting is the very raison d'être of the *ZAK.* It can, however, only be compared with *GER* for obvious reasons, and the following comparison was made on the basis of the last two mailings of *GER* and *ZAK* for the calendar year 1975; these were despatched according to the postmarks in December: *GER* 1975 (3), *ZAK* 27–29 and in March, *ZAK,* 30–33 and April, *GER* 1975 (4), of 1976. In the following list the journal issues cited by *both* are named in the centre column with the issues excerpted listed in the outer columns:

GER 1975 (3)	journal	ZAK 1975 (27–29)
1974,3	AION	1974,3
1974,4–1975,3	Akzente	1975,4
1974,3–75,1	Arcadia	1975,2
1975	Aurora	1975
1974–75,2.3	GLL	1975,3
1975,2–3	GR	1975,3
1974–75	Heine Jb	1975,1
1975,2	Mod. Spr	1975,2
1974,8–75,3.4	Mosaic	1975,3
1975,1.2	Mutterspr.	1975,2
1974,4–75,2	Seminar	1975,2
1975,1	Stud. Neoph.	1973,2–1975,1
1975,4–6	WB	1975,5

GER 1975 (4)	journal	ZAK 1975 (30–33)
1975,2	LWU	1975,2
1975,3	ZDP	1975,3
1975,1	Leu B.	1975,1
1975,3	Neuph M.	1975,3
1975,4–5	Akz	1975,5
1975,2	EG	1973,1
1975,38.39	Ling Ber	1975,37
1974,3–1975,5	DU	1974,9
1975,7–9	WB	1974,8–1975,6
1974,3–1975,2	ZDL	1975,2
1972–1973	LJb	1973
1974,14–16	LiLi	1974,13–14
1975,3	MDU	1975,3
1973,2–1974,6	SuF	1975,4
1975,3	Seminar	1975,3
1975,1–10	Merkur	1975,9–10
1975,3–4	Mutterspr.	1975,3
1975,53–55	STZ	1975,53
1975,96–99	LK	1975,99
1974,3	Fab	1974,3

From this list it would appear that *ZAK* is slightly ahead of *GER*. In December 1975, for example, it has already listed items from *Akzente* 1975,4 and *Arcadia* 1975,2 while *GER* is only up to 1975,3 and 1975,1 respectively. Presumably the earlier issues have been covered by earlier cards from *ZAK*. It is true that *GER* is one issue ahead of *ZAK* with *Mosaic* and *Weimarer Beiträge*, but in both cases earlier issues are also dealt with, in the case of *WB* including an issue that has presumably appeared some time before in *ZAK*. It seems in fact that *GER* tackles in the majority of cases two or more issues at once, e.g. *GLL* 1975, 2–3, *GR* 1975,2–3, and so forth. (The only anomaly of this kind in *ZAK* is the coverage of *Stud. Neophil.* from 1973,2 to 1975,1.) The same kind of "leapfrog" relationship is evidenced by spot checking *ZAK* against other items in the 1975/3 issue of *GER*. Kleist items 4371 and 4378 had appeared earlier in *ZAK*, but 4637, 4370, and 4373 had not yet appeared. Keller item 4477 and Kafka item 4689 had also been received earlier, but not Kafka item 4687.

A very similar relationship with similar anomalies is evidenced by the second set of figures. Here, however, it must be borne in mind that the publication date of *ZAK* was a full month ahead of *GER*. These figures will therefore be used to make an additional point about timeliness. From the user's point of view the publication date is of much less significance than the date of receipt of any issue of a periodical or of a bibliographical reference, while the purported date of publication, that is, the date printed on the cover of the periodical may be quite illusory. The second set of statistics includes, for example, the third (September) issue of *Seminar*. They might also have included the fourth (November) issue, if publication of this issue had not been delayed by postal strikes until January of 1976. The only items mentioned here for which local accession dates could be traced are the following.

ZDP	1975	(3)	received January 1976
Leuw. B.	1975	(1)	received January 1976
Mutt.	1975	(3)	received October 1975
		(4)	received January 1976
Fab.	1974	(3)	received January 1976

The point to make here is that, although there is *apparently* a lengthy time-lag between publication and bibliographical coverage, *in fact* there is only a time-lag of 3 to 4 months between the appearance of the journal and the bibliographical references — with the single exception of *Mutt., 1975,3.* This is admittedly not a large statistical basis on which to base definitive statements, but a more detailed study would have to be carried out over a long period of time and include an analysis of numerous factors, such as postal services, handling procedures, and so on.

The present situation as regards bibliographical sources for the study of German literature is therefore approximately as follows. There exists a vast number of sources for retrospective searches both in primary and secondary literature. There are also comprehensive guides to these sources, at least to the kinds of sources available and the names of the more important ones. For the most part these guides are restricted to sources of primary, secondary, and essential reference materials of the last two hundred years, that is to say, since the development of the study of German literature as an independent discipline in the latter half of the eighteenth century.

While the sources for retrospective searching, inadequate or inaccurate as they may often be, can therefore be located by the searcher without any great difficulty, he or she faces a much greater problem in what today is a more critical area, namely in keeping up with current or recent research. Comprehensive retrospective bibliographies exist for a bewildering variety of topics and for many individual authors; but the number of topics and authors *not* covered is far greater. Every such retrospective bibliography is in any case self-evidently out of date by the time it is published. Although the need to keep abreast of contemporary research in literary criticism should not be made a fetish, since it can reasonably be argued that no one is likely to suffer — as could well happen in fields such as medicine or agronomy — if a new discovery passes unnoticed, it is nevertheless clear that scholars have no desire to expend time and energy on fruitlessly repeating research that has already been undertaken and the results of which have already been published.

Guides to bibliographical sources provide the essential references to the appropriate bibliographies and indexes, by means of which the scholar can keep up with research, but these works do not from our studies appear to maintain the degree of currency that is necessary. They do not keep the scholar adequately informed about the sum total of research over the last two or three years. In a certain sense it can even be argued that rapid information about newly published material is more important in the humanities than in many other fields, because the time lag between the completion of research and the publication of the results of that research is already in many instances quite considerable. It is a rare event if a submitted manuscript is published a year later; more often it is a question of two, three, or even four years. To judge by the statistics available in this area (for example, in *PMLA* 1973),[10] the average delay in the field of German literature is approximately two years. One single example: the four items published in the last issue of *Seminar* for 1975 (November) were received by the editor on 14 June 1973 (Soudek), 19 July 1973 (Schmidt), 27 August 1973 (Neuse), 28 February 1974 (Stenberg). A scholar reading an article immediately after its appearance in print may therefore be reading results that have already been superseded by other material submitted over the past two years or more.

The problems that arise from publication delays of this nature are not properly within the sphere of bibliography, although they will be touched upon later. They do, however, point up the importance of informing the scholar with the least possible delay of the existence of material recently published. Unfortunately, as we have seen, existing bibliographies all fail to a lesser or greater extent to do just that.

The fastest service is provided by *ZAK,* although "fastest" probably means an average delay of six months. Its service is strictly limited to a specific number of journals and excludes the large number of books and other separately published materials. In a sense, though, this limitation is also a strength, since, quite apart from the fact that it covers what may be considered as core literature, it enables the scholar to make arrangements to keep track of only those journals that are known *not* to be covered. The burden of keeping up with periodical literature can therefore be divided.

GER is probably on average somewhat slower than *ZAK,* a great deal slower with many lesser known works, but it is very much more comprehensive. Provided that one is interested primarily in all literature on a particular author or in a topic that fairly precisely matches one of its subject divisions, there are no great dangers or difficulties. Its major weakness is the lack of any subject indexing, which may make it virtually impossible, or at least an onerous task, to locate items of interest that may (or may not) turn up at various places in its classification system.

10   William Pell, "Facts of scholarly publishing," *PMLA,* 88 (1973), 639–70.

From this point of view *EPP* is very much better, since one can use the subject index as well as more conveniently locate specific items within the author sub-categories. However, it can hardly be said to provide up to date information. By the time it appears, the older material will be almost two years, the most recently listed almost one year old. It is therefore the primary basis for a retrospective search, and the fifteen-year cumulation currently in progress will be a great improvement.

Although it was stressed in our analysis of entries from *GER, EPP,* and *MLA* that each produced a number of unique items, one is forced to conclude that *MLA* in its current format is of no great value. Its almost total lack of organisation and the absence of any indexes make it awkward to use and its existence can hardly be justified by the addition of the occasional supplementary item to *GER* and *EPP,* both of which regularly appear very much sooner.

Little can be said at all for *YW,* for the comments on books, though useful, are not likely to be superior to lengthier reviews which may already have appeared. Above all the selection of items seems so extremely haphazard as to negate the claim of a deliberately and purposefully selective listing. There is certainly much to be gained from a critical survey of scholarship in every field and in every aspect of every field. To this the increasing number of *Forschungsberichte* bears witness. Regretfully, however, this is not something that can be adequately done except by an individual specialist working in a narrow field — and then a good deal of space is required in which to put forward the results. As it now stands, *YW* fails either to provide a reasonable selection or to comment adequately on general trends.

Even excluding popular magazines and newspapers and most publications in "exotic" languages, articles of interest to scholars in the field of German language and literature may be expected to appear in around 500 periodicals, more than half of which are devoted primarily to literature. Most libraries will not have more than 200—300 of these, many will have far less. The scholar is therefore forced to make use of bibliographical aids. Taking 31 December 1975 as a "Stichtag" a scholar would at that time have had at his or her disposal (always supposing these too were in the local library) *MLA* up to and including 1973, *EPP* to 1974, and issues of *GER* and *ZAK* up to 1975,3 and 1975,29 respectively, *provided* that he or she lived not far removed from the publication sources, i.e., in Europe (a four to eight-week delay must be added for North America). With all four a search could be made for literature from 1973; with *GER, EPP,* and *ZAK* a search could be made through 1974 which could be expected to produce as much as 90 % of items by including the issues of 1975. At the end of 1975, however, information for the current year could be obtained only for a limited proportion of periodicals and an insignificant fraction of monographs published during the first six months of the year (only 29 works published in 1975 had been reviewed by *GER* by the end of the year). For all practical purposes, therefore, the scholars' knowledge of recent research would be at least one year out of date, if based on bibliographical sources and not on direct perusal of the periodicals themselves.

That such is the case will hardly be news to the majority of scholars; it may not even be of interest to many. Given, nevertheless, that large sums of money and a vast amount of effort is invested annually in the production of what are individually repetitive and collectively ineffectual bibliographies; and given also that the volume of material seems at least for the present to be increasing rather than decreasing — it seems essential to question not only the form of current bibliographies, but the premises on which they are based. An attempt at considering these and related questions will be made in the final chapter.

Chapter 7:

Bibliographies in the future

Even if one does not accept the view expressed in the previous chapter that much is rotten in the current state of periodic bibliographical sources for the study of German literature (and most, if not all, of what is said in the following will apply to other areas of the humanities, in particular to other foreign languages), it can certainly not reasonably be maintained that we live in the best of all possible bibliographical worlds. Our present methods of organising and disseminating bibliographical information are very little different from those employed nearly three hundred years ago, while in other fields bibliographical procedures and methods of information dissemination have undergone radical changes. The following discussion is based upon an examination of most, if not all, of these new concepts; it is based also on personal experience in using and creating bibliographies and on a careful analysis of the features not only of current bibliographies but also of current scholarly publication practices.

At the outset, however, certain basic assumptions must be made, assumptions which may seem so sweeping as to be indefensible (though normally accepted implicitly as axiomatic), but which will subsequently be re-considered in the light of any suggested changes in bibliographical procedures. The first and most important assumptions are that the scholar requires access to *all* information on a given topic and desires *immediate* access to that information. Obviously the terms "all" and "immediate" are absolutes that are beyond the capacity of mortal ingenuity and must even at this stage be qualified to read "all important" and "as soon as possible." But such restrictions immediately create even greater problems inasmuch as the terms become relative. It is impossible to determine to everyone's satisfaction what is important, just as it is impossible to define what is or is not possible without first laying down the conditions to be observed.

Immediate access to all relevant information therefore means no more and no less than it has done in the past, namely, as much as is humanly possible as soon as is humanly possible. With this one difference: what are to be considered here are ways and means to disseminate *more* information *more* quickly and *more* effectively than hitherto. To what extent new methods, if applicable, can in any way bring us closer to the absolutes of "all" and "immediate" will depend in the final analysis as always on such inhibiting factors as costs, physical limitations of space, and so forth.

To this rather lengthy caveat one further word of caution must be added. What follows is almost entirely theory — at least as far as the humanities in general and German in particular are concerned. It is essential, however, to consider carefully what is possible as if it were desirable, because it is logically impossible to determine what is desirable without knowing what is possible. A scholar who has not seen *Germanistik* may be satisfied with the *Year's Work in Modern Language Studies;* a scholar who uses *Germanistik* cannot know whether or not a citation index to German studies would be a good idea, since no such thing exists at present and cannot therefore be examined. At this stage, then, any suggestion can be based only on theory although the theory is based wherever possible on existing materials in analogous situations. The final proof would still have to be the practical implementation of any theoretical model. That and only that can prove or disprove any theory. Finally, it will be taken for granted that we are concerned solely with the printed word and not with audio- or other forms of non-print materials — and that the printed word will not in the foreseeable future be replaced by anything else.[1]

Assuming then that the scholar wishes to have access to all possible information with all possible speed, it seems logical to discuss first the form in which the information is sought or to be provided, for the process by which information is imparted must depend on the nature or form of that information. If the process is too slow or too expensive, then the optimum form may have to be modified.

The nature of research currently being published, together with discussions of research trends and the form which *GER* and *EPP* now take, give us every reason to conclude that the scholar making a literature search — by which is meant nothing more than looking for material in a field where he or she is engaged in research activity — is looking for material on a specific and definable, albeit not always easily definable, topic. This topic or subject orientation means that the scholar is unlikely to be interested in *all* the recent work on Goethe or *all* recent work on Thomas Mann, but on a specific aspect of a given author's work or a specific aspect of the work of certain authors across centuries or across linguistic boundaries. The first point to make, therefore, is that the scholar needs to know whether any given item is relevant to his topic; he needs to know what it is about.

It may reasonably be assumed that every published piece of research is provided with a title which, nominally at least, indicates the content of the publication. This content, or perhaps merely the title, is also the basis upon which the individual item is assigned to a certain place in the arrangement of any bibliography. Access to the item is therefore first through the section of the classification scheme and from there to the individual item. A study of these schemes, however, makes it evident that they are so broad in

---

1   This does not mean that it is not recognised that a trend toward different forms of publication (e.g., microforms) already exists. The proposals made here would be consistent at least with those new forms that have been experimentally introduced so far.

sub-categorisation as to make the search for material on a topic of any degree of specificity tedious, if not impossible. There is also the not inconsiderable risk that the item has been assigned (if only in the view of the user) to an inappropriate section of the classification scheme. Finally there is the problem that any given item may relate to several topics (even in the title) and be listed under only one, perhaps two, but not all of them. To class items as is currently done is hardly adequate for today's volume and specificity of research.

A relatively simple method of providing access to the full information contained in *titles* is the KWIC index (*key word in context*).[2] Each significant word in the title becomes in turn the alphabetical "lead" item by which it is entered (although this word need not necessarily appear at the beginning of the line in the alphabetical arrangement). An item such as the following: Karl E. Webb, "Themes in transition. Girls and love in Rilke's *Buch der Bilder*" would appear in a KWIC index as:

BILDER.   THEMES IN TRANSITION. GIRLS AND LOVE IN RILKE'S *BUCH DER*
BUCH DER BILDER.   THEMES IN TRANSITION. GIRLS AND LOVE IN RILKE'S
GIRLS AND LOVE IN RILKE'S *BUCH DER BILDER.*   THEMES IN TRANSITION.
LOVE IN RILKE'S *BUCH DER BILDER.*   THEMES IN TRANSITION. GIRLS AND
RILKE'S *BUCH DER BILDER.*   THEMES IN TRANSITION. GIRLS AND LOVE IN
THEMES IN TRANSITION. GIRLS AND LOVE IN RILKE'S *BUCH DER BILDER.*
TRANSITION. GIRLS AND LOVE IN RILKE'S *BUCH DER BILDER.*   THEMES IN

Integrated with other items, this particular item is then juxtaposed with other references in titles to the *Buch der Bilder,* to girls, to love, etc. The advantage of this system is its relative simplicity. It allows the key (alphabeticised) word to be seen in context and thus better understood – at least in so far as the title is clearly formulated. It is also a strictly mechanical process that can easily be computerized and it works well in many scientific and technical fields, where titles are precise and largely unambiguous.

In German studies the value of a KWIC index would be greatly reduced by the vagueness and wordiness of titles, by the numerous colourful epitheta or catchwords, and by the citation of titles of works.[3] A glance through a few pages of any general bibliography should be sufficient to demonstrate not only that KWIC indexes are not suitable, but that titles generally are an insufficient guide to content in very many cases. For the same reason therefore also KWOC (Keyword out of context) and permuterm indexes have to be rejected, while "enriched" KWIC indexes or a KWIC form of permutation based on a statement abstracted from the item are essentially a primitive form of

---

2 For these and similar technical terms see the *Encyclopedia of Library and Information Science (ELIS)* referred to in the Introduction.
3 All problems are increased where more than one language is used, since the same topics will occur under different words.

"rotating" index similar to PRECIS, but without the advantage of PRECIS (discussed below).

If the title is an inadequate indicator of content, then the only other possible surrogate is the abstract. This immediately raises several problems. In the first place there are the questions: who is to produce the abstract? And who then is to verify its accuracy? The abstract is also much longer than the title which it accompanies, so that any bibliography which included abstracts would increase enormously in size. But perhaps most important is the problem of obtaining access to the abstract. If it is to be published in the same manner as a title, i.e., at a given point in a classification scheme, then it may explain the title, but it does not in any way assist in locating that title. In itself it does not contribute to the solution of the basic problem, namely the *locating* of items which could or are likely to be of interest. At most it can confirm or deny whatever has led to its being located, thus eliminating the necessity of the further stage of consulting the item itself.

This function is now served by the *MLA Abstracts of articles in scholarly journals* (1971– published in conjunction with the *MLA International bibliography* discussed in the previous chapter.[4] The abstracts are composed by the author and submitted with the article or requested on the acceptance of the article. The abstract is normally published with the article while the original together with the relevant bibliographical data are sent by the editor of the journal to the MLA bibliographical centre. The abstracts are printed virtually unedited and in the same order (and with the same number) as the titles in the bibliography. They are thus supplementary to the bibliography and appear even later. At the present time only a small proportion of items listed in the bibliography are represented by the abstracts. There are, for example, only 42 abstracts for the section "Nineteenth and early twentieth centuries" in the 1972 volume as against 846 entries in the bibliography. If, on the other hand, an abstract had been available for every item, the foreign literature section would have comprised well over 2,000 pages (at 9 abstracts per page)!

Authors are also asked, however, to supply index terms with their abstract. These terms are then modified by the bibliographical centre: "some terms are deleted . . . other terms are added on the basis of the abstract or, on occasion, on the basis of our reading of the article itself."[5] The terms thus created form the basis of the subject index printed with the parts of the *Abstracts* (beginning in 1972). This index, while it is to a limited extent analytical, is not very

---

4 For a summary of MLA procedures and plans see Walter S. Achtert, "Abstracting and bibliographical control in the modern languages and literatures," *Conference on Access to Knowledge in the Social Sciences and Humanities*, 1972 (Flushing, 1974), pp. 55–60. Notification was received in July 1976 that the abstracts programme would be discontinued.

5 From a letter to me from the Director of Research for the MLA Bibliographical Center, Walter S. Achtert.

detailed. Above all it is not contextual, i.e., it refers from one point to one item (or more) solely by number. For example, the first entry is simply "ABSURD 949, 3529" (capitals are used to reproduce the bold-face of the original). There are many such single-term entries, while other, less specific entries are broken down into sub-groups, for example, "CRITICISM" by countries and these countries by author. Sub-sub-division appears to be the limit of analysis, as in the following example:

> TECHNIQUE 10234
> Drama 1324 . . .
> Epiphanies 2856
> Leitmotifs 3311 . . .
> Narration 718 . . .
> Deceptive narrator 10093 . . .

The number of entries for individual items varies considerably. Of those checked (all between 10,000 and 10,999) one could not be found in the index and the remainder had from one to six entries. The following item: "Die Funktion von Motiven und stereotypen Wendungen in Schnitzlers Reigen" was entered as:

> SOCIETY – Schnitzler 10512
> STRUCTURAL ANALYSIS – Drama – Schnitzler 10512
> TECHNIQUE – Leitmotifs 10512

Further examples, together with the abstracts, are given in the appendix.

The weakness of this, as of any such index, is the lack of context. Society is a very broad term and could apply in one way or another to the whole of Schnitzler's work. The entry "Technique – leitmotifs" gives neither the author nor the work(s) nor even the genre. The index is consequently of limited value and its value is not likely to be enhanced by the implementation of machine searching as envisaged in the prefatory note. According to that note, "articles are indexed according to approach, themes, genres, and special techniques" and the Director of Research for the MLA (see note 5) reports that a thesaurus exists which may eventually also be made available to facilitate searching. However, the style of indexing is so uneven and inconsistent – what, for example, does one do with an (undivided) entry like MEDIEVAL? – that development along these lines seems unlikely to be fruitful. Probably the root cause of the disappointing nature of the index is the almost total inability of authors to understand the function of indexing terms and to apply them appropriately. The indexing would be far better left in the hands of those trained in the techniques. The use of abstracts will be discussed further below.[6]

---

6 This criticism of the index does not imply that the abstracts themselves are not a valuable adjunct to the bibliography (or to any bibliography). They serve as a valuable surrogate where quick reference is required.

If the title and the abstract are discounted, there remains only the subject indexing of items as a means of locating relevant materials. Indexes can of course be of various kinds, but with one exception all depend on the intellectual evaluation of content, the use of terms which define in some way or other the whole or part of the subject discussed in the item indexed. The one exception is a relatively new form of index which should be discussed first precisely because it does not in theory at least require the services of an indexer. I refer to the citation index.[7]

Citation indexes are based upon the (reasonable) assumption that the published results of any research will document the earlier stages of research on that specific topic by citing those works upon which the new, published work has been based.[8] There is therefore a (close) content relationship between citing and cited items. If all citations in all works in a given field are collected and organised by cited and citing items, then it should be possible to ascertain not only that X has cited A and B, but also that A and B have been cited by Y and Z, and so forth. By working back and forth through the index, starting usually with the citations from a recent item of known relevance, the user is able to locate other items that cite the same sources and are therefore likely also to be relevant. In this form of index the item cited is a surrogate for the index term, while the bibliographical data are the equivalent of the page reference in a conventional book-index.

Indexing by this method has received a good deal of publicity in recent years and there is much to be said for it. Certainly there is already a considerable body of critical literature both on the theory and on the practical applications.[9] The *Science Citation Index (SCI)* (442) has been in existence since 1963 and it has had a sufficiently good reception that a *Social Sciences Citation Index (SSCI)* (448) has now been started. While these may be studied as possible models for a Humanities Citation Index (HCI), it would be unwise to conclude that the success (or failure) of the *SCI* and the *SSCI* would provide valid grounds for expecting the same degree of success or failure for any projected HCI. There are several reasons for this.

It cannot be denied that the use of citations to gather a list of possibly relevant materials is already a familiar practice in the humanities. Academics regularly extract the citations from the latest known article on a topic, then

---

7 See the article by Melvin Weinstock in *ELIS* and the list of articles cited by Elizabeth Miller & Eugenia Truesdell, "Citation indexing: history and applications," *Drexel Library Quarterly*, 8 (1972), 159–72.

8 "A citation index is an ordered list of cited articles each of which is accompanied by a list of citing articles." (Garfield, "Science citation index" [175], p. 650).

9 See, for example, Eugene Garfield, "Science citation index – A new dimension in indexing," *Science*, 144 (May 1964), 649–54; John Martyn, "An examination of citation indexes," *ASLIB Proc.*, 17 (1965), 184–96; Morton V. Malin, "The Science Citation Index: A new concept in indexing," *Library Trends*, 16 (1968), 374–87.

extract from these cited items their citations and so forth. Nor can it be denied that it is *possible* to construct a CI on the basis of citations from any field in the humanities (and from any other field as long as there are citations). However, it can also not be overlooked that the footnotes (the term *footnote* is used but is understood to include "end-notes" and other forms of referential material appended to the text) in articles and books in the humanities are frequently not simple citations; the variety of content is very considerable. These notes may simply give a date or may contain a complete article in miniature; they may list all items relevant to the topic (correctly or incorrectly) or cite a work which has been proved (in the text) to be non-relevant or to contain false information. Not only would the citations therefore be in many cases irrelevant, superfluous, or even misleading, it would also often prove difficult to disentangle them from their context.

In a study carried out at the Toronto University Faculty of Library Science in 1974[10] the citations contained in foreign language articles in *PMLA, MLR*, and *AUMLA*[11] for the years 1971−73 (a total of almost 6,000 citations) were analysed and tabulated from various points of view. Although one of the basic arguments in favour of a CI is that it can be constructed by non-experts (clerical workers), it was found in this study that this was by no means the case. Since the total citations present (in whatever form) in any article may be viewed as a document file, the same procedures for evaluating the efficiency of the system and the same terminology can be used as in the evaluation of a document retrieval system.[12] Thus, for example, the total number of items retrieved from the total available is the resolution factor (with the minor difference in this case that the proportion here refers to the number of items whose *complete* bibliographical data were located). This factor was found to be .75, i.e. only 75 % of items cited were fully retrieved from the notes.

More important, however, is the question of the efficiency of the citation index in retrieving *relevant* items from the total of all citations (recall). This figure was rather higher, namely ca. 83 %. But it was offset by the very low pertinency factor (i.e. relevant items in the total items retrieved) of only 59 %, 49 %, and 37 % respectively.

These figures demonstrated that less than half of the total of all citations were relevant, since:

if the resolution is .75, only 75 items are retrieved per 100

---

10 Michael S. Batts, "On the feasibility of citation indexes in the humanities." Research report, Faculty of Library Science, University of Toronto.
11 Australasian Universities Modern Language Association − the title *AUMLA* was retained when the name of the sponsoring association changed to Australasian Universities' Language & Literature Association.
12 See, for example, J. W. Perry and A. Kent, *Documentation and Information Retrieval* (Western Reserve U. Press, 1957).

and, if the pertinency factor is .48 (average), there are only 36 pertinent items in the 75 (48 % x 75)
but, if the recall factor is .83, and there are 36 pertinent items in the 75 retrieved, then the total of pertinent items, i.e. 100 %, is 43
and there can therefore only be 7 pertinent items in the 25 % unretrieved.
The curious result of this situation is that an increase in the resolution factor, i.e. the retrieval of more items per se, would only *reduce* the pertinency factor since 36 per 75 is already a higher rate than 7 per 25.

At this point it is necessary to pause and consider what exactly is meant by relevant. In the study cited here all items of a critical nature were normally assigned to the relevant category on the basis of the title of the item and a knowledge of the contents of the citing article. As non-relevant were considered editions, translations, reference works such as dictionaries and biographies, peripheral materials which indicated the "broader background" of the topic or suggested parallels in other disciplines, and the sources of "decorative" quotations. To define relevance in any satisfactory manner is virtually impossible and it could well be argued that references to editions for instance, might be important; the author had to be guided largely by experience. As an indication of the method followed, however, the following "typical" example is offered (cited from the original study). The marginal numbers correspond to the citations as registered on the standard statistical sheet used in the study (reproduced in the appendix) and to the notes that follow. The words underlined are discussed after these notes.

Notes from Morton W. Bloomfield,
"The Man of Law's Tale:
A tragedy of victimization and a Christian Comedy,"
PMLA, 87 (1972), 384—90

* This essay in an earlier form has been published in Italian in *Strumenti critici,* 9 (June 1969), 195–207, and delivered in yet other forms at the English 3 meeting of the MLA Annual Convention, New York, 29 Dec. 1970, and at several universities.

1 ¹ I first heard this term applied to these tales by Robert W. Frank in a speech delivered at the MLA Annual Convention in Madison, Wis., 1957. Needless to say this category has no clear-cut limits. We could, for instance, add the Prioress' Tale to the list if we wish. Some pathetic tales are more pathetic than others and involve us emotionally more than the MLT does.

2 ² We might perhaps make an exception for the Second Nun's Tale as a Saint's life; or somewhat of an exception for the Clerk's Tale as part of the marriage group – if we can accept the marriage group hypothesis. But the latter is still more than vaguely discomforting even as an example of wifely patience and as a tale in the mouth of the clerk.

Back of the MLT lies a variant of The Maiden without Hands folktale type (Aarne/Thompson, No. 706). But the folklorist antecedents of the tale are not my concern in this essay, in spite of the fact that they do help to explain some of the features of the present tale.

³ Cf. the remark attributed to Charles Chaplin, "Comedy is life in long shot and tragedy, life in close-up." We are both I's and he's – tragic from our own perspective and 3 comic to others. Cf. Brecht's suggestion that humor is a "Distanzgefühl" (referred to in *TLS,* 8 Aug. 1968, p. 838).

There is some parallel here to the emotional effect of 4 the grotesque. See Wolfgang Kayser, *Das Groteske: Seine* 5 *Gestaltung in Malerei und Dichtung* (Oldenburg: G. Stalling, 6 1957), trans. Ulrich Weisstein, *The Grotesque in Art and Literature* (Bloomington: Indiana Univ. Press, 1963), and Victor Erlich, "A Note on the Grotesque, Gogol: A Test Case." *To Honor Roman Jakobson: Essays on the Occasion of His Seventieth Birthday* (The Hague: Mouton, 1967), pp. 630–33.

⁴ For Constance's apostrophes, see ll. 274–87; 451–62; 639–44; 813–19; 826–33; 841–54; 855–57; 858–61; (841–61 Constance first to Mary, then to her son, and finally to the Constable, all, incidentally, Chaucer's additions): 1105–13.

⁵ A common Chaucerian gambit, the most famous example of which occurs in *Troilus* ll.666–85 when the persona answers the objection that Criseyde certainly fell in love with Troilus quickly. For further examples, see

Troilus iii.491 ff.. 1681 ff.: Knight's Tale, ll. 1881 ff.: **13**
Franklin's Tale. ll. 1493 ff.. etc.
  ⁶ Cf. the Yiddish folk figure of the *nebbish.*
7 ⁷ ii. 7. See the interesting discussion of this tale in Stavros
Deligiorgis. "Boccaccio and the Greek Romances." *CL.*
19 (1967). 97 ff. This tale is closely related to the MLT in
its spirit and organization in a mirror-image way: yet it
would not be classified as belonging to its folktale type.
Note Northrop Frye's definition of comedy: "normally
an erotic intrigue blocked by some opposition and resolved
by a twist in the plot known as 'discovery' or recognition":
8 "Comic Myth in Shakespeare." *Proceedings and Trans-*
actions of the Royal Society of Canada, 46, 3rd Ser. (June
1952). Sec. 2. p. 55. On the role of inversion and mirror
image in myths. see the brilliant remarks of Claude Lévi-
9 Strauss. *The Scope of Anthropology*, trans. Sherry Ortner
Paul and Robert A. Paul. Cape Editions. i (London:
Cape. 1967). 34–39.
  There is possibly a direct analogue to our tale in *The*
Decameron v. 2. about Gostanza. although not very close.
10 See Thomas H. McNeal. "Chaucer and the *Decameron*."
MLN. 53 (1938). 257–58.
  Miss Jeanne Krochalis points out to me the transfor-
mations of a similar victim theme in a large part of Chrétien
de Troyes's *Erec et Enide* where Enide endures much after
she and her husband leave the court until the end of the
story with its celebration of joy at the earthly (as opposed
to the heavenly) court. Here the concentration on Erec
rather than Enide. the absence of a rhetoricizing persona.
the downgrading of the persecution all give the tale a
happy. earthly ending. But I suspect that there is a parody
of the tragedy of the victim and saint's life lurking in the
background of part of Chrétien's poem.
11 ⁸ On the characteristics of the classical romance and its
related genre. the aretalogy, see Rosa Söder. *Die apo-*
kryphen Apostelgeschichten und die romanhafte Literatur
der Antike. Würzburger Studien zur Altertumswissenschaft.
iii (Stuttgart: W. Kohlhammer. 1932).
12 ⁹ *The Greek Romance* (New York: Doubleday. 1953).
Introd.. pp. 7–8.
  ¹⁰ Le cose tutte quante
    Hanno ordine tra loro. e questo è forma
    Che l'universo a Dio fa simigliante
            Dante. *Paradiso* i.103–05

13 ¹¹ See Robert T. Farrell. "Chaucer's Use of the Theme of
the Help of God in the *Man of Law's Tale*." *NM*, 71 (1970).
239–43. Farrell has put his finger on an important aspect
of the tale. related to saints' lives. but he uses the term
"figura" (p. 243) in an unusual fashion to describe Constance's role in this theme.
  ¹² Omitting the pathetic tales already mentioned. the
only other tales in *CT* which are stanzaic are Sir Thopas.
where the metrical unit varies and is parodic. and Monk's
Tale. which if not pathetic. certainly is linked to the contempt of the world tradition. *Troilus and Criseyde* seems to
be an exception to this principle. but I now think the meter
is another distancing device such as I discussed in my
14 article "Distance and Predestination in *Troilus and Cri-*
seyde." *PMLA*. 72 (1957). 14–26. However. in *Troilus*
Chaucer also brings us very close to the characters. whereas
in MLT he never allows us to approach the emotional.
15 ¹³ "Periodic Syntax and Flexible Meter in the *Divina*
Commedia." *Romance Philology*. 21 (1967–68). 17. I am
in general indebted to Scaglione's insights for some of my
metrical comments. To my colleague Professor Zeph
Stewart I am indebted for the observation that the run-
over effect is also more common in the *Aeneid* when emo-
tion rises.
  ¹⁴ Robinson edition. p. 691. See Robert Enzer· Lewis.
16 Chaucer's Artistic Use of Pope Innocent iii's *De miseria*
humane conditionis in the Man of Law's Prologue and Tale."
17 *PMLA.* 81 (1966). 485–92. Lewis sees the use of Innocent's
work mainly. though not entirely. in emphasizing the joy
after woe and woe after joy theme. which certainly plays
an important part in the tale.
  ¹⁵ The prologue is largely concerned with an apostrophe
to the hatefulness of poverty and thence by opposition
passes to rich merchants as a kind of preparation for the
merchants who appear in the first stanza of MLT. Most
scholars have found the connection between the prologue
and the tale only vaguely appropriate. I must say I do not
see how the theory set forth in this article will enable us
to solve this question.
18 Cf. John A. Yunck. "Religious Elements in Chaucer's
Man of Law's Tale." *ELH*. 27 (1960). 250. Yunck sees the
fundamentally religious quality of the tale (e.g.. "God.
then. in His providential care of His servants. is the
protagonist of the Man of Law's Tale." p. 259) although
I cannot fully understand why he calls it "A romantic
homily." See above. n. 11.

1 Although the author can be derived from the personal reference no title is given. Such
an item would normally fall under the heading of criticism but it has been assigned in
this case to the peripheral category, since it is evident that the material is merely an
earlier form of the present material and therefore of no significance.

2 An incomplete reference. Since the note speaks of the term being applied "to these
tales," it is assumed that the paper will have been on the same topic.

3 The reference is to Brecht; however, the source cited is not Brecht but a place where
Brecht is quoted. This "second-hand" source is incomplete inasmuch as neither author
nor title is given.

4/5 These are the same work in the original and in English translation. They are quoted in
order to provide a source for the discussion of the term grotesque and therefore are
placed under reference.

6 An example of the grotesque is derived from Russian literature which moves the
discussion too far away from Chaucer to be considered relevant; it has therefore been
assigned to the peripheral category.

7 Reference to the text revealed that the tale referred to is a "mirror image" of the Chaucerian tale under discussion. Although this would not seem to relate it very closely to the topic under discussion, it has been (perhaps generously) assigned to the category of criticism.

8 This citation is in the continuation of the note which produced item 7 and is a typical example of tangential reference. Moving from Chaucer to Boccaccio in the beginning of the note, the author now moves to a general discussion of comedy and exemplifies this from Shakespeare. This has therefore been considered only a peripheral citation.

9 The author now brings in the question of myths per se and cites in this connection the translation of a standard work on anthropology. This has therefore been listed under reference.

10 Still under note 7 the author returns to the Chaucer-Boccaccio relationship and cites a work which seems to be more closely related to his topic. This has therefore been included under criticism.

11 This is a typical example of the citation of background reference material.

12 Similar to item 11, but a split reference, since the author is cited only in the text. It should be noted that in the text the name of the author precedes a quotation at the end of which is the footnote number. One therefore has to look back several lines to find the author's name.

13 An evidently content-related citation.

14 A "self-citation." This has been assigned to the category of criticism as being possibly relevant.

15 Another split citation. In this case the citation has been assigned to criticism, even though the reference is to another literature. This (again perhaps generous) decision was based on the author's statement of indebtedness. However, it should be noted that the author introduces the topic of metrics only peripherally at the end of his essay.

16 This is a good example of a very confusing reference. The footnote simply says "Robinson edition, p. 691" and reference to the text reveals a quotation which is presumably derived from this Robinson edition. It would take some subject knowledge to determine whether or not the Robinson edition is an edition of Chaucer or an edition of Pope Innocent III, whose *Contempt of the World* is discussed in this paragraph. In any case Robinson is cited without initials.

17 This item was assigned without hesitation to the critical category.

18 This also could be assigned unhesitatingly to criticism.

Although 18 citations were derived from the 15 footnotes, there were other references in footnotes which might conceivably be considered as citations. These are the following.

Note 2: a brief identification of a reference source, in effect a classification number.

Note 3: a quotation attributed to Charles Chaplin with no reference as to the source.

Note 5: a reference to other works of Chaucer.

Note 7: a reference to Boccaccio's *Decameron,* but no edition cited.

In the same footnote, in the last paragraph, there is a discussion of a personal comment to the author regarding a work of Middle French literature (Chrétien de Troyes).

Note 10: a quotation from Dante's *Paradiso* has not been included as a citation. If it had been it would have been as an example of a "decorative" citation.
Note 13: another reference to personal information provided in regard to a similar phenomenon in the *Aeneid*.

In addition to these one should note that Pope Innocent III's *De contemptu mundi* is referred to in the text as a major source for Chaucer's work; there is, however, no reference to an edition of this (but see above the comment on item 16). Boccaccio's *Decameron* is also referred to in the text. It is unusual that no edition is cited of the work of the author under discussion.

Finally it should be noted that there is one reference to an Italian journal and one quotation in Italian; one German work is cited only in the original and a second is cited in the original and in translation. Of the 18 works recorded as citations, only the following (in order of precedence) would seem to be of any value to a potential index user using the citation method of locating material relevant to the topic discussed: 13, 17, 18; 14, 15; 7, 10.

It will certainly come as no surprise to many academics, particularly those who have editing experience, that such a large proportion of citations can be considered "irrelevant," i.e. not to refer to an item with related content. This factor alone might be sufficient to deter anyone from attempting to launch an HCI, but there are also other, more practical grounds for concern. In the first place research in science and technology is reported almost exclusively in periodicals. This is not the case in the humanities and the proportion of books to articles in the study cited was found to be in the region of three to one. It is naturally possible to construct an HCI which includes books along with articles, but the question arises as to the degree of relationship which may be considered to exist between citing article and cited book and the diffuseness of the body of citations collected on this basis. The fundamental assumption behind a CI is the *close* content relationship between cited and citing item, but this is hardly likely to be present between a citing article of five pages and a cited book of five hundred pages. True, a page reference is often included, but in many cases (an estimated 25 % of all book citations) there is none. And how is the book reference to be entered? Separately for each citation with page reference? A user looking for items that cite the same book could perhaps find those that refer to the same passage of the book; it is more likely that there would be too many that refer to different parts of the book or the book as a whole and would consequently not be genuinely relevant.

Another substantial difference between research in the humanities and in the sciences is the greater "life-expectancy" of critical work in the humanities. Critical writing on any literary work *may* derive from almost any period since the work was first written or published. In practice at least this means that a considerable proportion, if not the major proportion, of critical work cited is much older on average than the "half-life" of five years cited in literature on citations in the sciences.[13] In the study used here the median of average ages calculated per periodical item was approximately 28 years. The question therefore arises as to whether an HCI is *fully* effective that does not go back at least as far as that, since, if articles now cite items whose average age is 28 years, it is to be expected that in many cases a significant item may date at least that far back. Although obviously any index would have to start with contemporary work the user would eventually probably expect to be able to consult a thirty-year run of any citation index in order to be able to cover the field fully. This would, however, be a cumbersome procedure. Some study is clearly needed of the *relative* value of older and more recent citations.

Finally there are the strictly practical but not insignificant problems, referred to above, in creating the index without expert help. In the first place footnotes are often lengthy and abstruse and have citations buried in them, sometimes with the bibliographical data in different parts of the note. Notes of 10 or 20 lines in length are common; one article examined had 748 lines of notes (in smaller type) for 754 lines of text. The notes often refer back and forth or assume a degree of familiarity with the field. The proportion of items cited in foreign languages too is by no means negligible, besides the fact that the article itself may be in English or German if the topic is German and the source an English publication.[14] The proportion of foreign language citations in articles in *PMLA, MLR,* and *AUMLA* was calculated at 30 %, 55 %, and 63 %. In view of these and similar problems it is difficult to imagine how an HCI could be effectively constructed by anyone without substantial training in foreign languages and in the field covered.

One counter-argument to objections raised to an HCI is similar to that made at the beginning of this chapter, namely that one cannot logically argue that something is desirable or not desirable until it is known whether or not it is possible. *If* an HCI were created and *if* it found at least tentative or trial acceptance, it is possible that citation practices would change or could be adapted so that they would make the construction of the HCI simpler and its effectiveness greater. Writers could be asked, for example, to supply a list of references considered germane to the topic, just as they are asked now to supply an abstract and/or index terms. It is extremely unlikely, however, that even in this eventuality the resultant end-product would be effective. Experience shows – if this rather imprecise reasoning can be accepted – that many items cited by scholars in the humanities are not genuinely relevant to the topic under discussion precisely because the topic itself is neither easily

---

13 See, for example, J. Margolis, "Citation indexing and evaluation of scientific papers," *Science,* 155 (March, 1967), 1213–19.
14 In this connection see Michael S. Batts, "Citations in the humanities: a study in citation patterns in literary criticism in English, French and German," *IPLO Quarterly,* 14 (1972), 20–40.

definable nor susceptible to the kind of proof that is possible in the pure sciences. To give a simple example: a new interpretation of a monologue in *Hamlet* may owe something to earlier interpretations without being based on them, and many more may be cited than have been used. Any one of them could have provided the spark that led to the new study; but the relationship between the two is not necessarily significant, even if comprehensible.

In summary, then, it does not seem that a CI in a field such as German studies (and such an index would probably need to include other fields as well in order to be practicable) would be viable under present conditions, since it would require highly trained subject experts to elucidate and process the citations. Even if citation practices were modifed to meet the exigencies of an HCI, the viability would still be questionable on account of the high proportion of apparently irrelevant citations. And even if these could be eliminated, for example, by the use of subject experts, there would still be the major problem of determining the value and comprehensiveness of any supposed relevant citations. A considerable amount of study has been directed towards establishing the reasons for citations in the sciences, and a little work has been done in the humanities.[15] The results obtained in scientific fields cannot necessarily, however, be applied to the situation in the humanities. The nature of the topics treated in the humanities and the manner of their treatment are fundamentally different from the situation in the sciences, and a direct content relationship between citing and cited item can consequently not be assumed; or the relationship may be entirely different for author and reader. The listing of earlier work is also often for reference only rather than an indication of indebtedness. A study of the reasons behind current citation practices would make fascinating reading and would certainly be an essential pre-condition for any HCI; however, it is a task that is clearly well beyond the limits of the present work.

The only other major alternative method of access to information of the kind envisaged is the index, and this brings us back first of all to the discussion in the previous chapter. The bibliographies discussed there are indexes only to the extent that it is possible to look up an author or a broad topic, e.g. Goethe or "Vergleichende Literaturgeschichte." These terms and other, slightly narrower ones do not, however, index the items listed but are an index to an ideal whole which is the sum total of German studies in language and literature. The "index term" "Toposforschung" has not been derived from the items there listed; it is the larger term by which German studies are indexed and under which the various items have been subsumed.

---

15 For example, W. C. Simonton, "Characteristics of the Research Literature of the Fine Arts during the Period 1948–1957" (Diss. Illinois, 1960). I have not seen Carolyn O. Frost "Use of Scholarly Materials in German Literary Research . . ." (Diss. Chicago, July 1975).

The *ZAK* on the other hand is a true index in that the terms are derived from the individual items, and the first question to be considered is therefore whether this form of index could represent a viable solution if present objections could be answered. There are essentially three objections; two of these have already been discussed, namely the limited scope and the time-lag. A possible third objection is the class organisation.

There is no doubt but that the *ZAK* could be expanded without difficulty beyond its present limitation of 115 periodicals. It is questionable, however, whether the increase in scope, for example, to twice the size, would substantially increase its value. The journals currently listed are those in which the majority of serious work in German studies is reported.[16] The doubling of the journals indexed would increase the bulk without necessarily achieving a corresponding increase in value – there would be a much higher level of irrelevance – while nothing would be done to reduce the time-lag. On the contrary it would inevitably be increased. The greater volume would reduce also what value there currently is in the classification scheme, since browsing would be too slow a process with greatly increased numbers of cards. In fact it would probably be more profitable to list every item alphabetically, leaving the class numbers, if at all, as an appendage, much as the author (subject) entries have appended numbers, indicating the broad area of the item. In short, one can visualize a greatly expanded version of the *ZAK*, preferably in a single alphabetical sequence, but the bulk would rapidly become a major problem and would almost certainly preclude any faster processing. There would also remain the problem of monograph materials.

A monograph can be indexed as well as any article, though *possibly* requiring the use of more terms. That this is not *necessarily* the case is evident from the fact that some articles may have as many as one or two hundred pages, some monographs as few as fifty or even twenty-five pages. Again, however, there is the question of bulk. The addition of all monographs to the index, even assuming an average of only four entries per item, would mean a further 6000 cards per annum (for an estimated 1500 books). Certainly nothing would be done to speed up the publication process, since a book of average length, no matter how few index terms are eventually applied, cannot be scanned as rapidly as an article, although indexing would perhaps be faster than reviewing. There is moreover the problem that descriptors of the kind employed by the *ZAK* are less suitable for works of a general or broad nature. The article has as a rule a fairly specific though not always immediately intelligible title. The relationship between the index term and this title should be evident; the relationship is likely to be much less evident between an index term and a book title.

---

16 It is by no means easy to establish the core journals in any discipline and I have no information about the procedures used in the case of *ZAK*.

Since the questions of bulk and timelag have loomed so large in the discussion hitherto and only the question of time-lag has been analysed to any extent, something should be said at this juncture of physical bulk as opposed simply to the volume of entries. *GER* listed in 1974 5883 items; the unbound issues take up 8 cm of normal shelf space (standard 23 x15 cm format). *EPP* appears in annual hardbound volumes of the same format, the last of which (1973) is 4 cm thick. *MLA* adheres to its traditionally inconvenient large format with double columns on a page size of 27 x 19 cm and thus manages to include its biliography of all foreign literature in a volume 2 cm thick (1973); it requires of course a higher shelf. Since all three bibliographies are needed, the five year period 1969–73 will require shelf space 60 cm in length, 30 cm in height and ca. 25 cm depth (earlier volumes are slightly thinner; totals *GER* 34 cm, *EPP* 16 cm, *MLA* 10 cm; *GER* and *MLA* have been measured unbound).

In the same period the *ZAK* can be assumed to have added about 2500 cards per annum. At 40 cards per cm. that equals 62.5 cm. of drawer space or two drawers. If the same number of items were handled in *ZAK* as in *EPP* and *GER*, i.e. 6000, with an average of four cards per item, the annual volume of entries, namely 24,000, would require 600 cm of drawer space and the five year cumulation 3,000 cm or 30 metres. Since the average card drawer is about 35 cm long, a cabinet of 90 drawers would be required for the five year cumulation. This works out to approximately 100 times the volume of the bookshelf for the bibliographies. While this may seem grossly out of proportion with the bibliographies, it must be remembered that the user of *ZAK* would need to look in only one place for any given subject and would find the full bibliographical information at every point. The bibliography user would have to look in thirty different volumes (excluding cross references), i.e. 20 x *GER*, 5 x *EPP*, 5 x *MLA*.

There is one further point which presents itself in connection with bulk, but which will not be discussed at this stage, namely the extent to which the user has any interest in a bibliography as a whole or is interested only in a particular section of it. Since by their very format none of the bibliographies discussed so far lends itself to compartmentalisation, this topic will be left until later.

The weakness of the card index lies in its extremely inefficient use of the available space. Each card carries a descriptor, a numerical notation, and the bibliographical data on a surface area of 94sq. cm. The same information uses up a fraction of this space, namely 3–4 lines, in *GER* or *EPP*, and even less in *MLA*, at most perhaps 20sq. cm. Moreover precisely the same bibliographical data must appear with other index terms. This is essential so that a) the context in which the term appears may be seen and b) an additional step is not required to locate the item. However, the elimination of any information could not in any case reduce the size of the card, which is the major problem. There seems therefore to be an impasse; either cumulability must be sacrificed for the sake of economy of space or compactness must be sacrificed for the sake of cumulability – unless an alternative method of production can be found which will satisfy both demands.

The only possible solution would seem to lie in the application of computer technology in production and the use of a contextual form of indexing that would eliminate much of the volume of text. The latter point should perhaps be discussed first. In a basically single-term index such as *ZAK* it is essential to have the item listed with the term, since a single word out of context may mean little or at least be ambiguous where natural language is concerned. Words like "Epos" and "Metaphor" or even "Farbsymbolik" or "Reisebeschreibung" need another term to complement them, i.e. to place them in context. This context is supplied in *ZAK* by the title. However, to list all descriptors applied to any given item and omit the entry would not greatly assist the user, because these terms are not necessarily inter-related; they are not created for that purpose. Take, for example, the items cited above. It would be difficult to establish the connection between:

> Romantik
> Dialog
> Hoffmann, Kater Murr
> Novalis, Heinrich von Ofterdingen

or between:

> Mittelalter: Minnesang
> Minnesang
> Ritter: Tugendsystem
> werdekeit.

If on the other hand a *systematic* sequence of index terms were applied to any one item, the topic treated in that item could be sufficiently explicitly described so that the proper relationship could be derived from them. This would eliminate the necessity for providing the bibliographical data at each and every index point. A new system of this kind has recently been developed in the UK and is currently being employed for the entries in the *British National Bibliography (BNB)*.[17] Called PRECIS (*Pre*served *c*ontext *i*ndex *s*ystem), it is based on the fact that the broader and narrower aspects of any work are normally related in varying ways and can be expressed in a sequential series that will make this relationship apparent. Each work normally has one focus, sometimes there are two foci, but rarely more than this, and the indexer by his analysis of the content of the book is able to place this focus in perspective and define its special application.[18]

17   Also by the *Australian National Bibliography* and others.
18   The basic work on PRECIS is now Derek Austin, *PRECIS: A manual of concept analysis and subject indexing* (London: Council of the BNB., 1974), cited as Austin (1974).

It is not possible and presumably not even desirable to enter in a work such as this into the details of this system. It must suffice that the system is entity-based, i.e. "that an entity or group of entities which can be identified as the key system must be present" (Austin [1974], p. 156) and that subordinate facets are related to the key system — and/or to sub-systems — in a variety of ways. The focus or observed system is broken down into elements 0–6, while the numerous sub-facets are related by what are called "operators" (designated by letters). A complete outline is included in the appendix. The observed system may be an object (1), an action (2) or an agent of transitive action (3). Some simple illustrations will make this clearer. A book on the migration of birds in the Pacific Northwest, for example, would be coded (0) Pacific Northwest (0 = environment), (1) birds, (2) migration. The fields 4, 5, and 6 are reserved for: viewpoint-as-form, sample population/study region, and target/form. A more complex example would be a book such as *A Survey of the frequency of children's visits to theatres in London* which would be analysed as (Austin, [1974], p. 163):

(0) London
(1) theatres
(2) visits by/to
(3) children
(p) frequency [part/property operator]
(6) surveys

Once such a "concept string" has been established, a "manipulation string" is created which transforms the concept string into a variety of entries in which natural language order is automatically generated for such aspects as (2) visits by/to. For example, a concept string (1) journals, (2) reading by/of (3) scientists (from *The reading of journals by scientists*) would produce entries as (Austin [1974], p. 166):

Journals
    Reading by scientists
Reading Journals
    By scientists
Scientists
    Reading of journals

The basic form of every entry consists of the "lead" item (alphabetical entry), the "qualifier" (to the right), and the "display" (below), thus:

Prior to this (and referred to below) is the same author's (with Peter Butcher), *PRECIS: a rotated subject index system* (London: Council of the B.N.B., 1969), cited as Austin (1969). A critical comment on PRECIS by Jack A. Gold and a rejoinder by Austin provide a useful explanation of the system for the layman in *Canadian Library Journal*, 29 (1972), 460–69.

                    LEAD qualifier
                    display

The basic entry is then "rotated" so that items from the display move up to the lead position, displacing the item(s) on the first line to the right. To take a fairly complex example, a book entitled *The wreck of the "Torrey Canyon"* was analysed as follows (Austin [1969], p. 71): Sea   pollution   oil
      tankers/wrecks/"Torrey Canyon" This produced the following entries:[19]

SEA
Pollution. Oil. Tankers. Wrecks. 'Torrey Canyon'
POLLUTION. Sea
      Oil. Tankers. Wrecks. 'Torrey Canyon'
OIL. Sea pollution
      Tankers. Wrecks. 'Torrey Canyon'
TANKERS. Oil. Sea pollution
      Wrecks. "Torrey Canyon"
WRECKS. Oil Tankers. Oil. Sea pollution
      "Torrey Canyon"
"TORREY CANYON". Wrecks. Oil tankers. Oil. Sea pollution.

In another example from the same source a book entitled *The Herculean hero in Marlowe, Chapman, Shakespeare* was analysed as: [Literature, English]/Drama/Tragedies, 1587—1625   Characters/Heroes.
      It appeared as:

DRAMA. English Literature
      Tragedies, 1587—1625. Characters. Heroes
TRAGEDIES. English Drama
      1587—1625. Characters. Heroes
CHARACTERS. Tragedies, 1587—1625. English drama
      Heroes
HEROES. Tragedies, 1587—1625. English drama.

The complex machinery by which the concept strings are translated into the various entries is of no great concern to the user of the index. The essential point is that the original entry can always be re-established by reading anti-clockwise, i.e., the upper line right to left and the lower line left to right; and the reader is therefore always in a position to comprehend the relationship of the chosen entry word to other parts of the entry. In addition this form of analytical indexing appears to lend itself to the indexing of articles, for, as Austin points out, it was designed from the outset to be capable of being carried to any desired depth. The only problem arises in transferring the

19   The manipulation string was written as follows:
      \$z101\$a sea \$z100\$a pollution \$z022\$a sea pollution \$z101\$a oil \$z100\$a tankers
      \$z002\$a oil tankers \$z101\$a wrecks \$z101\$c610 Field 610020 \$a "Torrey Canyon"

explicit relationships envisaged by PRECIS, primarily on the basis of technical
literature, to the less strictly definable relationships in language and literature
studies. Thus, to take one very simple example, it is clearly undesirable to view
an author as the *subject* carrying out the *activity* writing which produces the
product a play. On this basis the play *Hamlet* might be a part of a key system
Plays in English with the author qualifying as the agent. In fact, as far as one
can tell from the *BNB* indexes published to date, PRECIS accepts the literary
form as the principle sub-facet within the language facet, i.e., German literature
as a sub-facet of literature and drama in German as a sub-facet of drama. Drama
is then extended to include dramas and dramatists, while the literary work is
viewed as a sub-system within the context of the person.

While it seems that the PRECIS system has already been applied to
periodical items and to abstracts, its major application hitherto has been to the
BNB and its function there is rather different from that of an index within the
confines of a single discipline. The level of indexing in the *BNB* is exemplified
by the following recent entries.

832.912 — GERMAN DRAMA, 1900-1945
832'.9'12 — Drama in German, 1900-1945. *Texts*
  Brecht, Bertolt. The threepenny opera/ [by]
    Bertolt Brecht; translated by Hugh
    MacDiarmid. — London: Eyre Methuen, 197.
    — [4],67p; 21cm. — (A Methuen modern play

    Translation of 'Die Dreigroschenoper'. Berlin
    Suhrkamp, 1955.
    ISBN 0 413 29720 9 Pbk: £0.50
                                    (B73-13714)

  832'.9'12 — Drama in German. Brecht, Bertolt
        Critical studies
  Benjamin, Walter. Understanding Brecht/ [by
    Walter Benjamin; translated [from the German
    by Anna Bostock; introduction by Stanley
    Mitchell. — London (7 Carlisle St., W.1): NH
    1973. — xix,124p; 22cm.
    Translation of 'Versuche über Brecht'.
    Frankfurt am Main: Suhrkamp, 1966. — Bibl.
    122. — Index.
    ISBN 0 902308 54 8 : £2.25
                                    (B73-04 ??

832.914 — GERMAN DRAMA, 1945-
832'.9'14 — Drama in German, 1945-. *English texts*
Bauer, Wolfgang. All change & other plays/ [by]
Wolfgang Bauer; translated by Martin &
Renata Esslin, Herb Greer. — London: Calder
and Boyars, 1973. — 179p; 21cm. —
(Playscript; 56)
This collection originally published in German,
Köln [Cologne]: Kiepenheuer und Witsch,
1969. — Contents: All change - Party for six ·
Magic afternoon.
ISBN 0 7145 0945 0 : £2.60

(B73-21099)

The first item appears in the subject index as follows:

Drama in German
      1856–1945. Special subject: social conditions —
            Critical studies – Inaugural lectures[20]
Social conditions. Special subject. Drama in German, *1856–1945 – Critical studies –*
Inaugural lectures

Looking in the index under Brecht and Drama in German reveals also an item
listed from a quite different area of the classified section (016 instead of 832):

Brecht, Bertolt. Drama in German. Stock. Birkbeck
      College. Library – *Catalogues.*

There was an additional index entry for this item under Birkbeck College. It is
to be expected that books are more general in character than articles and one
should not necessarily expect a longer string of terms. Rather, indexing of a
narrowly circumscribed periodical article will require a longer string, but *only* if
it is to be included in a general index. The strings for both books and articles
can be reduced if the broader context can be assumed. Thus in an index of
work in literature the term literature is superfluous just as the term German
literature is superfluous if the index covers only that field.

The following examples are an attempt to show how the PRECIS indexing
system might be applied in the field of German studies. The items used are
taken from volume 7 of *Seminar* (1971). The titles are:

(1)   "Like and look alike: Symmetry and Irony in Storm's *Aquis submersus*"
(2)   "Ausgangspunkte und Dialektik der gesellschaftlichen Ansichten C. M. Wielands"
(3)   "Johann Beer's approach to the novel"

---

20   Italicised terms are form terms and do not appear as lead items.

(4) "Masterpieces in disguise: the radio plays of Friedrich Dürrenmatt"
(5) "Neidhart's tomb revisited"
(6) "The relationship between Eduard and Ottilie in Goethe's *Wahlverwandtschaften*"
(7) "Key symbols in Hesse's *Steppenwolf*"
(8) "Hölderlin in der Lyrik Günter Eichs"
(9) "A Note on Kriemhilde's three dreams"
(10) "Hölderlin in perspective: 1770–1970"
(11) "The enigma of *Der blonde Eckbert:* The significance of the end"
(12) "Mephistopheles: 'Ein Teil von jener Kraft, Die stets das Böse will und stets das Gute schafft' "
(13) "Hölderlin's 'Heidelberg' as poetic Myth"
(14) "Animal and nature references in F. Hebbel's *Maria Magdalena*"
(15) "C. F. Meyer's *Der Heilige:* the problem of Beckett's conversion
(16) "Die Gerichtsthematik bei Oskar Jellinek 1886–1949."

These titles provide adequate examples of vagueness. In (1) and (4) there are "captions" that catch the attention but give no clue as to content. In (4) there is no indication of the direction of the article, i.e., why masterpieces. The title of (3) is extremely vague and could equally well be the title of a book. There is no suggestion in (7) as to what the key symbols are; (8) and (10) are equally equivocal.

As an example of procedure – in article (8) the author points out that Eich cites Hölderlin in two specific poems but otherwise rejects the Hölderlin "cult." This was therefore analysed in the concept string as:

Poetry in German. Günter Eich. Latrine, Neue Postkarte 8. Influence of Hölderlin.

These elements would be coded in such a way that the total series of entries would read:

POETRY IN GERMAN
     Eich, Günter. Latrine, Neue Postkarte 8. Influence of Hölderlin, Friedrich
EICH, GÜNTER. Poetry in German
     Latrine, Neue Postkarte 8. Influence of Hölderlin, Friedrich
LATRINE, NEUE POSTKARTE 8. Eich, Günter. Poetry in German
     Influence of Hölderlin, Friedrich
HÖLDERLIN, FRIEDRICH. Influence on Latrine, Neue Postkarte 8. Eich, Günter. Poetry in German

An additional entry could have been added for Neue Postkarte 8 (this would repeat the third entry with the poems in reverse order or enter each separately).

Bearing in mind the requirements of an index that is to provide analysis of content from what might be termed an "uncommitted" viewpoint, but including at least the generic (discipline) designation, the following are the preliminary content analyses and the resulting concept strings for the first seven items. Further examples are given in the appendix along with the abstracts, the entries from *ZAK*, etc.[21]

(1)   Symmetrical structure — Johannisnacht episode — results in ironic contrast
(2)   happiness of individual in relation to demands of state — constitutionalism
(3)   theory of the novel as genre based on comments in Willenhag novels
(4)   structural pattern — success despite neglect of accepted rules of genre
(5)   legend of translatio supported by discovery of 14th century document
(6)   central theme — form of chemical attraction and change
(7)   positive rather than pessimistic interpretation based on Jungian analysis of symbols of wolf, mirror, flowers, laughter

Concept strings

(1)   Prose in German, Novellas. Storm, Theodor. Aquis submersus. Structure and irony
(2)   Prose in German. Wieland, Christoph Martin. Philosophy. Sociological aspects
(3)   Prose in German. Beer, Johann. Willenhag novels. Theory of Novel
(4)   Drama in German. Dürrenmatt, Friedrich. Radio plays. Technique of writing
(5)   Poetry in German. Lyric poetry, 1150–1300. Neidhart von Reuental. Reburial
(6)   Prose in German. Novels. Goethe, Johann Wolfgang von. Wahlverwandtschaften. Character studies: Eduard & Ottilie
(7)   Prose in German. Hesse, Hermann. Steppenwolf. Jungian symbols.

Omitted from consideration are of course the cross references from and to general and specific alternative and related terms. These would depend entirely on the form and scope of the index as a whole.

These concept strings may seem — they no doubt are — relatively simple; it may seem in fact nothing more than a simple hierarchical sequence from the general to the particular. There are, however, important distinctions. As far as possible natural language is used, and used in a natural sequence of words, especially in regard to the most specific elements. There is moreover no restriction on the kind of relationship that may be invoked between any or all elements, something that is normally pre-determined in a genuinely hierarchical system. It should also be noted that these are advisedly not complex examples and all are from the literary field; in the language field the relationships are less apparently hierarchic. Finally it would be possible to go into greater detail, for example, to list the individual key symbols in article (7), but this is a question of policy. It would be up to the indexer to decide what level of specificity is appropriate, given the agreed nature of the index. For our purposes, which are primarily comparative and exemplary, this level seems sufficient. The main purpose is to demonstrate the flexibility of the system and the manner in which the context of any entry term may be seen at any point, e.g., that the theory of the novel [in (3)] is derived from the Willenhag novels and not vice

---

21 Examples of the use of the PRECIS system in foreign languages are given by Austin in (1974), p. 503ff.

versa (which would have been the case, had Beer's theory in general been discussed and exemplified on the basis of the Willenhag novels).

The essential feature of the index as a whole is then the bringing together of items related by a particular facet, e.g. the "character studies: Eduard and Ottilie" will be juxtaposed with character studies in other articles; sociological aspects from various works will be juxtaposed. The works in which these facets occur may be quite different and may, from the user's point of view, not be relevant; but the user can immediately see from the context in which they appear whether or not they are relevant. The full *bibliographical* data need therefore be given at only one point, probably in a numbered alphabetical sequence, since a subject order would be less appropriate within a disciplinary index. (The *BNB* is arranged by Dewey decimal classification.) Each entry in the subject index would therefore have the number of the "main" entry attached to it. Assuming a two-line bibliographical entry of the style of the *MLA* and an average of four two-line index entries for a total of 10 lines per item, and assuming further a maximum annual output of 6000 items, the whole index for a year could be accommodated on 400 pages of the *MLA* format. Given the clearer form of the index entries it would in fact be possible to use much smaller type as in the case of the *BNB*.

Since computer operations are essential to such an indexing system, i.e., to generate and integrate entries, the cumulated entries would presumably be printed more economically by computer governed photo-setting equipment. Given the expected volume of 5000 to 6000 items per annum, the most useful type of product would probably be the monthly listing, cumulated quarterly (March, June, October) and annually. Any desired form of multi-annual cumulation would also be possible.

Such a proposal is far from utopian. The technology and experience exist and are constantly being refined and expanded. The two questions left open are first the familiar problem of time-lag and secondly the question, who is to be responsible for the indexing process. Both of these questions will be discussed in a different context subsequently; for the time being it is necessary to return to the question raised above of the extent to which the individual requires a complete index to all work in the whole field and to consider one other alternative or possible supplement to the system suggested.

That system foresees as an end-product a printed annual index to all work in German language and literature. While this may be an essential reference work for libraries, the vast majority of scholars work in a restricted field, at most within a certain definable broad area. A scholar may teach and study, for example, within the broad area from Goethe to the present day and wish to be generally informed about all new work in this area; but he is unlikely then to be interested also in Old High German, Gothic, etc. to the extent of acquiring an index to or bibliography of work in these and related fields. For the individual, then, a complete list of work in a narrow area is desirable, but not normally a complete bibliography of the whole field. It is true that the system suggested would reduce the number of indexes to one and that this would be, it is hoped, more up to date. It could, however, still be bulky and expensive for the individual in addition to providing a considerable quantity of unwanted material.

Compartmentalisation of a bibliography such as that suggested is a possibility, particularly since it would necessarily be computer-based. Printed sections of the bibliography for individuals or small groups would, however, be prohibitively expensive on account of the inevitable degree of overlap. There are two possible alternatives for individual service, namely an SDI system (*selective dissemination of information*) or direct access to the computer file. In either case it is likely that abstracts would be needed.

It would presumably be no more difficult to construct a profile for searching PRECIS-type entries than for any other form of index. The main question is the form of output. The most useful form would be a printout of the full bibliographical (numbered) entry for all items located, but it is conceivable that index entries or simply a list of numbers could be provided, assuming that the recipient had a copy of the full bibliography within easy reach. Direct access assumes local terminals on-line to the computer file. This would enable the user to consult the file on an ad hoc basis, applying the normal procedures of Boolean logic. Items located could be either studied visually or printed out at the terminal.

In both cases it would seem logical to make use of abstracts, if only because it is highly unlikely that all or even most of the works cited will be available locally. Assuming, then, that there is a computer file of abstracts, numbered in the same way as the bibliographical file, then the SDI service would send out copies of the abstracts (in microfiche form) of articles located on the basis of the profile. The on-line facility would enable the user to read the abstract in visual display and, if need be, to produce a printout.

Given, however, that an abstract file would be highly desirable, it would be more economical to separate this *and* the related functions from the main file. Thus, either the concept string could be added to the abstract before it is filed, or key words tagged for searching, so that both SDI and direct searching could be done from this file. In the first item, for example, the words "Novella," *"Aquis submersus,"* "symmetrical patterning," and "irony" all occur in the abstract. If this system were used, it would be necessary to publish a list of all such keywords, much as in the *ZAK* system.

On-line facilities of this nature are not new, although rarely employed in the humanities. The major problem for a subject such as German is the international nature of the materials and their sources. On-line facilities are therefore out of the question (unless duplicate files were made available to national centres) and the most that could be hoped for is one central computer which would serve all countries. This would not affect the SDI service, but specific search requests would have to be mailed in, after having been formulated (as with SDI profiles) by local experts in information retrieval. The replies, printout, etc., would again be returned by mail. Such an arrangement involves international cooperation and would not preclude the possibility of considerable delays. It raises two basic questions. In the first place is it desirable to organise bibliographical services in this comprehensive manner and in the second is it possible?

The first point in favour of a genuinely comprehensive bibliographical record is the fact that all work, whether good or bad, has in theory at least a function. A selection of material, no matter how judicious or unbiased, inevitably falsifies the true historical record. Both the good and the bad (and their relative proportions) are characteristic for the time – and who are we to make judgments for the future? The more practical point in favour of total coverage is the perhaps regrettable fact that it is cheaper to record the existence of material than to evaluate it. Critical sifting and selecting, even if it *should* be done and *could* be done, is prohibitively expensive.

The major objection to total coverage is the burden that it places on the user who must make the necessary evaluation of the undesirably large mass of material that is recorded. There are several reasons why this is not such a great burden as might at first appear. In the first place most scholars soon learn to recognise what may be expected from given scholars just as they are aware of the policies of specific journals or the policies, standards, and so forth of presses. Right or wrong, they make a priori judgments in many cases. The evaluation process is also aided to a considerable extent in the scheme suggested here by the provision of a more informative indexing system and possibly also of abstracts. The negative cost factor is overridden in part by the practical consideration just mentioned and by the fact that the individual should be able to make arrangements to be informed of only those matters which are of primary interest.

While the point may reasonably be stressed – as it has been – that the majority of individuals do not want to be burdened with masses of information about publications in fields other than their own (not to mention disciplines other than their own as in the case of the *MLA International bibliography*), this does not mean that there might not also still be a place in a future bibliographical world for an index of the type of ZAK. There is no reason to suppose that Bradford's law will be superseded in the foreseeable future, and there is also no reason to suppose that there will not equally continue to be those to whom a limited selection of the more important material is more desirable than an exhaustive listing. To provide such a selective listing on a regular basis would be a very small task for the computer. The product would be based on an agreed list of core journals (it would be difficult to include monograph materials) and represent merely a subset of the master file. It would presumably appear at approximately the same time intervals as the major publication, but it could not in the nature of things have that advantage of earlier publication which is enjoyed by *ZAK* over its more comprehensive and consequently slower competitors. Only if the comprehensive listing were found to be so difficult as to result in delays, would a "preferential" listing of items from core journals be conceivable, i.e., they would be given priority in handling. Such a development is, however, unlikely, since it may be supposed that those whose interests are more general are less concerned about the speed with which they are informed.

In view of these and related minor considerations such as the saving of space through amalgamation and selective dissemination of information, it is evident that a unified index to German studies offers great advantages. Looking again at the present situation, it is clear that there is duplication on two levels. Scholarly journals are indexed on the one hand to some extent by national, general periodical indexes and on the other by internationally-oriented (scholarly) organisations. *Seminar,* for example, the Canadian journal of Germanic studies, is not (yet) indexed by the *Canadian periodical index,* but it is indexed by *ZAK* and *GER,* and then subsequently by *EPP,* and by *MLA.* The same or a similar situation obtains in other countries and with other journals. The major producers of bibliographical sources for "Germanistik" are therefore duplicating each other's work and including only a very few minor items of usually local significance that are not included elsewhere. Above all they provide with the exception of *ZAK* far more material than the individual requires while not providing the necessary degree of access which would enable the individual to make the best use of the part in which he or she is interested. What is needed is less publication and a higher, more flexible degree of access to the stored information.

It is difficult to know *how* such an arrangement could be brought about, but it would clearly be logical, at least in language and literature studies, for the bibliographical organisation to be centred in the (or a) country where the "study language" is native. Thus German bibliography should be centred in Germany (French studies in France, etc.). If nothing else, these countries have — or should have — a vested interest in the encouragement of the cultural interchange represented by international studies in "their" language and literature. It is not to be expected on the other hand that "foreign" studies, e.g., of German literature in non-German countries should be bibliographically assessed from the country of the source language, since every country has also a particular interest in the "foreign" studies carried out within its borders. The most logical arrangement would therefore be one whereby national professional associations accept the responsibility for collecting the material published within the borders of their country and for forwarding this to the central agency in the proper form and with the minimum of delay. In the rare cases where no professional organisation exists the task could be transferred, if not to a suitable bibliographical agency, then to a group from a neighbouring state or to the central agency. Bibliography would therefore be organised primarily on a national level with one country — in our case Germany — functioning as the international bibliographical centre.

The major question which still has to be answered is: would such a procedure be more efficient? The answer is of course an unequivocal yes. Existing procedures are inefficient insofar as they duplicate each other and because they work at too great a distance from the sources. This latter problem is the cause of many delays and the system as outlined here should be capable of providing information more quickly and without greater economic strain. It is one of the anomalies of scholarly publishing that there should be such great interest in the latest research and yet such laxness about publishing schedules. Perhaps it is in part at least a result of the lack of any real financial incentive for publishers. At all events it is not uncommon for journals to appear months after the cover date, or for books to be mailed out for review months, even a year or more, after the date of publication. When it comes to popular literature, however, a review can appear the very day on which a novel is published.

There is in fact no reason at all why a bibliographer or a reviewer should receive the finished product only weeks or months after it becomes available to the general public. The author or editor knows at the latest by the page proof stage when the item will appear and in precisely what form. The text is there and the abstract is there; both have been proofread and paged. It is at this stage that the local bibliographic process should begin.[22] Either the editor/publisher should be able to assign PRECIS index terms, or a copy of the page proofs and abstract should be sent to the national representative who is trained in these procedures. It is not a difficult task and could be assigned to a member of the professional organisation or to a member of the national library staff. At all events it should be possible to have the complete material forwarded to the central agency *before* the date of publication.

At the processing and publishing stage speed will depend primarily on the available financial resources. Given, however, that the indexing has already been done, it should be a much less expensive operation than, for example, the "manual" indexing currently done for *ZAK*. The main function of the staff would be spot-checking for accuracy and translating the concept strings into manipulation strings for processing. Also the printing process would be determined by economic factors which cannot be discussed here. All that can be said is that computer-governed photo-setting machines, such as the Mergenthaler VIP, are very fast and very flexible. It should be possible to produce monthly issues not later than one month after receipt of the material, and, since these would be throw-away issues, they would not need to be on

22 It is at this stage that the CIP process begins and there seems to be little difficulty about preparing catalogue material for inclusion in the finished product.

expensive paper or carefully bound. Entering the abstracts into the computer file, supposing such a system to be included, is purely a clerical function. An outline of the procedure is on the opposite page.

To the average scholar in German studies such a proposal may sound less utopian than like flying in the face of nature, for it is the nature of humanists to be, or to want to seem to be, slow, ponderous and disorganised. To the scholar in the sciences and to a large extent also in the social sciences this is familiar terrain. Pre-print indexing, computerized SDI services, on-line links to computerized data banks are a commonplace today and already a factor, if a minor one, in the humanities. Sporadic attempts are being made to utilise the computer for bibliographical work, for example the abstract/index terms of the MLA or the computerisation plans of *ZAK,* but a major deterrent to progress on a broad scale seems to be the lack of any international co-operation of the kind achieved in the area of cataloguing, book numbering and so forth. There seem to be only two alternatives. Either a supra-national organisation such as the IVG or FILLM must take the initiative (which is unlikely for financial reasons) or an existing "national" group such as the DFG or the MLA must seek the means to start such an international co-operative programme, i.e. initiate planning and seek funding. A related kind of project has already been started in linguistics (Language Information Network and Clearinghouse System [LINCS]) and there is no reason to suppose that the system proposed here is beyond the reach of humanists. Certainly, it is likely that humanists will have to continue to bear their cross of inefficiency for some time yet, but fortunately or unfortunately the time seems not far distant when the luxury of inefficiency will no longer be affordable.

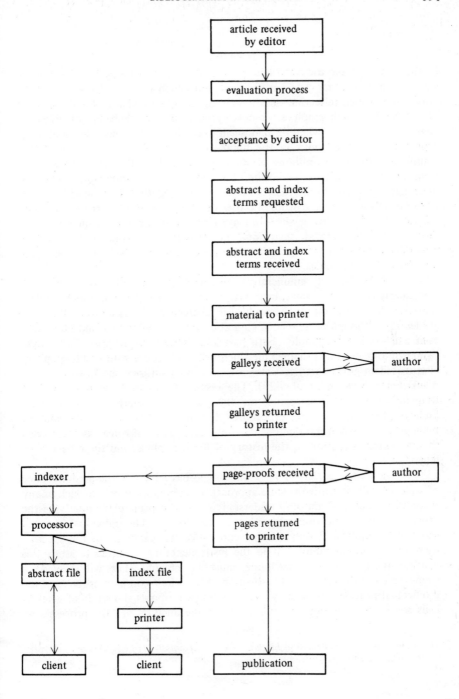

Conclusion

In the course of the thousand and more years of bibliography that have been surveyed here a great deal has changed, but much of that change has been purely superficial, reflecting variations in opinion as to what material ought to be included in bibliographies, or developments in the mechanics of printing, distribution, etc. But whatever may seem to be the gap between the simple one page listing of the books in the library of St. Kilian in Würzburg and the computer storage of millions of items that can be examined through the medium of a cathode ray tube, the function of bibliography remains unchanged, namely, to mediate between or bring together the item of "graphic communication" and the would-be user of that item. Rather, therefore, than attempt — probably fruitlessly — to make a critical summation of the history of bibliography to date, I shall look in conclusion in some detail at this relationship between bibliography and research, between the bibliographer and the user of bibliographies.

The work of the enumerative bibliographer has all too often, and particularly in modern times, been viewed by scholars as being something less than scholarly, something basically for professional hacks rather than for academics, although most scholars are also only too willing to find fault with each and every bibliography, both past and present. As Koppitz (299) says: "Zwar betont man allenthalben die Unentbehrlichkeit der guten Bibliographen, aber trotzdem gibt es wenige Kategorien von Buchautoren, die so gern und so oft kritisiert werden" (col. 829). The result of this attitude is not only a frequently displayed ignorance on the part of scholarly critics of basic bibliographical sources and procedures, but also a blindness to the value of bibliographies as cultural documents. Only the occasional voice has been raised to urge closer attention to the history of bibliographies, and these have been largely unheeded.

One such voice is that of Jesse Shera who has lamented the predominance of what he calls the microcosmic approach to communication, the lack of any theoretical approach and any understanding of the principles underlying the *process* of communication rather than its end-result.[1] The individual or group is normally interested only in this end-result, for example, in the specific, user-oriented bibliography, not in the instrumentality. In order to study this instrumentality, "a new discipline must be created that will provide a framework for the effective investigation of the whole complex problem of the intellectual processes of society" (p. 27). Shera proposes the study of what he calls social epistemology. By this is meant the analysis of "the processes by

---

1 Shera's essays are collected in *Libraries and the Organisation of Knowledge* (444); page references are to this work.

which society *as a whole* seeks to achieve a perceptive or understanding relation to the total environment" (p. 27), that is to say, "the analysis of the production, distribution, and utilization of intellectual products" (p. 29). Since society records its reaction to the environment primarily in the form of "graphic communication," i.e., written records ("intellectual products"), such a proposal is effectively the foundation of a new general theory of bibliography, and the essay in which Shera most clearly outlines this new discipline (mentioned in several articles in various ways) is in fact entitled "Foundations of a theory of bibliography."[2]

In Germany a rather more general plea for increased attention to bibliographies was made by Koppitz. He stresses in particular the value of bibliographies as an indication of contemporary knowledge, cultural climate, etc. He refers to, among other specific examples, the existence of enormous numbers of unlisted theses and to theatre programmes. Both of these kinds of material are important sources for the history of knowledge and yet neither has been bibliographically recorded. The major thrust of his article is therefore less in the direction of the development of a theory of bibliography, and more toward creating retrospectively the kind of bibliographies that are so lamentably lacking in Germany and on which a cultural history might be based. Koppitz' views fall short of the theoretical considerations raised by Shera; he views bibliographies as summary statistical quantities, so to speak, as succinct quantifications of available knowledge rather than as information carriers within the framework of the communication process.

On this side of the Atlantic again a rather different concept has been put forward by the main proponent of citation indexes, Eugene Garfield. In several articles Garfield has proposed the study of "historio-bibliography," based on analyses of the inter-relationships of all recorded knowledge as evidenced in the network of citations (chiefly 172, 174, 176, 173). Cited and citing works are related in infinitely variable degrees, so that it would theoretically be possible to construct a map of the whole of human knowledge as expressed in published records, a map in which the most significant "mentefacts" would stand out by the frequency with which they have been cited. Although this idea can be seen as representing an aspect of, or an approach to, social epistemology, much of what has been written about citation indexing serves only to justify Shera's complaint about the overriding concern for the end rather than the process, for much of what even Garfield has written is concerned with the *pragmatic* aspects of this idea, with, for example, the function of bibliographic relationships as sociometrical indicators or as a basis for prognostication. It nevertheless seems clear that the underlying concept of historio-bibliography is related to Shera's social epistemology.

---

2 Pp. 18–33; co-author Margaret Egan; originally in *Library Quarterly*, 22 (1952), 125–37.

Shera's idea has more recently been reiterated by Brookes (92), who has linked it with, among other things, Goffmann's theory (196/7) of the epidemic nature of intellectual communication. Very briefly this draws a parallel between the spread of an infectious disease and the transmission of knowledge, where the idea contained in an item of information reaches a susceptible individual and creates knowledge. A genuine "outbreak" of knowledge can not take place until a certain threshhold has been reached, until there is a sufficient number of individuals available, susceptible to infection and able to act in turn as carriers. Perhaps these widely scattered articles on social epistemology and historio-bibliography are themselves a demonstration of the validity of this theory, at least for the negative aspect, for there seems to have been as yet no general or widespread reaction to these stimuli, no indication that the threshold has been reached at which the ideas will communicate themselves rapidly and effectively through the community (of librarians and bibliographers). From the particular point of view of the individual bibliographer, however, it seems essential to develop such a broad theoretical approach and to integrate bibliographical concepts into a comprehensive theory of communication, so that the role of bibliographies within the communication process may be better appreciated.

The communication flow passes from creator (author) via the created work (mentefact) to the receptor (reader). If, using the analogy referred to above, the receptor is susceptible to the information carried by the work, then knowledge is created. Knowledge is not created or only partially created, if the reader is immune or only partially susceptible to the communicated idea. If the receptor has received the work *directly,* whether passively or as the result of actively seeking direct access to it, then the only barriers to direct communication between author and reader are the language on the one hand and the reader's preconceptions on the other.

The situation is quite different, however, if the receptor comes to the item via a bibliography. It is true that a bibliography may also be read in a sense "passively," i.e. that the reader may not necessarily be looking for anything; but it is much more likely that the reader uses the bibliography with intent, that is, he or she is looking for something relevant to his or her interests. The preconception is therefore already present; but much more important is the fact that the bibliography itself is a "secondary" creation of the bibliographer. It is − to quote our own definition − an "organised listing" of which each item forms an integral part. The user of a bibliography therefore comes to the item located through a bibliography not only with his own preconceptions, but also with the consciousness of its context *as defined by the bibliography.* The reception of the item, when located, is thus to a certain extent preconditioned by the process through which it is located.

What is involved here is the fundamental problem of the supposed inter-relationship of all knowledge. Ever since the extent of knowledge began to exceed the ability of the individual to comprehend it and knowledge began to be replaced by an accumulation of written records, attempts have been made to organise knowledge, to develop a taxonomy that reflects man's perception of knowledge and of the inter-relationship of areas of knowledge. This historical-genealogical, latterly almost Darwinistic approach has found expression in the organisation of libraries and on a smaller scale in the organisation of bibliographies. However, it is apparent that the creation of an epistemological framework, whether based on a supposedly abstract philosophy or on extant research in the form of written records, is not without its dangers. Collections of items of knowledge, like other kinds of collections, tend to become self-perpetuating, to develop an impetus (or inertia) that maintains growth (or the status quo) but inhibits change. Libraries are not in fact living organisms but take on in effect the character of organisms, and nowhere is this more evident than in their structure. Once established, these structures are difficult to change and possess a not inconsiderable influence on their own future. Above all the nature of the structure, i.e. the organisation of the books as based on their intellectual content, exerts a powerful influence on the users of those books.

In bibliographies, much as in libraries, the user may come to an item via the classification scheme or via a subject term (descriptor). In the former case the item, if found in the expected place, may reinforce the preconceived expectation of relevance; alternatively the item may be found in an unexpected context and the preconceived notion thus modified. In the latter case, where the item is located via an index term, the influence of a pre-determined contextual relationship seems at first less, inasmuch as it is accepted that each term is one of a number of descriptors that may be applied. However, such terms may be a strong influence, if they are not precisely those with which the search began. The user may have turned or been referred to a term which is not identical but (more or less) closely related. The search is thus diverted or the issue confused by association with related concepts.

The index term is notwithstanding less tainted than the classification statement, since despite all the subtleties of colon classification systems and the like, a given work is assigned to a fixed position in what is inevitably (by design or not) a pre-conceived order; it stands in relation to others by virtue of its classification even though it may be assigned more than one (possible) position. The link between works that are "indexed," i.e. to which subject terms have been applied, is, however, multi-variant and independent of any established intellectual order. Given on the one hand the growing volume and variety of publication and the consequently decreasing possibilities of physically locating together disparate forms of material (books, periodicals, microforms, etc.) that may be considered intellectually related; and given on the other hand the increasing volume of specialised and/or cross-disciplinary research; given further that research materials are increasingly being stored in non-print form, it seems evident that indexing rather than classification will be the primary, if not the sole method of access to research material in the future.

The main concern in the future must remain, however, precisely that referred to above, namely the inhibiting effect of traditional concepts in the indexing process. While the individual index term does not define the content of a work in the way that classification does, yet the danger still exists of assigning index terms on the basis of transmitted concepts rather than on the basis of the new material. To some extent this is a linguistic or semantic problem (as discussed above in relation to citation indexing), but it will become an increasingly serious problem as ever greater reliance is placed on indexes and on computer storage. Searching is normally done on a basis of two or more terms. One inadequate term will make a search difficult; several such terms would probably frustrate the search entirely. Moreover, if material is indexed and stored (e.g. in the case of abstracts) in a computer memory, then the material is available only via the terms *and* the processes which governed search strategy at the time of entry of the material. If large quantities of research material are stored in computer memories, then it seems there will be the very real danger that these data banks will become like the older libraries they replace — vast storehouses of inaccessible information, because their organisation may be based on principles that become outmoded with time. Far from being a stimulus to research they could easily become an obstacle if and when research interests and modes change.

This problem will not easily be solved, if at all. It is not raised on the other hand as a deterrent either to indexing or to computer data storage. Each age questions the intellectual values and priorities of the preceding ages and the next will presumably be no different. What should be urged, however, and this especially in the humanities, is the attempt in the bibliographical treatment of current research to analyse all work as far as possible disinterestedly, without commitment to past or present views as to the natural order of things. Each work should be treated rather as offering points of departure for further research. This after all is the prime function of bibliography. The fact that in so doing the bibliographer faithfully creates a record of his time is only added value.

Appendix

1. Sample abstracts and indexing terms from *MLA*, PRECIS, *ZAK*
2. PRECIS outline
3. Sample of analysis of footnotes

10351. Plater, Edward M. "The Banquet of Life: Conrad Ferdinand Meyer's *Die Versuchung des Pescara.*" *Seminar* 8 : 8–98

Allegorical and symbolic configurations are an integral part of *Conrad Ferdinand Meyer's* narratives. Some of these configurations have gone unnoticed such as the fresco of the feeding of the multitude described at the beginning of *Die Versuchung des Pescara.* The many parallels that exist between the biblical accounts of the *feeding of the multitude* and the story of Pescara give this fresco potential anticipatory force. The fresco's individual details and general composition correspond to the characters, events, and outcome of the story. While it is acceptable for its concrete reality alone it also suggests, without any external reference, a meaning beyond itself. It is a variation of one of Meyer's *symbolic motifs,* the banquet of life. The meaning it suggests corresponds to the ambivalent feelings toward life of the hero of the novella. The hidden significance of the fresco reveals certain ironies that point up the need to approach Meyer's work with a particularly open and discerning mind.

Underlined words: *Conrad Ferdinand Meyer, Die Versuchung des Pescara, feeding of the multitude, symbolic motifs.*
Precis terms:
FICTION IN GERMAN
     Meyer, Conrad Ferdinand   "Versuchung des Pescara"   frescos   alle-
     gory and symbolism
MLA Index terms:
ALLEGORY – Meyer, Conrad F.
ARTS – painting – Meyer, Conrad F.
BIBLICAL ALLUSIONS – Meyer, Conrad F.
IRONY – prose fiction – Meyer, Conrad F.
PROSE – novella – Meyer, Conrad F.
SYMBOLISM – miscellaneous – fresco

* All terms (including both allegory and symbolism) would appear as lead terms

10487. Webb, Karl E. "R. M. Rilke's 'Lied des Aussätzigen': A Personal Dilemma." *Seminar* 8: 31–41.

Michael Hamburger in his book Truth in Poetry (1969) makes a strong case for considering the modern poets from Baudelaire to the present as writers who maintain both an "ivory tower" stance toward society and an "engagiert" approach toward social change. *Rainer Maria Rilke* seems particularly representative of this thesis. On the one hand, he demonstrates a concern for the poor and dejected and complains about the *social conditions* of the big *city*. On the other, he denies in his letters and diaries that he is in any way concerned with social change and denounces those poets who are. In *"Die Stimmen,"* a cycle of poems in Buch der Bilder, Rilke portrays this dichotomy of view and creates primarily as a result of the tensions involved a powerful and poetic biographical statement.

Underlined words: *Rainer Maria Rilke, Die Stimmen, city, social conditions*
Precis terms:
POETRY IN GERMAN
      Rilke, Rainer Maria   "Die Stimmen"   city life   social conditions
MLA Index terms:
LETTERS – Rilke, Rainer M.
SOCIETY – Rilke, Rainer M.

It is not easy to be certain that the appropriate entries in *ZAK* have all been located. No entry could be found, for example, for the Rilke item just cited. Only one entry was found for the Meyer item which was simply listed under:
                  Meyer, Conrad Ferdinand: 5
                  Die Versuchung des Pescara.
Better examples are the following:
   "Like and look alike: Symmetry and irony in Storm's *Aquis submersus"*
ZAK
C3   Storm, Theodor: 4
         Ironie
       Storm, Theodor: 4
         Maerchen [Motiv]
       Storm, Theodor: 5
         Aquis submersus
       Storm, Theodor: 5
         Johannisnacht
Suggested Precis entry (above, p. 184)
PROSE IN GERMAN, NOVELLAS

   Storm, Theodor. Aquis submersus. Structure and irony
"Masterpieces in disguise: The radio-plays of Friedrich Dürrenmatt"
ZAK
C 2,49 Hoerspiel
C 3   Duerrenmatt, Friedrich: 5
        Hoerspiel
Suggested Precis entry:
DRAMA IN GERMAN.
   Dürrenmatt, Friedrich. Radio plays. Technique of writing

Appendix 1. Role operators

Main line operators

Environment of observed system	0 Location
Observed system (Core operators)	1 Key system: *object of transitive action, agent of intransitive action*
	2 Action/Effect
	3 Agent of transitive action; Aspects; Factors

A ——————————————————————————————

Data relating to observer	4 View point-as-form
Selected instance	5 Sample population/Study region
Presentation of data	6 Target/Form

Interposed operators

Dependent elements	p Part/Property
	q Member of quasi-generic group
	r Aggregate
Concept interlinks	s Role definer
	t Author attributed association
Coordinate concepts	g Coordinate concept

B ——————————————————————————————

Differencing operators	h Non-lead direct difference
(prefixed by $)	i Lead direct difference
	j Salient difference
	k Non-lead indirect difference
	m Lead indirect difference
	n Non-lead parenthetical difference
	o Lead parenthetical difference
	d Date as a difference

Connectives

(Components of linking phrases; prefixed by $)	v Downward reading component
	w Upward reading component

C ——————————————————————————————

Theme interlinks	x First element in coordinate theme
	y Subsequent element in coordinate theme
	z Element of common theme

Journal	date	topic Eng. lit	language	pages	notes	citations	comments			
PMLA	1972/3/2	(Chaucer)	English	6.5	15	18				
		← FORM				**CONTENT →**				
ref. no.	publ. type	date	comp. inc. split	page no. s	lang.	edition etc.	criticism	reference	peripheral	neg. ref.
1	art	1969	com	13	I	(trans)			√ (same paper)	
2	ppr	1957	inc	0	E		√ (no title)			
3	art	1968	inc	1	E		√ (no author/title — "derived" quotation)			
4	bk	1957	com	0	G			√		
5	bk	1963	com	0	E			√ (trans of 4)		
6	bk	1967	com	4	E				√	
7	art	1967	com	ff	E		√*			
8	art	1952	com	1	E				√	
9	bk	1967	com	6	E	(<F)		√		
10	art	1938	com	2	E		√*			
11	bk	1932	com	0	G			√		
12	bk	1953	spl	2	E			√		
13	art	1970	com	5	E		√*			
14	art	1957	com	13	E		√*			
15	art	1968	spl	1	E		√			
16	bk	–	inc	1	E	ed √	√*			
17	art	1966	com	8	E		√*			
18	art	1960	com	1	E		√			
19										
Total 18	bk 7 / art 10 / ppr 1	1353	com 13 / inc 3 / spl 2	0/4 / 59/13	E 15 / G 2	1	9/6	5	3	0

Works cited and consulted

It would be futile to attempt to include in this list all the numerous bibliographies, reference works, and critical studies that have been examined and/or consulted. It would be equally futile to attempt to divide bibliographies from critical studies or to categorise these works in any way, since many appear as bibliographies that are also "critical works" in respect of other bibliographies, while some critical studies contain useful "bibliographies." Included in this list are therefore only those works that have been cited and some few of the more useful works that have been consulted.

Since this is also an exercise in enumerative rather than descriptive bibliography, no attempt has been made to reproduce titles and imprints exactly. Many of the longer titles are not cited in full and punctuation and capitalisation have been modified on occasion or abbreviations resolved. The place of publication is given in the English form (e.g., Munich) and the publisher's name is cited without Christian names or initials except in the case of common names. Dates are normally given in Arabic numerals. Only when a colophon is cited or there might be doubt as to the correct German form of the latinised name is the original form of the imprint reproduced.

It is perhaps worth stressing, however, that, with the exception of those few instances indicated, all works listed here have been examined in the original, although not necessarily all editions.

The spelling of many of the authors' names in the older period varies considerably and causes no little confusion. Although this study has been based upon the British Library collection, it was nevertheless thought advisable to adhere as closely as possible to the forms of name used in the L.C. and N.U.C. catalogues. There are, however, some exceptions, such as the spelling Gessner (on the basis of recent research) rather than Gesner. The actual style of entry conforms largely to the principles laid down in the *MLA Style Sheet*.

1   *AUMLA. Journal of the Australasian Universities' Language and Literature* [formerly *Modern Languages*] *Association.* Christchurch, 1953–

2   Abeling, Theodor. *Das Nibelungenlied und seine Literatur,* Teutonia, 7 + Suppl. Leipzig: Avenarius, 1907, 1909; *Zu den Nibelungen; Beiträge und Materialien von Max Ortner und Theodor Abeling.* Leipzig: Bass, 1920

3   *Acta eruditorum,* ed. Otto Mencke. Leipzig, 1682–1731
    Adelung, J.C. – see *Allgemeines Verzeichnis*

4   Albrecht, Günter, ed. *Internationale Bibliographie zur Geschichte der deutschen Literatur von den Anfängen bis zu Gegenwart,* 3 vols. Munich-Pullach: Verlag Dokumentation, 1969–72

5   Alcuin. *Monumenta alcuiniana,* ed. W. Wattenbach & E. Dümmler, Bibliotheca rerum germanicarum, VI. Berlin: Weidmann, 1873; repr. Aalen: Scientia, 1964

6 *Allgemeine Bibliographie für Deutschland.* Leipzig 1836–42; preceded by *Bibliographie von Deutschland,* q.v.; succeeded by *Wöchentliches Verzeichnis . . .* q.v.

7 *Allgemeine deutsche Bibliothek,* ed. Christian Friedrich Nicolai. Berlin, 1765–96; continued by *Neue allgemeine deutsche Bibliothek.*

8 *Allgemeine deutsche Biographie,* ed. Historische Commission bei der Königl. Akademie der Wissenschaften (Bavaria), 56 vols. Leipzig: Duncker & Humblot, 1875–1912

9 *Allgemeines Verzeichnis neuer Bücher mit kurzen Anmerkungen,* ed. Johann Christoph Adelung. Leipzig, 1776–84

10 Almeloveen, Theodoor Jansson van. *Bibliotheca promissa et latens. Huic subjunguntur Georgii Hieronymii Velschii De scriptis suis ineditis Epistolae.* Gaudae: apud Justum ab Hoeve, 1688

11 *Altdeutsche Blätter,* ed. Moriz Haupt. Leipzig, 1836–40

12 *Altdeutsche Wälder,* ed. J. L. C. & W. Grimm. Kassel (Frankfurt), 1813–16

13 "American bibliography," 1921–. In *PMLA,* 37– (1922); succeeded by *MLA International Bibliography,* q.v.

14 *The American college dictionary.* New York: Random House, 1958

15 *Anglo-Saxon poetry,* selected and translated by R. K. Gordon. Everyman's Library, 794. London: J. M. Dent, 1962

16 *Anzeiger für deutsches Altertum und deutsche Literatur,* ed. Elias Steinmeyer. Berlin, 1876–

17 Arber, Edward. *A Transcript of the registers of the Company of Stationers of London, 1554–1640 A.D.* London: privately printed, 1875–77; Birmingham, 1894; repr. New York: Peter Smith, 1950

18 Arnim, Max. *Internationale Personalbibliographie 1850–1935.* Leipzig: K. W. Hiersemann, 1936; . . . *1800–1943.* I Leipzig: Hiersemann, 1944, II Stuttgart: Hiersemann, 1952; III *Fortgeführt von Gerhard Bock & Franz Hodes (1944–59) und Nachträge zur 2. Auflage von Band I–II.* Stuttgart: Hiersemann, 1963

19 Arnold, Klaus. *Johannes Trithemius (1462–1516).* Würzburg: Schöningh, 1971

20 Arnold, Robert Franz. *Allgemeine Bücherkunde zur neueren deutschen Literaturgeschichte.* Strasburg: K. J. Trübner, 1910; [2]1919; Berlin: de Gruyter, [3]1931; [4]1966

21 Augsburg (library): Henisch, Georg. *Bibliothecae inclytae Reipub. Augustanae utriusque tum graecae tum latinae librorum & impressorum & manu exaratorum catalogus.* Augsburg: per Valentinum Schönigk, 1600

22 Augsburg (library): Hoeschel, David. *Catalogus graecorum codicum qui sunt in bibliotheca Reip. Augustanae vindelicae, Quadruplo quàm antea auctior.* Augsburg: ad insigne pignus, 1595

23 Augsburg (library): Wolff, Hieronymus. *Catalogus Graecorum librorum, manuscriptorum, Augustanae bibliothecae . . .* Augsburg: ex officina Michaelis Mangeri, 1574

24 Augsburg (library): *Index manuscriptorum bibliothecae Augustanae cum adpendice duplici, praemissus historiae literariae & librariae ibid. à M. Antonio Reisero N. T. illustris reipubl. bibliothecario & c.* Sumtu Theophili Goebelii typo Jacobi Koppmaieri, 1675

25 *Aurora; Eichendorff Almanach* [etc.]. Neumarkt, 1929–

26 Austin, Derek. *PRECIS: A manual of concept analysis and subject indexing.* London: Council of the B.N.B., 1974

27   Austin, Derek & Butcher, Peter. *PRECIS: A rotated subject index system.* London:
     Council of the B.N.B., 1969
28   Bacon, Francis. *The twoo bookes of Francis Bacon. Of the proficience and
     advancement of learning, divine and humane.* London: Henri Tomes, 1605
29   Bahder, Karl. *Die deutsche Philologie im Grundriss.* Paderborn: F. Schöningh, 1863
30   Baillet, Adrien. *Auteurs deguisez sous des noms étrangers; empruntez, supposez,
     feints à plaisir, chiffrez, renversez, retournez, ou changez d'une langue en une
     autre.* Paris: A. Dezallier, 1690
31   Bale, John. *Illustrium maioris Britanniae . . . scriptorum, hoc est Angliae, Cambriae, ac
     Scotiae summarium . . .* Excudebatur praesens opus Wesaliae per Theodoricum
     Plateanum, 1548; 2nd edition, Basle: Oporinus, 1557, 1559; a modern edition
     by R. L. Poole and Mary Bateson, Oxford: Clarendon, 1902 (from the original
     autograph)
32   Basse, Nicolaus. *Collectio in unum corpus, omnium librorum hebraeorum, graecorum,
     latinorum necnon germanice, italice, gallicè, & hispanicè scriptorum, qui in
     nundinis Francofurtensibus ab anno 1564 usque ad nundinas autumnales anni
     1592 partim novi, partim nova forma, & diversis in locis editi, venales extiterunt:
     desumpta ex omnibus Catalogis Willerianis singularum nundinarum, & in tres
     tomos distincta, meliorique ratione quàm hactenus disposita, universis & singulis
     disciplinarum omnium & facultatum professoribus ac studiosis, theologis,
     jurisconsultis, medicis, &c. necessaria & utilis . . .* Frankfurt: Ex officina
     Typographica Nicolai Bassaei, 1592
33   Batts, Michael Stanley. "Citations in the humanities: a study in citation patterns in
     literary criticism in English, French and German." *IPLO Quarterly,* 14 (1972),
     20–40
34   –   "The 18th century concept of the rare book." *The Book Collector,* 24 (1975),
     381–400
35   –   "The International current awareness service of the German Research Council."
     Research Quarterly, 12 (1973), 19–22
36   –   "On the feasibility of citation indexes in the humanities." Research report
     (typescript), Faculty of Library Science, University of Toronto, 1974
     Bauer, Martin Jacob – see *Literarisches Wochenblatt*
37   Bauerhorst, Kurt. *Bibliographie der Stoff- und Motivgeschichte der deutschen
     Literatur.* Berlin: de Gruyter, 1932
38   Baumgarten, Siegmund Jakob. *Nachricht(en) von einer hallischen Bibliothek.* Halle,
     1748–58
39   Becker, Gustav Heinrich. *Catalogi bibliothecarum antiqui.* Bonn: Cohen, 1885; repr.
     Hildesheim: Olms, 1973
40   Becker, Joseph & Hayes, Robert M. *Information storage and retrieval tools, elements,
     theories.* New York: John Wiley, 1963
41   Beddie, James Stuart. "Ancient classics in medieval libraries." *Speculum,* 5 (1930),
     17–20
42   –   *Libraries in the twelfth century; their catalogues and contents.* Boston:
     Houghton Mifflin, 1929
43   Bede, The Venerable. *The ecclesiastical history of the English nation.* Translated by J.
     Stevens. Everyman's Library, 479. London: J. M. Dent, 1963

44 Beier, Adrian. *Kurtzer Bericht von der nützlichen und fürtrefflichen Buchhandlung und deroselben Privilegien.* Jena: J. Meyer, 1690

Beiträge — see Beyträge

Bertius, P. — see Leiden (library)

45 Bestermann, Theodore. *The Beginnings of systematic bibliography.* Oxford University Press, 1935, [2]1940

46 — *A World bibliography of bibliographies.* London: Oxford University Press, 1939–40, [2]1947–49; Lausanne: Societas bibliographica, [3]1955–56, [4]1965–66

47 Beughem, Cornelius à. *Apparatus ad historiam literariam novissimam, variis conspectibus exhibendus, quorum nunc primus prodit, qui est bibliographia eruditorum critico-curiosa, seu dispositio harmonica scriptorum, operumque, quorum summaria & contenta in actis & ephemeridibus eruditorum universae fermè Europae exhibentur,* 5 vols. [varying titles]. Amsterdam: Jansson-Waesberg, 1689–1710

48 — *Incunabula typographiae sive catalogus librorum scriptorumque proximis ab inventione typographiae annis, usque ad annum Christi MD inclusive, in quavis linguâ editorum . . .* Amsterdam: J. Wolters, 1688

49 — *La France sçavante; id est Gallia erudita, critica et experimentalis novissima . . .* Amsterdam: Abraham Wolfgang, 1683

50 Beutler, Johann Heinrich Christian. *Allgemeines Sachregister über die wichtigsten deutschen Zeit- und Wochenschriften. Voran als Anleitung ein raisonnierendes litterarisches Verzeichniß aller in diesem Jahrhundert bis jetzt erschienenen periodischen Blätter, nach Dezennien gearbeitet und mit einem Namenverzeichniß aller dabei befindlichen Mitarbeiter.* Leipzig: Weygand, 1790

51 *Beyträge zur critischen Historie der deutschen Sprache, Poesie und Beredsamkeit,* ed. Johann Christoph Gottsched. Leipzig: Breitkopf, 1732–44

52 *Beyträge zur Historie und Aufnahme des Theaters,* ed. G. E. Lessing & C. Mylius. Stuttgart, 1750

53 *The Bibliographic index. A cumulative bibliography of bibliographies.* New York, 1938–

54 *Bibliographie der Bibliographien . . . ,* 1966–. Leipzig, 1966–; preceded by *Bibliographie der deutschen Bibliographien,* q.v.

55 *Bibliographie der deutschen Bibliographien. Jahresverzeichnis der selbständig erschienenen und der in deutschsprachigen Büchern und Zeitschriften enthaltenen versteckten Bibliographien,* 1954–. Leipzig, 1957–; succeeded by *Bibliographie der Bibliographien,* q.v.

Bibliographie der Deutschen Bibliothek — see *Deutsche Bibliographie*

Bibliographie der deutschen Zeitschriftenliteratur . . . see *Internationale Bibliographie der Zeitschriftenliteratur*

Bibliographie der fremdsprachigen . . . — see *Internationale Bibliographie der Zeitschriftenliteratur*

Bibliographie der Rezensionen — see *Internationale Bibliographie der Zeitschriftenliteratur*

56 *Bibliographie der versteckten Bibliographien aus deutschsprachigen Büchern und Zeitschriften 1930–1953.* Leipzig: Deutsche Bücherei, 1956

57 *Bibliographie des Bibliotheks- und Buchwesens* (supplement to *Zentralblatt für Bibliothekswesen*). Leipzig, 1904–12, 1922–25; succeeded by *Internationale* . . . , q.v.

58 *Bibliographie und Buchhandel. Festschrift zur Einweihung des Neubaus der Deutschen Bibliothek.* Frankfurt: Börsenverein, 1959

59 *Bibliographie von Deutschland, oder wöchentliches vollständiges Verzeichnis der in Deutschland erscheinenden, neuen Bücher, Musikalien und Kunstsachen.* Leipzig, 1826–; succeeded by *Allgemeine Bibliographie für Deutschland,* 1836–, q.v.

60 *Bibliographische Berichte* (in *Zs. für Bibliothekswesen und Bibliographie,* 1954–). Frankfurt, 1959–

61 "Bibliographische Übersicht über die Erscheinungen auf dem Gebiet der germanischen Philologie," 1862–69/70. In *Germania,* 1863–71

62 *Bibliographisches Bulletin der Schweiz.* Berne, 1901–; succeeded by *Das Schweizer Buch,* q.v.

63 *Bibliothek des Instituts für Weltwirtschaft Kiel.* Boston: G. K. Hall, 1967

64 *Bibliothek des Instituts für Zeitgeschichte München.* Boston: G. K. Hall, 1967

Bibliothèque nationale – see Paris: Bibliothèque nationale

65 Biesius, Antonius (sale catalogue). *Catalogus plurimorum insignium librorum ex bibliotheca . . . D. Antonii Biesii . . . quorum auctio fiet Leydae, die xv Decembris & sequentibus: apud Ioannem Maire bibliopolam.* Leiden: Ioannes a Dorp, 1607

66 *Bio-bibliographisches Literaturlexikon Österreichs von den Anfängen bis zur Gegenwart,* ed. Hans Giebisch & Gustav Gugitz. Vienna: Hollinek, 1963

67 Blackall, Erich. *The emergence of German as a literary language 1700–1775.* Cambridge University Press, 1959

68 Blankenburg, Friedrich von. *Literarische Zusätze zu Johann George Sulzers allgemeiner Theorie der schönen Künste* . . . Leipzig: Weidmann, 1796–98

69 Blount, Thomas Pope. *Censura celebriorum authorum.* London: Richard Chiswell, 1690

70 Blum, Rudolf. "Bibliographie: eine Wort- und begriffsgeschichtliche Untersuchung." *Archiv für Geschichte des Buchwesens,* 9 (1969), 1017–1246; also separately Frankfurt, 1969

71 – "Vor- und Frühgeschichte der nationalen Allgemeinbibliographie." *Archiv für Geschichte des Buchwesens,* 2 (1959), 233–303; also separately Frankfurt, 1959

72 Bodleian Library. *Catalogus librorum impressorum Bibliothecae Bodleianae.* 4 vols. Oxford: Oxford University Press, 1843–51

73 *Börsenblatt für den deutschen Buchhandel.* Leipzig, 1834– See also *Tägliches Verzeichnis* and *Wöchentliches Verzeichnis*

74 Börsenverein der deutschen Buchhändler: Historische Kommission. *Geschichte des deutschen Buchhandels,* 4 vols., by Friedrich Kapp & Johann Adolf Goldfriedrich. Leipzig: Börsenverein, 1886–1913, *Register* 1923

75 Bohatta, Hanns. *Internationale Bibliographie der Bibliographien.* Frankfurt: Klostermann, 1939–50

76 Bolduanus, Paulus. *Bibliotheca historica* . . . Leipzig: Fridericus Lanckisius, 1620

77 – *Bibliotheca philosophica, sive elenchus scriptorum philosophicorum atque philologicorum illustrium, qui philosophiam ejusq; partes aut omnes aut*

praecipuas, quovis tempore idiomatéve usque in annum praesentem Redemptionis MDCXIV descripserunt, illustrarunt & exornarunt, secundum artes & disciplinas, tùm liberales tùm Mechanicas eorumáue titulos & locos communes, autorumáue nomina ordine alphabetico digesta ... Jena: Apud Joannem Weidnerum, Impensis Haeredum Thomae Schureri, Bibl. Lips., 1616

78   –   *Bibliotheca theologica* ... Jena: Joannes Weidnerus, 1614

79   Borchling, Conrad & Claussen, Bruno. *Niederdeutsche Bibliographie. Gesamtverzeichnis der niederdeutschen Drucke bis zum Jahre 1800,* 3 vols. Neumünster: Wachholtz, 1931–57

80   Borel, Pierre. *Bibliotheca chimica.* Paris: Carolus du Mesnil. 1654

     Boston, John, of Bury St. Edmunds. *Catalogus scriptorum ecclesiae* – see Savage, Ernest A.; Tanner, Thomas; Lehmann, Paul

81   Bouterwek, Friedrich. *Geschichte der Poesie und Beredsamkeit seit dem Ende des dreizehnten Jahrhunderts* (3. Abt. der *Geschichte der Künste und Wissenschaften* ...), 12 vols. [Germany 9–11]. Göttingen: Röwer, 1801–19

82   Bowers, Fredson. "Bibliography, pure bibliography, and literary studies." *Papers of the Bibliographical Society of America,* 46 (1952), 186–208

83   Bradford, Samuel Clement. *Documentation.* Washington: Public Affairs Press, 1950; London: Lockwood, [2]1953

84   Breitkopf, Johann Gottlob Immanuel. *Über Bibliographie und Bibliophilie.* Leipzig: Breitkopf, 1793.

85   Breul, Karl Hermann. *A handy bibliographical guide to the study of German language and literature for the use of students and teachers of German.* London/Paris: Hachette, 1895

86   Brieger, Lothar. *Ein Jahrhundert deutscher Erstausgaben. Die wichtigsten Erst- und Originalausgaben von etwa 1750 bis etwa 1880.* Stuttgart: J. Hoffmann, 1925

87   British Library, formerly British Museum. *British Museum. General catalogue of printed books. Photolithographic edition to 1955.* London: Trustees of the B.M., 1965–66; *Ten-Year Supplement 1956–65,* etc.

88   –   *Catalogue of the printed books in the library of the British Museum.* London: William Clowes, 1881–1900.

89   –   *Subject index of books published before* [*to*] *1880,* ed. R. A. Peddie. 4 vols. London; Grafton, 1933–48

90   –   *Subject index of the modern works added to the library* ... *1881–1900,* ed. G. K. Fortescue. 3 vols. London, 1902–3

     British Museum – see British Library

91   *The British National Bibliography.* London: Council of the B.N.B., 1950–

92   Brookes, B. C. "Jesse Shera and the theory of bibliography." *Journal of Librarianship,* 5 (1973), 233–245, 258

93   Brückmann, Franz Ernst. *Bibliotheca animalis,* 2 vols. Wolfenbüttel: no pub. 1743, 1747

94   Brümmer, Franz. *Lexikon der deutschen Dichter und Prosaisten vom Beginn des 19. Jahrhunderts bis zur Gegenwart.* Leipzig: Reclam, 1885 [6]1913

95   –   *Lexikon der deutschen Dichter und Prosaisten von den ältesten Zeiten bis zum Ende des 18. Jahrhunderts.* Leipzig: P. Reclam Junior, 1884

96   Brunfels, Otto. *Catalogus illustrium medicorum, sive de primis medicinae scriptoribus.* Strasburg: Schott, 1530

97 *Bücher aus der DDR.* Leipzig, 1972/73–; preceded by *Leipziger Bücherkatalog*

98 *Die Bücherei; Zeitschrift der Reichsstelle für volkstümliches Büchereiwesen.* Leipzig, 1934–44

99 *Bücher-Kunde* (Amt Schrifttumspflege). Bayreuth, 1934– [?]

100 *Bulletin bibliographique de la société internationale Arthurienne.* Paris, 1949–

101 *Bulletin de documentation bibliographique.* Paris, 1934–

102 Burger, Konrad. *Buchhändleranzeigen des 15. Jahrhunderts in getreuer Nachbildung.* Leipzig: Hiersemann, 1907

103 — *The Printers and publishers of the fifteenth century with lists of their works.* London: Sotheran, 1902; Berlin: Altman, 1926; Milan: Görlich, 1950

104 Burley, Walter. *Das buoch von dem Leben und Sitten der heydnischen Maister.* Augsburg: Anton Sorg, 1490

105 — *Libellus de vita et moribus philosophorum.* Augsburg: Anton Koberger, 1472

106 — *Liber de vita et moribus philosophorum mit einer altspanischen Übersetzung der Eskurialbibliothek,* ed. Hermann Knust. Tübingen: Literarischer Verein, 1886; repr. Frankfurt: Minerva, 1964

107 Caius, John. *Historiae Cantebrigiensis Academiae ab urbe condita.* London: John Day, 1574

108 *Cambridge History of English Literature.* 15 vols. Cambridge University Press, 1907–27

109 Camerarius, Joachim, the younger. *De re rustica opuscula nonnulla, lectu cum iucunda, tum utilia, iam primum partim composita, partim edita a D. Ioachimo I. F. Camerario, medico noribergensi.* Nuremberg: In officina Catharinae Gerlachin & Haeredum Iohannis Montani, 1577

110 — ΕΚΛΕΚΤΑ' ΓΕΩΡΓΙΚΑ',*sive opuscula quaedam De re rustica... Editio iterata auctior.* Nuremberg: Excudebat Paulus Kaufmann, 1596

111 Cardan, Jerome. *De sapientia libri quinque... Eiusdem, de libris propriis, liber unus. Omnia locupleti indice decorata.* Data xiii. kalendas Octobri anni à salute MDXLIII Mediolani: Excusum Norimbergae apud Johan. Petreum

112 *Catalogus verschiedener Juristischer/ Historischer und Philologischer... Bücher... welche... durch eine kleine Lotterey von 701. Lossen... distrahiret werden sollen.* Hamburg: F. C. Greflinger, 1714

113 Champier, Symphorien. *De medicine claris scriptoribus.* Lyons: J. de Campis, 1506

114 Chrétien de Troyes. *Cligés* [= *Les romans,* II], ed. A. Micha. Paris: Honoré Champion, 1957

115 Clessius, Joannes. *Unius seculi eiusque virorum literatorum monumentis tum florentissimi, tum fertilissimi: ab Anno Dom. 1500. ad 1602. Nundinarum autumnalium inclusive, elenchus consummatissimus librorum; Hebraei, Graeci, Latini, Germani, aliorumque Europae idiomatum: typorum aeternitati consecratorum... Desumptus partim ex singularum nundinarum catalogis, partim ex instructissimis ubiq; locorum bibliothecis: atque in tomos duos partitus; quorum utilitas, & dispositionis ratio in praefatione habetur.* Frankfurt: Ex officina typographica Ioannis Savrii, impensis Petri Kopfij. 1602

116 *The Concise Oxford dictionary of the English language,* fourth edition. Oxford: Clarendon, 1954

Conrad of Hirsau — see Whitbread, L. G.

117   Conring, Hermann. *De bibliotheca Augusta quae est in arce Wolfenbuttelensi ad illustr. et generosum. Joannem Christianum L. Bar. a Boineburg epistola qua simul de omni re bibliothecaria disseritur.* Helmstadt: Henning Müller, 1661

118   Constantin, Robert. *Nomenclator insignium scriptorum, quorum libri extant vel manuscripti, vel impreßi: ex bibliothecis Galliae, & Angliae: Indexque totius bibliothecae atque pandectarum doctißimi atque ingeniosißimi viri C. Gesneri.* Paris: Apud Andream Wechelum, 1555

119   Copinger, Walter Arthur. *Supplement to Hain's Repertorium bibliographicum.* London: Sotheran, 1895–1902; Berlin: Altman, 1926; Milan: Görlich, 1950

120   Curtius, Ernst Robert. *Europäische Literatur und lateinisches Mittelalter,* 4th ed. Berne: Francke, 1963

121   Delisle, Léopold. *Le cabinet des manuscrits de la bibliothèque impériale [nationale].* 3 vols. Paris: Imprimerie royale [nationale], 1886–81

122   Denis, Michael. *Annalium typographicorum.* Vienna: Joseph de Kurzbek, 1789

123   –   *Einleitung in die Bücherkunde.* 2 vols. Vienna J. T. von Trattner, 1777–78

124   *Deutsche Bibliographie. Fünfjahresverzeichnis 1951–1955. Bücher und Karten [Deutsche Bibliographie 1945–1950].* Frankfurt, 1957–. Preceded by *Deutsches Bücherverzeichnis,* q.v.

125   *Deutsche Bibliographie. Halbjahresverzeichnis [Bibliographie der Deutschen Bibliothek. Halbjahres-Verzeichnis, 1951–52], 1953–.* Frankfurt, 1953–. Preceded by *Halbjahresverzeichnis . . . ;* cf. *Jahresverzeichnis des deutschen Schrifttums*

126   *Deutsche Bibliographie. Hochschulschriftenverzeichnis, 1971–.* Frankfurt, 1972–; preceded by *Jahresverzeichnis der deutschen Hochschulschriften,* q.v.; cf. *Jahresverzeichnis der Hochschulschriften . . .*

127   *Deutsche Bibliographie. Wöchentliches Verzeichnis [Bibliographie der Deutschen Bibliothek, 1947–52], 1953–.* Frankfurt, 1953–. Preceded by *Deutsche Nationalbibliographie.* Since 1965 in three parts: Reihe A *Erscheinungen des Buchhandels* (weekly), Reihe B *Erscheinungen außerhalb des Buchhandels* (monthly), Reihe C *Karten* (twice yearly). Since 1975 in addition: *Neuerscheinungen-Sofortdienst (CIP)* (weekly) and *Neuerscheinungen-Monatsverzeichnis (CIP).*

128   *Deutsche Bibliophilie in drei Jahrzehnten. Verzeichnis der Veröffentlichungen der deutschen bibliophilen Gesellschaften und der ihnen gewidmeten Gaben 1898–1930.* Leipzig: Freunde der Deutschen Bücherei, 1931

Die deutsche Bibliothek – see Köster, Kurt

129   *Deutsche Bücherei 1912–1962. Festschrift zum fünfzigjährigen Bestehen der deutschen Nationalbibliothek,* ed. Helmut Rötzsch et alia. Leipzig: no pub., 1962

130   *Deutsche Literatur des Mittelalters. Verfasserlexikon,* ed. Wolfgang Stammler. 5 vols. Berlin: de Gruyter, 1933–55

131   *Deutsche Musikbibliographie* (continues *Hofmeisters Musikalisch-literarischer Monatsbericht,* 1829– *[Handbuch der musikalischen Literatur* 1817–28], 1943–. Leipzig, 1943–

132   *Deutsche Nationalbibliographie: Reihe A Neuerscheinungen des Buchhandels, Reihe B Neuerscheinungen außerhalb des Buchhandels, Reihe C Dissertationen und Habilitationsschriften.* Leipzig, 1931–. Preceded by *Wöchentliches Verzeichnis,* q.v.

Das deutsche wissenschaftliche Schrifttum – see *Jahresberichte des literarischen Zentralblattes.*

133 *Deutscher Gesamtkatalog*, vols. 1–8. Berlin: Preussische Druckerei- und Verlags-AG, 1931– (= *Gesamtkatalog der preussischen Bibliotheken)*

134 *Deutsches Bücherverzeichnis*, 1911–. Leipzig, 1916–. Quinquennial cumulations of *Halbjahresverzeichnis der Neuerscheinungen* ... q.v. Preceded by Hinrichs *Bücher-Katalog*, q.v. Cf. *Deutsche Bibliographie. Fünfjahresverzeichnis.*

135 Diesch, Carl Hermann. *Bibliographie der germanistischen Zeitschriften.* Leipzig: Hiersemann, 1927

136 – Der Goedeke. *Werdegang eines wissenschaftlichen Unternehmens.* Dresden: Ehlermann, 1941

"Dietrich" – see *Internationale Bibliographie der Zeitschriftenliteratur*

137 Doni, Antonio Francesco. *La libraria del Doni Fiorentino. Nella quale sono scritti tutti gl' autori vulgari con cento discorsi sopra quelli. Tutte le tradutioni fatte all' altre lingue, nella nostra & una tavola generalmente come si costuma fra librari.* In Vinegia appresso Gabriel Giolito de Ferrari, 1550

138 Draud, Georg. *Bibliotheca classica* ... Frankfurt: P. Kopff, 1611

139 – *Bibliotheca exotica* ... Frankfurt: P. Kopff, 1610

140 – *Bibliotheca librorum germanicorum classica. Das ist: Verzeichnuß aller und jeder Bücher / so fast bey denchlichen Jaren / bis auffs Jahr nach Christi Geburt 1625 in Teutscher Sprach von allerhand Materien hin und wieder in Truck außgangen* ... Frankfurt: bey Egenolff Emmeln / in Verlegung Balthasaris Ostern, 1625

141 – *Bibliotheca librorum germanicorum classica. Das ist: Verzeichnuß aller und jeder Bücher / so fast bey dencklichen Jaren in Teutscher Spraach von allerhand Materien hin und wider in Truck außgangen / und noch den mehrertheil in Buchläden gefunden werden* ... Frankfurt: durch Johann Saurn / in Verlegung Peter Kopffen, 1611

142 Ebert, Friedrich Adolf. *Allgemeines bibliographisches Lexikon,* 2 vols. Leipzig: Brockhaus, 1821–30; repr. Hildesheim: Olms, 1965

143 – "Über die Geschichte der literarischen Waarenkunde." Preface to C. G. Kayser, *Deutscher Bücherkunde,* q.v.

144 Edwards, Edward. *Memoirs of libraries.* London: Trübner, 1859; London 1901; repr. New York: Burt Franklin, n.d. [1964?]

145 Ehrismann, Gustav. *Geschichte der deutschen Literatur bis zum Ausgang des Mittelalters.* Munich: Beck, 1918–, ²1932–

146 Eichhorn, Johann Gottfried. *Litterärgeschichte der drey letzten Jahrhunderte.* Göttingen: Vandenhoeck & Ruprecht, 1814

Einblattdrucke des 15. Jahrhunderts – see Kommission für den Gesamtkatalog

147 *Einblattdrucke des 15. Jahrhunderts,* ed. Paul Heitz. Strasburg, J. H. E. Heitz, 1901–

148 *Encyclopedia of Library and Information Science.* New York: Marcel Dekker, 1968–

Engelmann, Wilhelm – see Enslin, T. C. F.

149 Engelsing, Rolf. "Ein bibliographischer Plan aus dem Jahr 1826." *Archiv für Geschichte des Buchwesens,* 6 (1969), 1409–12

150 Enslin, Theodor Christian Friedrich. *Bibliothek der schönen Wissenschaften oder Verzeichniß der vorzüglichsten, in älterer und neuerer Zeit, bis zur Mitte des Jahres 1836 in Deutschland erschienenen Romane, Gedichte, Schauspiele und*

anderer zur schönen Literatur gehöriger Werke, so wie der besten deutschen Uebersetzungen poetischer Werke aus lebenden fremden Sprachen . . . zweite Auflage, by Wilhelm Engelmann. Leipzig: Engelmann, 1837. Title varies in earlier editions: Stuttgart: Loeflund, 1821; Berlin: Chade, 1823

151 Eppelsheimer, Hanns W., ed. *Bibliographie der deutschen [Sprache und] Literaturwissenschaft* (ed. Köttelwelsch, 1969–). Frankfurt: Klostermann, 1957–

152 Erasmus Desiderius. *Catalogus omnium Erasmi Roterodami lucubrationum, ipso autore cum aliis nonnullis.* [Colophon] Basileae, tertio Calend. Febru. An. à Christo nato MDXXIII

153 Ernst, Heinrich. *Variarum observationum libri duo. Ad Christianum Frisium Regis Daniae Cancellarium.* Amsterdam: J. Jansson, 1636

154 Ersch, Johann Samuel. *Allgemeines Repertorium der Literatur für die Jahre 1785 bis 1790.* Jena: Expedition der allgemeinen Literatur-Zeitung, 1793–94

155 — *Handbuch der deutschen Literatur seit der Mitte des achtzehnten Jahrhunderts bis auf die neueste Zeit.* Amsterdam: Kunst- und Industrie Comptoir, 1812; later editions Leipzig: Brockhaus

156 Estienne, Henri. *Francofordiense emporium, sive Francofordienses nundinae.* Excudebat Henricus Stephanus, 1574

157 Evelyn, John. *The Diary of John Evelyn,* ed. E. S. de Beer. 6 vols. Oxford: Clarendon, 1955. See also Naudé, G.

158 Everett, George A. *A Select bibliography of Günter Grass (From 1956 to 1973), including the works, editions, translations, and critical literature.* No place: Burt Franklin, 1974

Fabian, Bernhard. – see *Die Messkataloge*

159 Fabricius, Johann Albert. *Bibliographia antiquaria.* Hamburg: C. Liebezeit, 1713

160 Ferguson, John. *Some Aspects of Bibliography.* Edinburgh: George P. Johnston, 1900

Festschrift für Georg Leidinger – see Hartmann, Albert

Feyerabend, Sigmund – see Pallmann, Heinrich

161 Fischer, Walter. "Die Abwanderung des Buchhandels von der Frankfurter Messe nach Leipzig." Diss. Frankfurt, 1934

162 Fontius, Martin. "Zur literarhistorischen Bedeutung der Messekataloge im 18. Jahrhundert." *Weimarer Beiträge,* 7 (1961), 607–16

163 Foresti, Jacobus Philippus. *De plurimis claris scelestisque mulieribus. Opus prope divinuz novissime congestum* . . . [colophon] Opera 4 impensa Magistri Laurentii de rubeis de Valentia. tertio Kal'. maias anno salutis n̄re. 1497

La France scavante – see Beughem, Cornelius à

164 Franeker (library): *Catalogus librorum bibliothecae publicae, quae est in illustrium Frisiae ordinum academia Franekerana* . . . Franeker: Excudit Idzardus Alberti, 1656

165 Frels, Wilhelm. *Deutsche Dichterhandschriften von 1400 bis 1900. Gesamtkatalog der eigenhändigen Handschriften deutscher Dichter in den Bibliotheken und Archiven Deutschlands, Österreichs, der Schweiz und der ČSR.* Leipzig: Hiersemann, 1934; repr. Stuttgart: Hiersemann 1970

166 Friedrichs, Elisabeth. *Literarische Lokalgrößen 1700–1900. Verzeichnis der in regionalen Lexika und Sammelwerken aufgeführten Schriftsteller.* Repertorien zur deutschen Literaturgeschichte, 3. Stuttgart: Metzler, 1967

167 Frisius, Johann Jacob. *Bibliotheca philosophorum classicorum authorum chronologica in qua veterum philosophorum origo, successio, aetas, & doctrina compendiosa, ab origine mundi, usq; ad nostram aetatem proponitur* . . . Zürich: apud Ioannem Wolphium typis Frosch., 1592

168 Frömmichen, [Karl Heinrich?] "Einige Bemerkungen welche sich über den deutschen Meßkatalogus machen lassen." *Deutsches Museum,* 7 (1780), 176–87

169a Fromm, Hans. *Germanistische Bibliographie seit 1945, Theorie und Kritik.* Stuttgart: Metzler, 1960.

169b Frost, Carolyn O. "Use of Scholarly Materials in German Library Research: An Analysis of Reference Citations in Publications about Literary Works Written in the German Language." Diss. Chicago, 1975 [not seen]

170 Galen. *Galeni Pergameni omnia, quae extant, in Latinum sermonem conversa.* . . . *His accedunt nunc primum Con. Gesneri Praefatio & Prolegomena tripartita, De vita Galeni, eiusque libris & interpretibus.* Ex III. officin. Frobenianae Editione, 1562

Gallus – see Le Coq

171 Garfield, Eugene. "Can citation indexing be automated? " *Proceedings of the Symposium on statistical association methods for mechanized documentation,* Washington D.C. 1964, ed. Mary Elizabeth Stevens, U.S. National Bureau of Standards Miscellaneous Publications, 269 (Washington: U.S. Govt. Printing Office, 1965), 189–92

172 – "Citation indexes in sociological and historical research." *American Documentation,* 14 (1963), 289–291

173 – "Citation indexing, historio-bibliography, and the sociology of science." *Proceedings of the third international congress of medical librarianship, Amsterdam, 5–9 May, 1969,* ed. K. Ellison & W. D. Sweeney (Amsterdam: Excerpta medica, 1970), 187–204.

174 – "Primordial concepts, citation indexing, and historio-bibliography." *Journal of Library History,* 2 (1967), 235–249

175 – "Science Citation Index – A new dimension in indexing." *Science,* 144 (May 1964), 649–54

176 – " 'World brain' or 'Memex'? Mechanical and intellectual requirements for universal bibliographical control." *The Foundations of access to knowledge* (Syracuse: Syracuse University Press, 1968), 169–196

177 Geissler, Friedrich. *Disputatio de nominum mutatione et anonymis scriptoribus.* Leipzig: J. E. Hahn, 1669, 1671, 1679

178 Georg, Karl. *Schlagwort-Katalog. Verzeichnis der [im deutschen Buchhandel erschienenen] Bücher und Landkarten in sachlicher Anordnung,* 7 vols. Hannover: Lemmermann, 1889–1913 (publisher varies)

179 Georgi, Theophilus. *Allgemeines europäisches Bücher-Lexikon, in welchem nach Ordnung des Dictionarii die allermeisten Autores oder Gattungen von Büchern zu finden welche . . . noch vor dem Aufgang des XVI. Seculi bis 1739 inclusive . . . in dem europäischen Theile der Welt gedruckt worden.* Leipzig: Georgi, 1742–58

180 *Germania,* ed. Friedrich Heinrich von der Hagen. Berlin, 1836–53

181 *Germania. Vierteljahrschrift für deutsche Alterthumskunde,* ed. F. Pfeiffer. Vienna, 1856–92

182 *Germanistik. Internationales Referatenorgan mit bibliographischen Hinweisen.* Tübingen, 1960–

183 Germany: Reichsministerium des Innern. *Monatliches Verzeichnis der reichsdeutschen Amtsschriften.* Berlin, 1928–

184 Gervinus, Georg Gottfried. *Geschichte der poetischen National-Literatur der Deutschen,* 5 vols. (= *Historische Schriften* Band 2–). Leipzig: Engelmann, 1835–42
     Gesamtkatalog der preussischen Bibliotheken – see *Deutscher Gesamtkatalog*
     Gesamtkatalog der Wiegendrucke – see Kommission für den Gesamtkatalog

185 *Geschichte der deutschen Nationalliteratur von den Anfängen bis zur Gegenwart.* Berlin: Volk und Wissen, 1960; see also Albrecht, Günter

186 Gessner, Konrad. *Appendix bibliothecae Conradi Gesneri. Typographus lectori. Quoniam bibliothecae Conradi Gesneri epitome Basileae primum superioribus annis per Conradum Lycosthenem, deinde nunc apud nos per Iosiam Simlerum multò auctior aedita est . . .* Zürich: Froschouer, 1555

187 –   *Bibliotheca universalis, sive catalogus omnium scriptorum locupletissimus, in tribus linguis, Latina, Graeca, & Hebraica: extantium & non extantium, veterum & recentiorum in hunc usqz diem, doctorum & indoctorum, publicatorum & in bibliothecis latentium . . .* Zürich: Froschouer, 1545; repr. (with Simler's *Epitome*) Osnabrück: Zeller, 1966

188 –   *Elenchus scriptorum omnium. . . Ante annos aliquot a . . . C. Gesnero . . . editus, nunc vero . . . in compendium redactus . . . per Conradum Lycosthenem Rubeaquensem.* Basle: Oporinus, 1551

189 –   *Epitome bibliothecae Conradi Gesneri, conscripta primum à plus quàm bis mille authorum accessione (qui omnes asterico signati sunt) locupletata per Josiam Simlerum Tigurinum.* Zürich: Froschouer, 1555

190 –   *Mithridates: De differentiis linguarum, tum veterum, tum quae hodie apud diversas nationes in toto orbe terrarum in usu sunt.* Zürich: Froschouer, 1555

191 –   *Pandectarum sive partitionum universalium Conradi Gesneri Tigurini, medici & philosophiae professoris, libri XXI.* Zürich: Froschouer, 1548

192 –   *Partitiones theologicae, pandectarum universalium Conradi Gesneri liber ultimus . . .* Zürich: Froschouer, 1549
     –   – see also Constantin, Robert; Hofmann, Max; Simler, Josias

193 Goedeke, Karl. *Grundriss zur Geschichte der deutschen Dichtung.* Hannover: Ehlermann, 1857–

194 Goette, Arthur. "Der Ehrenbrief des Jakob Püterich von Reichertshausen an die Erzherzogin Mechthild." Diss. Strasburg, 1899

195 *Göttingische Zeitungen von gelehrten Sachen* (title varies). Göttingen, 1739–

196 Goffman, W. & Newill, V. A. "Communication and epidemic processes." *Proceedings of the Royal Society of London, Series A,* 298 (1967), 316–334

197 –   "Generalization of epidemic theory: an application to the transmission of ideas." *Nature,* 204 (1964), 225–228

198 Gold, Jack A. "PRECIS: An analysis." *Canadian Library Journal,* 29 (1972), 460–469
     Goldfriedrich, Johann Adolf – see Börsenverein: Historische Kommission

199 Gottfried von Strasburg. *Tristan und Isold,* ed. Friedrich Ranke. Berlin: Weidmann, 1949

200 Gottlieb, Theodor. *Über mittelalterliche Bibliotheken.* Leipzig: Harrassowitz, 1890; repr. Graz: Akademische Druck- und Verlagsanstalt, 1955

201 Graesse, Johann Georg Theodor. *Handbuch der allgemeinen Literaturgeschichte...*
     Dresden/Leipzig: Arnoldische Buchhandlung, 1845–50

202 — *Lehrbuch einer allgemeinen Literärgeschichte aller bekannten Völker der Welt
     von der ältesten bis auf die neueste Zeit.* Dresden/Leipzig: Arnoldische
     Buchhandlung, 1837–59

203 Grisebach, Eduard Rudolf Anton. *Katalog der Bücher eines deutschen Bibliophilen mit
     litterarischen und bibliographischen Anmerkungen.* Leipzig: Drugulin, 1894

204 Grosse, Hennig. *Catalogus librorum quos Henningus Grosius Lipsiae hactenus suis
     sumptibus imprimi curavit. Verzeichnis der Bücher / so von Henningo Grossen
     Buchhendlern in Leipzig vorlegt / und bey ihm zu bekommen sein.* Typis
     Grosianis gedruckt zu Eisleben, 1600

205 — *Elenchi seu indicis quinquennalis, continuatio tertia in qua continentur libri
     omnes, qui anno MDC nundinalis autumnalibus vel recens in lucem prodierunt,
     vel aucti aut perpurgati locupletiones exiverunt...* Ex officine Grosiana, 1600

206 — *Elenchus seu index generalis in quo continentur libri omnes, qui ultimo seculi
     1500. lustro, post annum 1593. vsq; ad annum 1600. in S. Romano Imperio &
     vicinis regionibus novi auctivè prodiêrunt. Allgemeine Verzeichniss...* in
     typographio suo, procurante Hennigo Grosio. Leipzig, 1600

207 Growoll, Adolf. *Three centuries of English booktrade bibliography.* New York: The
     Dibdin Club, 1903

208 Haan, Wilhelm. *Allgemeines sächsisches Schriftsteller-Lexicon. Ein Verzeichnis der von
     den im Königreiche Sachsen dermalen lebenden Gelehrten aller academischen
     Facultäten, auf dem Gebiete des Handels, der Industrie und Gewerbe, des Berg-
     und Ackerbaus, des Militärs, des Theaters, der Journalistik u.s.w. im Druck
     erschienenen Schriften...* Leipzig: R. Schaefer, 1875

209 Hagen, Friedrich Heinrich von der & Büsching, Johann Gustav. *Literarischer Grundriss
     zur Geschichte der deutschen Poesie von der ältesten Zeit bis in das sechzehnte
     Jahrhundert.* Berlin: Duncker & Humblot, 1812
     — — see also *Germania*

210 Hain, Ludwig Friedrich Theodor. *Repertorium bibliographicum, in quo libri omnes ab
     arte typographica inventa usque ad annum MD typis expressi ordine alphabetico
     vel simpliciter enumerantur vel adcuratius recensentur.* 2 vols. Stuttgart: Cotta,
     1826–38; repr. Leipzig: Brockhaus, 1925; Milan: Görlich, 1948

211 *Halbjahresverzeichnis der Neuerscheinungen des deutschen Buchhandels,* 1916–
     (Börsenverein); 1931– (Deutsche Bücherei). Leipzig 1916–44. Preceded by
     Hinrichs *Verzeichnis,* q.v. Succeeded by *Deutsche Bibliographie. Halbjahres-
     verzeichnis,* q.v. Cf. *Jahresverzeichnis des deutschen Schrifttums*
     Halbmonatliches Verzeichnis von Aufsätzen — see *Internationale Bibliographie der
     Zeitschriftenliteratur*

212 Hallam, Henry. *Introduction to the literature of Europe.* London: J. Murray, 1837–39

213 Hamberger, Georg Christoph. *Das gelehrte Teutschland oder Lexikon der jetzt-
     lebenden teutschen Schriftsteller.* Lemgo: Meyer, 1767

214 *Handbuch der Literaturwissenschaft,* ed. Oskar Walzel. Berlin: Akademische Verlags-
     gesellschaft Athenaion, 1923–
     Handl, Jacob — see Le Coq

215 Hankamer, Paul. *Deutsche Gegenreformation und deutsches Barock. Die deutsche Literatur im Zeitraum des 17. Jahrhunderts.* Epochen der deutschen Literatur, 3. Stuttgart: Metzler, 1935, [2]1947, [3]1964 (without bibliography)

216 Hansel, Johannes. *Bücherkunde für Germanisten. Studienausgabe,* bearbeitet von Lydia Tschakot, 6. vermehrte Auflage. Berlin: Erich Schmidt, 1972

217 –   *Bücherkunde für Germanisten. Wie sammelt man das Schrifttum nach dem neuesten Forschungsstand?* Berlin: Erich Schmidt, 1959

218 –   *Personalbibliographie zur deutschen Literaturgeschichte. Studienausgabe.* Berlin: Erich Schmidt, 1967, [2]1974

219 Harder, Michael. *Mess-Memorial des Frankfurter Buchhändlers Michael Harder Fastenmesse 1569,* ed. Ernst Kelchner & Richard Wülcker. Frankfurt/Paris: Joseph Baer, 1873

220 Hartmann, Albert, ed. *Festschrift für Georg Leidinger zum 60. Geburtstag am 30. Dezember 1930.* Munich: Hugo Schmidt, 1930

221 Harvard University (library). *German literature.* Widener Shelflist, 49, 50. Cambridge, Mass.: Harvard University Library, 1974

222 Haude, Ambrosius. *Catalogus von alt- und neuen Büchern / welche aus der Franckfurter und Leipziger Michaelis-Messe 1731. Mitgebracht, und nebst vielen andern zu haben sind . . .* Berlin: Ambrosius Haude, 1731

223 –   *Verzeichniß derer Bücher, welche Ambr. Haude, Buchhändler in Berlin, entweder selbst verleget, oder in Menge bey ihm zu finden.* No place: no pub., 1729

     Haupt, Moriz – see *Altdeutsche Blätter*

224 Hayn, Hugo. *Bibliotheca erotica et curiosa monacensis. Verzeichniss französischer, italienischer* [etc] *Erotica und Curiosa, von welchen keine deutschen Übersetzungen bekannt sind.* Berlin: M. Harrwitz, 1889

225 Hayn, Hugo & Gotendorf, Alfred N. *Bibliotheca Germanorum erotica & curiosa. Verzeichnis der gesamten deutschen erotischen Literatur mit Einschluß der Übersetzungen, nebst Beifügung der Originale.* München: G. Müller, 1919–29; earlier edition Leipzig: Unflad, 1885; 1st ed. by N. Hay [!] Leipzig: n.p., 1875 (title varies)

226 Heidegger, Bookseller, Zürich. *Catalogus dererjenigen Jurid. Medic. Philos. Mathem. Histor. Philolog. und anderer alten und neuen Bücher, welche um beygesetzte Preise in Gulden und Creutzer zu haben sind in Zürich bey Heidegger und Compagnie, Buchhändler,* Zürich, 1759

227 Heinsius, Johann Samuel. *Catalogus novus universalis, derer Bücher, welche vor den beygesetzten Preiss zu haben sind bey dem Buchhändler Joh. Sam. Heinsius.* Leipzig, 1748

228 Heinsius, Wilhelm. *Allgemeines Bücher-Lexikon oder alphabetisches Verzeichnis der in Deutschland und den angrenzenden Ländern gedruckten Bücher, nebst beygesetzten Verlegern und Preisen.* Leipzig: Heinsius, 1793–98

229 –   *Allgemeines Bücher-Lexikon oder vollständiges alphabetisches Verzeichnis aller von 1700 bis zu Ende 1810 erschienenen Bücher, welche in Deutschland und in den durch Sprache und Literatur damit verwandten Ländern gedruckt worden sind. Nebst Angabe der Druckorte, der Verleger und der Preise.* 4 vols. Leipzig: Gleditsch, 1812; continued until vol. 19 for 1889–92 (1893–94)

230 Heitz, Paul und Ritter, F. *Versuch einer Zusammenstellung der Deutschen Volks-bücher des 15. und 16. Jahrhunderts nebst deren späteren Ausgaben und Literatur.* Strasburg: Heitz, 1924

231 Hendreich, Christoph. *Pandectae Brandenburgicae, continentes I. Bibliothecam, seu magnam, &, si additamenta accesserint, maximam auctorum inpressorum & manuscr. partem: quibus adduntur auctorum quorundam vitae, delectus; nomina plurimorum anonymorum, pseudonymorum &c explicata. Idque in omnibus fere scientiis, & orbis terrarum linguis.II. Indicem materiarum praecipuarum, in iis contentarum: utrumque ordin. alphabetico.* Berlin: typis viduae Salfeldianis, 1699

Henisch, Georg — see Augsburg (library)

232 Herrmann, Carl Heinrich. [*Bibliothecae philologicae, 4 vols*] *Bibliotheca orientalis* (1870), *Bibliotheca scriptorum classicorum et graecorum et Latinorum* (1871), *Bibliotheca philologica* (1873), *Bibliotheca germanica* (1878). Halle: Herrmann.

233 Heumann, Christoph August. *De libris anonymis ac pseudonymis schediasma complectens observationes generales et spicilegium ad Vincentii Placcii theatrum anonymorum et pseudonymorum.* Jena: J. F. Bielcke, 1711

234 Hinrichs [Johann Conrad], firm, publishers, Leipzig. *Hinrichs Bücher-Katalog 1851–1865.* Leipzig, 1875. Preceded by Kirchhoff, q.v. Continues as *Hinrichs fünfjähriger Bücher-Catalog,* vol. 4 etc (title varies) until vol. 13 for 1910–12 (1913). Succeeded by *Deutsches Bücherverzeichnis,* q.v.

235 — firm, publishers, Leipzig. *Verzeichnis neuer Bücher die seit Michaelis 1797 bis Juli 1798 wirklich erschienen sind ... welche bei Reinicke und Hinrichs zu bekommen sind.* Leipzig, 1798–. Semi-annual until succeeded by *Halbjahres-verzeichnis,* q.v.

236 Hirschberg, Leopold. *Der Taschengoedeke.* Frankfurt: Tiedemann & Uzielli, 1924; Stuttgart: Cotta, ²1961; repr. Munich: dtv, 1970

237 Hirsching, Friedrich Karl Gottlob. *Versuch einer Beschreibung sehenswürdiger Bibliotheken Teutschlands nach alphabetischer Ordnung der Städte,* 5 vols. Erlangen: J. J. Palm, 1786–90; repr. Hildesheim: Olms, 1971

238 *Historisch-litterarish* [sic] *-bibliographisches Magazin. Errichtet von einer Gesellschaft litterarischer Freunde in und ausser Deutschland,* ed. Johann Georg Meusel. Zürich, 1788–

Hoeschel, David — see Augsburg (library)

239 Hoffmann von Fallersleben, August Heinrich. *Die deutsche Philologie im Grundriss. Ein Leitfaden zu Vorlesungen.* Breslau: Aderholz, 1836

240 — *Fundgruben für Geschichte deutscher Sprache und Literatur.* Breslau: Grass Barth & Co., 1830

241 Hofmann, Johann Jacob. *Lexikon universale historico-geographico-chronologico-poetico-philologicum, continens historiam omnis aevi, geographiam omnium locorum, genealogiam principum familiarum, additâ ubique chronologia tum veteri tum recentiore, mythologiam insuper omnium fabularum, discussionem philologicam illustrium circa haec occurrentium difficultatum; aliaqua plurima scitu dignissima. Cum indicibus...* Basle: impensis Iohan. Herman. Widerhold, Bibliop. Genevensis. Typis Jacobi Bertschii & Joh. Rodolphi Genathii, 1677, 1683; repr. Leiden: J. Hackius, 1698

242 Hofmann, Max, ed. *Conrad Gessner, 1516–1565; Universalgelehrter, Naturforscher, Arzt. Mit Beiträgen von Hans Fischer, Georges Petit, Joachim Staedtke, Rudolf Steiger, Heinrich Zoller.* Zürich: Füessli, 1967

243 *Hofmeisters Jahresverzeichnis sämtlicher Musikalien, Musikbücher, Zeitschriften, Abbildungen und plastischen Darstellungen, die in Deutschland und in den deutschsprachigen Ländern erschienen sind.* Leipzig: Hofmeister, 1852–; succeeded by *Jahresverzeichnis der deutschen Musikalien*, q.v.

244 *Hofmeisters musikalisch-literarischer Monatsbericht neuer Musikalien, musikalischer Schriften und Abbildungen für das Jahr 1829* etc. Leipzig: Hofmeister, 1830–; succeeded by *Deutsche Musikbibliographie*, q.v.

245 Holzmann, Michael & Bohatta, Hanns. *Deutsches Anonymen-Lexikon 1501–1850. Aus den Quellen bearbeitet.* 7 vols. Weimar: Gesellschaft der Bibliophilen, 1902–28

246 Holzmann, Michael & Bohatta, Hanns. *Deutsches Pseudonymen Lexikon. Aus den Quellen bearbeitet.* Wien/Leipzig: Akademischer Verlag, 1906

247 Horn, Franz. *Die Poesie und Beredsamkeit der Deutschen, von Luthers Zeit bis zur Gegenwart.* 4 vols. Berlin: T. Enslin, 1822–29

248 Hottinger, Johann Heinrich. *Bibliothecarius quadripartitus.* Zürich: Melchior Stauffacher, 1664

249 –   *Schola tigurinorum Carolina: Id est, demonstratio historica; ostendens Illust. & Per-antiquae Reipub. Tigurinae scholam, à Carolo Magno deducendam ... Accedunt I Bibliotheca Tigurina, sive catalogus librorum ante & post reformationem à Tigurinis scriptorum ...* Zürich: Typis Joh. Henrici Hambergeri, impensis Joh. Henrici Wyssii, 1664

250 Hughes, Andrew. *Medieval Music, the sixth liberal art.* University of Toronto Press, 1974

251 Hugo von Trimberg. *Registrum multorum auctorum,* ed. Karl Langosch, Germanische Studien, 235. Berlin: Ebering, 1942

252 –   *Der Renner,* ed. G. Ehrismann, BLVS, 247, 248, 252, 256. Tübingen: Literarischer Verein, 1908–11

253 *Index auctorum, et librorum, qui tanquam haeretici, aut suspecti, aut perniciosi, ab officio S. Ro. Inquisitionis reprobantur, et in universa Christiana republica interdicuntur.* Rome: apud Antonium Bladum Impressorem Cameralem, 1557

254 *Index bibliographicus* (sub-title varies). Geneva: League of Nations, Committee on Intellectual Co-operation, 1925; Berlin: de Gruyter (for International Institute for Intellectual Co-operation), [2]1931; Paris/The Hague: UNESCO/IFD, [3]1952; The Hague: IFD, [4]1959

255 *Index Expressionismus. Bibliographie der Beiträge in den Zeitschriften und Jahrbüchern des literarischen Expressionismus 1910–25,* ed. Paul Raabe. 18 vols. Nendeln, Liechtenstein: Kraus Thomson, 1972

256 *Index op de Nederlandse periodieken.* The Hague: Nijhoff, 1909–

     International Bibliography (Modern Language Association of America) – see *MLA International Bibliography*

257 *Internationale Bibliographie der Zeitschriftenliteratur aus allen Gebieten des Wissens (IBZ),* 1963/64–. Osnabrück, 1965– & *Internationale Bibliographie der Rezensionen wissenschaftlicher Literatur (IBR),* Osnabrück, 1971: Preceded by *Inter-*

nationale Bibliographie der Zeitschriftenliteratur mit Einschluß von Sammel-werken und Zeitungen: Abteilung A Bibliographie der deutschen Zeitschriften-literatur (1896–), *Abteilung B Bibliographie der fremdsprachigen Zeitschriften Literatur* (1911–), *Abteilung C Bibliographie der Rezensionen* (1913–), *Halb-monatliches* [etc] *Verzeichnis von Aufsätzen aus deutschen Zeitungen in sach-lich-alphabetischer Anordnung* (1908–44) [Osnabrück: Dietrich]

258 *Internationale Bibliographie des Buch- und Bibliothekswesens mit besonderer Berück-sichtigung der Bibliographie.* Leipzig, 1926–40 (successor to *Bibliographie des...* q.v.)

259 *Internationale Bibliographie zur deutschen Klassik 1750–1850.* Weimar, 1960–

260 *Internationaler Jahresbericht der Bibliographie,* ed. J. Vorstius. Leipzig, 1930–40

261 Jacob, Louis. *Traicté des plus belles bibliotheques publiques et particulières, qui ont esté, & qui sont à present dans le monde.* Paris: Rolet le Duc, 1644; *Traitté...* Paris: Louis Chamhoudry, 1655

262 *Jahresbericht für deutsche Sprache und Literatur,* 1940–50. 2 vols. Berlin: Akademie, 1960–66

263 *Jahresbericht über die Erscheinungen auf dem Gebiet der germanischen Philologie* (continues "Bibliographie des Jahres 1876/1877/1878" in *Zeitschrift für deutsche Philologie* 1876–78), 1879–. Berlin, 1880–, Neue Folge, 1924–; succeeded by *Jahresbericht für deutsche Sprache und Literatur,* q.v.

264 *Jahresbericht über die wissenschaftlichen Erscheinungen auf dem Gebiete der neueren deutschen Literatur* (continues *Jahresberichte für neuere...*), 1921–. Berlin 1924–; succeeded by *Jahresbericht für deutsche Sprache und Literatur,* q.v.

265 *Jahresberichte des literarischen Zentralblattes über die wichtigsten wissenschaftlichen Neuerscheinungen des gesamten deutschen Sprachgebietes* (later: *Das deutsche wissenschaftliche Schrifttum*), 1924–. Leipzig, 1925–

266 *Jahresberichte für neuere deutsche Literaturgeschichte,* 1890–. Stuttgart, 1892– succeeded by *Jahresberichte über die wissenschaftlichen Erscheinungen,* q.v.

267 *Jahresverzeichnis der an den deutschen Schulanstalten erschienenen Abhandlungen* (Königl. later [Preussische] Staatsbibliothek). Berlin, 1889–

268 *Jahresverzeichnis der [an den deutschen Universitäten und Hochschulen erschienenen Schriften] deutschen Hochschulschriften.* Leipzig, 1885–; succeeded by *Deutsche Bibliographie: Hochschulschriften-Verzeichnis,* q.v. and *Jahresver-zeichnis der Hochschulschriften,* q.v.

269 *Jahresverzeichnis der deutschen Musikalien und Musikschriften.* Leipzig, 1943–. Preceded by *Hofmeisters Jahresverzeichnis,* q.v.

270 *Jahresverzeichnis der Hochschulschriften der DDR, der BRD und Westberlins,* 1971–. Leipzig, 1973; preceded by *Jahresverzeichnis der deutschen Hochschulschriften,* q.v. Cf. *Deutsche Bibliographie: Hochschulschriften-Verzeichnis.*

271 *Jahresverzeichnis der Verlagsschriften und einer Auswahl der außerhalb des Buch-handels erschienenen Veröffentlichungen der DDR, der BRD und Westberlins sowie der deutschsprachigen Werke anderer Länder,* 1968–. Leipzig, 1972–; preceded by *Jahresverzeichnis des deutschen Schrifttums,* q.v. Based on weekly issues of *Deutsche Nationalbibliographie,* q.v.

272 *Jahresverzeichnis des deutschen Schrifttums,* 1945–. Leipzig, 1947–. Based on weekly issues of *Deutsche Nationalbibliographie,* q.v.; preceded by *Halbjahresverzeich-nis,* q.v.; succeeded by *Jahresverzeichnis der Verlagsschriften,* q.v.

273   Jentzsch, Rudolf. *Der deutsch-lateinische Büchermarkt nach den Leipziger Oster-meßkatalogen von 1740, 1770 und 1800 in seiner Gliederung und Wandlung.* Beiträge zur Kultur- und Universalgeschichte, 22. Leipzig: Voigtländer, 1912

274   Jerome, Saint. *S. Eusebii Hieronymi stridonensis presbyteri De viris illustribus liber* [Greek and Latin] *Patrologiae latinae,* xxiii (Paris, 1883), col. 631−768

275   Jöcher, Christian Gottlieb. *Allgemeines Gelehrten Lexikon.* Leipzig: Gleditsch, 1750−51

276   Josephson, Aksel Gustav Salomon. *Bibliographies of bibliographies chronologically arranged with occasional notes and an index.* Chicago: Bibliographical Soc., 1901, [2]1901−13

277   Jugler, Johann Friedrich. *Bibliotheca historiae litterariae selecta.* Jena: Cuno, 1754−63

278   Juncker, Christian. *Schediasma historicum, de ephemeridibus sive diariis eruditorum, in nobilioribus Europae partibus hactenus publicatis . . .* Leipzig: Gleditsch, 1692

279   Junker, Carl & Jellinek, Arthur L. *Österreichische Bibliographie,* vols. 1−3. Vienna: Verein der österreichischen Buchhändler, 1899−1901

280   Junker, Carl. *Über den Stand der Bibliographie in Österreich. Bericht erstattet der zweiten internationalen bibliographischen Conferenz.* Vienna: Holder, 1897

281   Kaplan, Norman. "The norms of citation behaviour: Prolegomena to the footnote." *American documentation,* 16 (1965), 179−84

      Kapp, Friedrich − see Börsenverein: Historische Kommission

282   Kayser, Christian Gottlob. *Deutscher Bücherkunde oder alphabetisches Verzeichnis der von 1750 bis Ende 1823 erschienenen Bücher, welche in Deutschland und in den durch Sprache und Literatur damit verwandten Ländern, gedruckt worden sind. Nebst Angabe der Druckorte, der Verleger und Preise.* Leipzig: Gleditsch, 1825−27

283   −   *Index locupletissimus . . . Vollständiges Bücher-Lexikon enthaltend alle von 1750 bis zu Ende des Jahres 1832 gedruckten Bücher in alphabetischer Reihenfolge, mit einer vollständigen Übersicht aller Autoren, der anonymen sowohl der pseudonymen, und einer genauen Angabe der Kupfer und Karten . . .* Leipzig: Ludwig Schumann, 1834−36. Multiannually until vol. 36, 1907−10 (1911−12); succeeded by *Deutsches Bücherverzeichnis,* q.v.

284   Kelchner, Ernst. "Verlagskataloge deutscher Buchdrucker vor 1500. Ein Beitrag zur Geschichte des Buchhandels und der Buchdruckerkunst." *Buchhändlerakademie,* 1 (1884), 560−88

285   Kienitz, Werner. "Formen literarischer Ankündigungen im 15. und 16. Jahrhundert." Diss. Cologne, 1930.

286   Kirchhoff, Albrecht. *Albrecht Kirchhoff's Bücher-Katalog. Verzeichniss der in der zweiten Hälfte des neunzehnten Jahrhunderts im deutschen Buchhandel er-schienenen Bücher und Landkarten, erster Band 1851−55.* Leipzig: Kirchhoff & Wigand, 1856; continued by Hinrichs, q.v.

287   Kirchner, Joachim. *Bibliographie der Zeitschriften des deutschen Sprachgebiets bis 1900.* 3 vols. Stuttgart: Hiersemann, 1969-

288   −   *Die Grundlagen des deutschen Zeitschriftenwesens. Mit einer Gesamt-bibliographie der deutschen Zeitschriften bis zum Jahre 1790.* Leipzig: Hierse-mann, 1928−31

289 Koch, Erdwin Julius. *Compendium der deutschen Literatur-Geschichte von den ältesten Zeiten bis auf das Jahr 1781.* Berlin: Im Verlag der Buchhandlung der Königl. Realschule, 1790;. . . *bis auf Lessings Tod,* [2]1795

290 Köhring, Hans. *Bibliographie der Almanache, Kalender und Taschenbücher für die Zeit von ca. 1750–1860.* Hamburg: Hermann Weber, 1929

291 König, Georg Matthias. *Bibliotheca vetus et nova, in qua Hebraeorum, Chaldaeorum, Syrorum, Arabum, Persarum, Aegyptiorum, Graecorum & Latinorum per universum terrarum orbem scriptorum, . . . patria, aetas, nomina, libri, saepiùs etiam eruditorum de iis elogia, testimonia & judicia summa fide atq; diligentia ex quotidianâ autorum lectione depromta à prima mundi origine ad annum usqúe MDCLXXIIX ordine alphabetico digesta gratissima brevitate recensentur & exhibentur.* Altdorfi impensis Wolffgangi Mauritii & Haeredum Johannis Andreae Endterorum, Bibliopol. Norimb. Typis Henrici Meyeri, Typographi Acad., 1678

292 König, Robert. *Deutsche Litteraturgeschichte.* Bielefeld: Velhagen & Klasing, 1878

293 Körner, Josef. *Bibliographisches Handbuch des deutschen Schrifttums, dritte völlig umgearbeitete und wesentlich vermehrte Auflage.* Berne: Francke, 1949. Earlier editions in Scherer's *Geschichte der deutschen Literatur,* q.v.

294 Köster, Kurt, ed. *Die deutsche Bibliothek 1945–65; Festgabe für Hanns Wilhelm Eppelsheimer zum 75. Geburtstag.* Frankfurt: Klostermann, 1966

295 Köttelwelsch, Clemens, ed. *Handbuch der deutschen Literaturwissenschaft 1945–69.* Frankfurt: Klostermann, 1973–
   –   – see also Eppelsheimer

296 Kommission für den Gesamtkatalog der Wiegendrucke. *Einblattdrucke des XV. Jahrhunderts; ein bibliographisches Verzeichnis.* Sammlung bibliothekswissenschaftlicher Arbeiten 35/36. Halle: Karras, 1914

297 Kommission für den Gesamtkatalog der Wiegendrucke. *Gesamtkatalog der Wiegendrucke.* Leipzig: Hiersemann, 1925– (vol. 7 1938 [to Eigenschaften], vol. 8 1972–)

298 Kommission für den Gesamtkatalog der Wiegendrucke. *Nachträge zu Hain's Repertorium bibliographicum und seinen Fortsetzungen.* Leipzig: Rudolf Haupt, 1910.

299 Koppitz, Hans-Joachim. "Bibliographien als geistes- und kulturgeschichtliche Quellen im deutschen Sprachgebiet." *Archiv für Geschichte des Buchwesens,* 5 (1962–64), 827–848

300 –   "Zur Bibliographie der deutschen Buchproduktion des 18. Jahrhunderts." *Zeitschrift für Bibliothekswesen und Bibliographie,* 9 (1962), 18–30

301 Kosch, Wilhelm. *Deutsches Literatur-Lexikon. Biographisches und bibliographisches Handbuch.* Halle: Niemeyer, 1927–30; Berne: Francke, [2]1947–58; condensed one-volume ed. 1963; [3]1968–

302 Kossmann, Bernhard. "Deutsche Universallexika des 18. Jahrhunderts." *Archiv für Geschichte des Buchwesens,* 9 (1967–69), 1553–96

303 Krüger, Hermann Anders. *Deutsches Literatur-Lexikon. Biographisches und bibliographisches Handbuch mit Motivübersichten und Quellennachweisen.* Munich: Beck, 1914

304 Küpper, Heinz. *Bibliographie zur Tristansage.* Deutsche Arbeiten der Universität Köln, 17. Jena: Diederichs, 1941

305   "Kürschner." *Allgemeiner deutscher Literaturkalender* . . . Bremen: H. Fischer, 1879; *Kürschners deutscher Literatur-Kalender 1973,* 56th ed. Berlin: de Gruyter, 1974

306   Kurz, Dora. "Verluste auf dem Gebiet der mittelhochdeutschen höfischen Erzähldichtung." Diss. Tübingen, 1950

307   Labbé, Philippe. *Bibliotheca bibliothecarum curis secundis auctior* . . . Paris: Ludovicus Billaine, 1664; [3] 1672; etc

308   —   *Nova bibliotheca MSS. librorum, sive specimen antiquarum lectionum latinarum et graecarum. In quatuor partes tributarum, cum coronide duplici, poetica et libraria.* Paris: Ioannes Henault, 1653

309   Lambek, Peter. *Liber primus prodromi historiae literariae; nec non libri secundi capita quatuor priora, cum appendice, qui sciagraphiam continet, sive primam delinationem praecipuarum personarum ac rerum, de quibus, volente Deo, reliquis triginta duobus ejusdem libri capitibus pleniùs ac accuratiûs agetur. Accedunt insuper tabulae duae* . . . Hamburg: sumptibus autoris, Typis Michaelis Piperi, 1659

310   Lamberg, Abraham. *Catalogus singularis omnium librorum, qui in electoratu et ducatu Saxoniae hoc semestri typis excusi sunt* . . . [not seen]

311   Lang, Johannes (sale catalogue). *Catalogus bibliothecae Eximiae B. Dn. M. Johannis Langii . . . qui auctionis ritu V. D. in aedibus defuncti . . . die 7. Februarii & seqq. Anni MDCCI divendendi exponentur.* Hamburg: Joach. Reumann, n.d.

312   Lawätz, Heinrich Wilhelm. *Handbuch für Bücherfreunde und Bibliothekare.* 7 vols. Halle: Gebauer, 1788—94

313   Le Coq, Paschalis. *Bibliotheca medica. Sive catalogus illorum, qui ex professo artem medicam in hunc usque annum scriptis illustrârunt* . . . Basle: Conradus Waldkirch, 1590

314   Lehmann, Paul. *Erforschung des Mittelalters; ausgewählte Abhandlungen und Aufsätze.* 5 vols. Stuttgart: Hiersemann, 1941; repr. 1959

315   Leiden (library): Bertius, Petrus. *Nomenclator autorum omnium, quorum libri vel manuscripti, vel typis expreßi exstant in Bibliotheca academiae Lugduno-Batavae.* Leiden: Apud Franciscum Raphelengium, 1595

316   Library of Congress. *A Catalog of books represented by Library of Congress printed cards issued to July 31, 1942.* Ann Arbor: Edwards, 1943

317   Linder, LeRoy Harold. *The rise of current complete national bibliography.* New York: Scarecrow, 1959

318   Lipen, Martin. *Bibliotheca realis universalis omnium materiarum, rerum et titulorum, in theologia, jurisprudentia, medicina et philosophia occurrentium melioris ordinis, commoditatis & distinctionis causa, respectu IV facultatum in IV partes, seu specialis bibliothecas theologicam, juridicam, medicam et philosophicam divisa, ordine alphabetico ita disposita, ut primo statim aspectu tituli . . . 4 pts.* Frankfurt: Cura & sumptibus Johan. Friderici, literis Johannis Görlini, 1685 (1679, 1679, 1682, 1685)

319   *Literarisches Centralblatt für Deutschland,* ed. F. Zarncke. Leipzig, 1850—1944

320   *Literarisches Wochenblat, oder gelehrte Anzeigen mit Abhandlungen.* Nuremberg: Martin Jacob Bauer, 1770— [1769—]

321   Loewenthal, Fritz. *Bibliographisches Handbuch zur deutschen Philologie.* Halle: Niemeyer, 1932

322 Loosaeus, Cornelius. *Illustrium Germaniae scriptorum catalogus quo doctrina simul et pietate illustrium vita, & operae celebrantur*... Mainz: apud Casparum Behem, 1582

323 Lowe, E. A. "An eighth century list of books in a Bodleian MS from Würzburg and its probable relation to the Laudian *Acts.*" *Speculum*, 3 (1928), 3–15

324 Luther, Arthur. *Deutsche Geschichte in deutscher Erzählung. Ein literarisches Lexikon.* Leipzig: Hiersemann, 1940, ²1943

325 – *Deutsches Land in deutscher Erzählung, ein literarisches Ortslexikon.* Leipzig: Hiersemann, 1936, ²1937

326 – *Land und Leute in deutscher Erzählung.* Stuttgart: Hiersemann, ³1954 (combination of *Deutsche Geschichte* and *Deutsches Land*)

Lycosthenes, Conrad – see Gessner, Konrad

327 *MLA Abstracts of articles in scholarly journals,* 1971–. New York: MLA, 1973–

328 *MLA International Bibliography (Annual Bibliography* 1956–63), 1956–. Modern Languages Association, 1957–; preceded by "American Bibliography," q.v.

329 Mader, Joachim Johann. *De bibliothecis atque archivis virorum clarissimorum, quos aversa monstrat pagina, libelli et commentationes. Cum praefatione de scriptis et bibliothecis antediluvianis.* Helmstadt: Henning Müller, 1666

330 Maittaire, Michael. *Annales typographici ab artis inventae origine ad annum MD.* 5 vols. The Hague: Isaacus Vaillant, 1719 (–41)

331 Malclès, Louise Noëlle. *Manuel de bibliographie,* 2d. ed. Paris: Presses universitaires, 1969

332 – *Les sources du travail bibliographique.* Geneva: Droz, 1950–58

333 Malin, Morton V. "The Science Citation Index: A new concept in indexing." *Library trends,* 16 (January 1968), 374–87

334 Mallon, Otto. *Brentano-Bibliographie.* Berlin: Fraenkel, 1926

335 Margolis, J. "Citation indexing and evaluation of scientific papers." *Science,* 155 (March 1967), 1213–19

336 Martyn, John. "An examination of citation indexes." *ASLIB Proceedings,* 17 (June 1965), 184–96

337 Mencke(n), Johann Burkhard. *Bibliotheca Menckeniana, quae autores praecipue veteres graecos et lat. historiae item literariae, eccl. et civilis, antiquitatum ac rei nummariae scriptores, philologos, oratores, poetas et codices Mss complectitur, ab Ottone et Jo. Burchardo Menckeniis, patre et filio, multorum annorum spatio studiose collecta*... Leipzig: Gleditsch, 1723

338 – *Compendiöses Gelehrten-Lexicon, darinnen die Gelehrten, als Fürsten und Staats-Leute, die in der Literatur erfahren, Theologi, Prediger, Juristen, Politici, Medici ... an der Zahl über 20 000 ... beschrieben werden*... Leipzig: Gleditsch, 1715

339 Merker, Paul. *Neuere deutsche Literaturgeschichte.* Wissenschaftliche Forschungsberichte, 8. Stuttgart-Gotha: Perthes, 1922

340 Merryweather, Frederick Sommer. *Bibliomania in the Middle Ages.* London: Merryweather, 1849; New York: Meyer, 1900; etc

341 *Die Meßkataloge des sechzehnten Jahrhunderts,* ed. Bernhard Fabian: *I Die Meßkataloge Georg Willers: Herbstmesse 1564 bis Herbstmesse 1573; II ... Fastenmesse 1574 bis Herbstmesse 1580.* Hildesheim: Olms, 1972, 1973

Meßkataloge – see also Fontius, M; Frömmichen; Müller, Hans von; Schroeder, Felix von; Schwetschke, Gustav

Meulen, Jan van der – see Molanus, Johannes

342 Meusel, Johann Georg. *Das gelehrte Teutschland . . . Angefangen von Georg Christoph Hamberger . . . Fortgesetzt von Johann Georg Meusel . . . Vierte, durchaus vermehrte und verbesserte Ausgabe.* Lemgo: Mayer, 1783

343 –   *Leitfaden zur Geschichte der Gelehrsamkeit.* Leipzig: G. Fleischer, 1799–1800

344 –   *Lexikon der vom Jahr 1750 bis 1800 verstorbenen teutschen Schriftsteller.* Lemgo: Meyer, 1802–16

345 Meyer, F. Hermann. "Vertriebsmittel der ältesten Buchhändler." *Archiv für Geschichte des Buchwesens,* 14 (1891), 1–9

346 Meyer, Friedrich Heinrich Albert. *Maler-Müller-Bibliographie.* Leipzig: F. Meyer, 1912

347 Meyer, Richard Moritz. *Deutsche Literatur des 19. Jahrhunderts.* Berlin: Bondi, 1900

348 –   *Grundriss der neueren deutschen Literaturgeschichte.* Berlin: Bondi, 1902, ²1907

349 *Meyers Konversations-Lexikon. Encyklopädie des allgemeinen Wissens,* 4th ed. Leipzig: Bibliographisches Institut, 1885–90

350 Milkau, Fritz. *Handbuch der Bibliothekswissenschaft.* 4 vols. Leipzig: Harrassowitz, 1931–42; 2nd ed., F. Milkau and Georg Leyh, 1950–65

351 Miller, Elizabeth & Truesdell, Eugenia. "Citation indexing: history and applications." *Drexel Library Quarterly,* 8 (April 1972), 159–72

352 Mineur, B. W. "Relations in chains." *Journal of librarianship,* 5 (1973), 175–202

353 *Miscellanea curiosa [sive, Ephemeridum] medico-physica [rum Germanicarum].* Nuremberg, 1670–1706

354a *Mittelalterliche Bibliothekskataloge Deutschlands und der Schweiz,* ed. Königliche Bayerische Akademie der Wissenschaften. 3 vols. Munich: Beck, 1918–39; repr. 1961–69

354b *Modern Language Review,* published by the Modern Humanities Research Association, 1905–

355 Molanus, Johannes. *Bibliotheca materiarum quae, a quibus auctoribus, cum antiquis, tum recentioribus sint pertractatae docentibus, concionantibus, ac scriptoribus pernecessaria . . .* Cologne: apud Joannem Kinchium, 1618

356 Moller, Johannes. *Homonymoscopia historico-philologico-critica, sive schediasma* ΠΑΡΕΡΓΙΚΟΝ *de scriptoribus homonymis quadripartitum . . .* Hamburg: Liebezeit, 1696

    – – see also Morhof, D. G.

357 Monath, George Peter. *Neuer volständiger Catalogus aller Bücher welche bei George Peter Monath Buchhändlern in Nürnberg und Altdorf um beigesezten richtigen Preisen zu haben sind nebst Anzeige der neuesten Editionen und jezigen Verlegern bis zu Ende des Jahres 1780 fortgesezt allen Gelehrten Bücherfreunden und Buchhändlern brauchbar.* Nuremberg: no pub. 1782–86

358 *Monatliche Unterredungen einiger guten Freunde von allerhand Büchern und andern annehmlichen Geschichten: allen Liebhabern der Curiositäten zur Ergetzligkeit und Nachsinnen,* ed. W. E. Tentzel. Leipzig, 1689–98

    Monatliches Verzeichnis der reichsdeutschen Amtsschriften – see Germany: Reichsministerium des Innern

359   Montag & Weiss. *Monatliche Anzeige ganz neuer Bücher, welche in der Montag- und Weissischen Buchhandlung in Regensburg um die beygesetzten Preise zu haben sind,* Zwölfter Jahrgang, 1814 (no place or publisher).

360   Morhof, Daniel Georg. *Polyhistor, sive de notitia auctorum et rerum commentarii. Quibus praeterea varia ad omnes disciplines concilia et subsidia proponuntur.* Lübeck: Böckmann, 1688 [2] 1695–98; posthumous editions: Lübeck: Böckmann, 1708, [2] 1714, etc

361   —   *Polyhistor, literarius, philosophicus et practicus cum accessionibus virorum clarissimorum Ioannis Frickii et Iohannis Molleri, Flensburgensis. Editio quarta. Cui praefationem, notitiamque diariorum litterrariorum Europae praemisit Io. Albertus Fabricius . . .* Lübeck: Petrus Boeckmann, 1747

362   —   *Unterricht von der teutschen Sprache und Poesie.* Kiel: Reumann, 1682

363   Müller, Hans von. "Die Messkataloge als Quelle für die Literaturgeschichte. An dem Beispiel E. T. A. Hoffmanns dargelegt." *Von Büchern und Bibliotheken* (Festschrift Ernst Kuhnert), ed. Gustav Abb (Berlin: Struppe & Winckler, 1928; 2nd ed. Darmstadt: Wissenschaftliche Buchgesellschaft, 1964), pp. 97–107

364   —   *Zehn Generationen deutscher Dichter und Denker. Die Geburtsjahrgänge 1561–1892 in 45 Altersgruppen zusammengestellt.* Berlin: Frankfurter Verlags-Anstalt, 1928

365   Mylius, Johann Christoph. *Bibliotheca anonymorum et pseudonymorum.* Hamburg: C. W. Brandt, 1740

366   *National Union Catalogue; Pre-1956 Imprints.* London/Chicago: Mansell, 1968–

367   Naudé, Gabriel. *Advis pour dresser une bibliothèque.* Paris: François Targa, 1627

368   —   *Bibliographia militaris.* Jena: Ex officina Nisiana, 1683

369   —   *Bibliographia politica.* Venice: F. Baba, 1633

370   —   *Bibliothecae Cordesianae Catalogus.* Paris: A. Vitray, 1643

371   —   *Instructions concerning erecting a library: presented to My Lord the President de Mesme. By Gabriel Naudeus, P. and now interpreted by Jo. Evelyn, Esquire.* London: printed for G. Bedle, and T. Collins, at the Middle-Temple Gate, and J. Crook in St. Pauls Church-yard, 1661

372   Neander, Michael. *De bibliothecis deperditis ac noviter instructis.* In Mader, *De bibliothecis,* q.v.

373   *Nekrolog zu Kürschners Literatur-Kalender,* ed G. Lüdtke. Berlin/Leipzig: de Gruyter, 1936; *Nekrolog 1936–70.* Berlin: de Gruyter, 1973

374   *Neue deutsche Biographie,* ed. Historische Kommission bei der Bayerischen Akademie der Wissenschaften. Berlin: Duncker & Humblot, 1953-

375   *Neuer Bücher-Saal der gelehrten Welt oder ausführliche Nachrichten von allerhand neuen Büchern und andern zur heutigen Historie der Gelehrsamkeit gehörigen Sachen,* ed. J. G. Krause. Leipzig 1710–17

376   Nevizzano, Giovanni. *Inventarium librorum in utroque iure . . .* Finem sumpsit Lugduni MDXXII in calce Augusti

377   Nicolai, Christoph Friedrich. *Verzeichniß einer Handbibliothek der nützlichsten deutschen Schriften zum Vergnügen und Unterricht . . . welche um beygesetzte Preise zu haben sind bey Friedrich Nicolai.* Berlin, 1787; Berlin, [5] 1811

Nicolai, C. F. — see also *Allgemeine deutsche Bibliothek*

378   Nollen, John Scholte. *A chronological and practical bibliography of modern German literature.* Chicago: Scott-Foresman, 1903

379   Norris, Dorothy May: *A History of Cataloguing Methods 1100–1850, with an Introductory Survey of Ancient Times.* London: Grafton, 1939

      Nuremberg (library) — see Saubert, Johannes

380   Obenaus, Sibylle. "Die deutschen allgemeinen kritischen Zeitschriften in der 1. Hälfte des 19. Jahrhunderts." *Archiv für Geschichte des Buchwesens,* 14 (1973), 1–122; also separately Frankfurt, 1973

381   *Österreichische Bibliographie.* Wien, 1945–
      —   — see also Junker, Carl

382   Oporinus, Johannes. *Librorum per Ioannem Oporinum partim excusorum hactenus, partim in eiusdem officina venalium, index . . .* Basle: Oporinus, 1552

      Ortner, Max — see Abeling, Theodor

383   *PMLA* Publications of the Modern Language Association [of America], 1884–

384   Pallmann, Heinrich. "Ein Meßregister Sigmund Feyerabend's aus dem Jahre 1565." *Archiv für Geschichte des Buchwesens,* 9 (1884), 5–46

385   —   *Sigmund Feyerabend, sein Leben und seine geschäftlichen Verbindungen nach archivalischen Quellen bearbeitet.* Archiv für Frankfurts Geschichte und Kunst, N.F., 7. Frankfurt: K. Th. Völcker, 1881

386   Panzer, Friedrich Wilhelm. *Bibliographie zu Wolfram von Eschenbach.* Munich: Ackermann, 1897

387   Panzer, Georg Wolfgang Franz. *Annalen der älteren deutschen Litteratur oder Anzeige und Beschreibung derjenigen Bücher welche von Erfindung der Buchdrucker-kunst bis MDXX in deutscher Sprache gedruckt worden sind.* Nuremberg: Grattenauer, 1788; *Zusätze* Nuremberg: Hempel, 1802; *Zweyter Band* [1521–26] Nuremberg: Lechner, 1805

388   —   *Annales typographici ab artis inventae origine ad annum MD . . .* Nuremberg: J. E. Zeh, 1793–97 (I–V), 1798–1803 (VI–XI)

      Papal index — see *Index auctorum*

389   Paris: Bibliothèque nationale. *Catalogue général des imprimés de la bibliothèque nationale.* Paris: Imprimerie Nationale, 1897–; repr. Paris: Paul Catin, 1924–

      Paris (library) — see also Delisle, Léopold

390   Pataky, Sophie. *Lexikon deutscher Frauen der Feder. Eine Zusammenstellung der seit dem Jahre 1840 erschienenen Werke weiblicher Autoren, nebst Biographien der lebenden und einem Verzeichnis der Pseudonyme.* Berlin: Carl Pataky, 1898; repr. Berne: Lang, 1971

391   Paulli, Simon. *Bibliotheca portatilis seu librorum omnium facultatum catalogus in usum philobiblorum congestus.* Strasburg: Simon Paulli, 1669

392   —   *Catologi librorum in bibliopolio argentinensi Simonis Paulli venalium,* pars 1, 2, 3, 4. Strasburg, 1670

393   —   *Historia litteraria sive Dispositio librorum omnium facultatum ac artium, secundum materias, in usum philobiblorum congesta.* Strasburg: sumptibus auctoris, 1671

394   Peddie, Robert Alexander. *National Bibliographies: A descriptive catalogue of the works which register the books published in each country.* London: Grafton, 1912

395   Pell, William. "Facts of scholarly publishing." *PMLA,* 88 (1973), 639–70

396   Perry, James Whitney & Kent, Allen. *Documentation and information retrieval.* Western Reserve University Press, 1957

397 Petzholdt, Julius. *Bibliotheca bibliographica; kritisches Verzeichniss der das Gesamt-gebiet der Bibliographie betreffenden Litteratur des In- und Auslandes in systematischer Ordnung.* Leipzig: Engelmann, 1866

398 Placcius, Vincent. *De scriptis & scriptoribus anonymis atque pseudonymis syntagma...* Hamburg: Sumptibus Christiani Guthii, 1674

399 —   *Theatrum anonymorum et pseudonymorum, ex symbolis & collatione virorum per Europam doctissimorum ac celeberrimorum, post syntagma dudum editum...* Hamburg: sumptibus viduae Gothofredi Liebernickelii, typis Spieringianis, 1708
     —   — see also Heumann, C. A; Mylius, J. C.

400 Poccianti, Michele. *Catalogus scriptorum Florentinorum omnis generis* Florence: P. Iuncta, 1589

401 Pollard, Graham & Ehrman, Albert. *The Distribution of Books by Catalogue from the Invention of Printing to A.D. 1800: Based on Material in the Broxbourne Library.* Cambridge: Roxburghe Club, 1965

402 Poole, William Frederick. *Index to periodical literature,* 1802–81. Revised edition Boston: Houghton Mifflin, 1893; supplements 1882–1906, 5 vols. New York: P. Smith, 1938

403 Prachner, Georg. "Zur Geschichte der österreichischen Bibliographie." *Biblos,* 4 (1955), 136–42

404 Proctor, Robert. G. C. *An index of German books 1501–1520 in the British Museum = An index to the early printed books in the British Museum,* part 2, section 1. London: Holland, 1903

405 Prutz, Robert Eduard. "Der deutsche Journalismus...," in *Neue Schriften. Zur dt. Literatur und Kulturgeschichte,* 2 vols. (Halle: Schwetschke, 1854), I, 1–103

406 —   *Geschichte des deutschen Journalismus.* Hannover: Kius, 1845

407 Püterich von Reichertshausen, Jakob. *Der Ehrenbrief des P. von R.,* ed. Fritz Behrend & Rudolf Wolkan. Weimar: Gesellschaft der Bibliophilen, 1920
     Püterich von Reichertshausen, Jakob von — see also Goette, Arthur; Scherer, Wilhelm *(Die Anfänge)*

408 Pyritz, Hans. "Bibliographie zur deutschen Barockliteratur." In Paul Hankamer, *Deutsche Gegenreformation,* q.v.
     Quesnel, Joseph — see Thou, Jacques Auguste de

409 *The Random House dictionary of the English language.* New York: Random House, 1966

410 Raumer, Rudolf von. *Geschichte der germanischen Philologie, vorzugsweise in Deutschland.* Geschichte der Wissenschaften in Deutschland, 9. Munich: Königl. Akademie der Wissenschaften, 1864

411 *Reallexikon der deutschen Literaturgeschichte,* ed. Paul Merker & Wolfgang Stammler. Berlin: de Gruyter, 1925–31, [2]1958–
     Registrum anglie de libris doctorum et auctorum veterem — see Savage, Ernest A.; Tanner, Thomas

412 Reichling, Dietrich. *Appendices ad Hainii-Copingeri Repertorium bibliographicum.* Munich: Rosenthal, 1905–11, supplement 1914

413 Reimmann, Jacob Friedrich. *Versuch einer Einleitung in die Historiam Litterariam, so wohl insgemein, als auch in die Historiam Litterariam derer Teutschen insonderheit.* Halle: Renger, 1708–13

Reinicke, A. L. – see Hinrichs [J. C.], firm

414 Reusch, Franz Heinrich. *Die Indices librorum prohibitorum des sechzehnten Jahr-hunderts.* Nieuwkoop: B. de Graaf, 1961

415 Richter, Günter. "Die Sammlung von Drucker-, Verleger- und Buchführerkatalogen in den Akten der kaiserlichen Bücherkommission." *Festschrift für Josef Benzing zum sechzigsten Geburtstag 4. Februar 1964* (Wiesbaden: Guido Pressler, 1964), pp. 317–372

Rodenberg, J. – see *Deutsche Bibliophilie*

416 Rosenbaum, Alfred. *Bibliographie der in den Jahren 1914 bis 1918 erschienenen Zeitschriftenaufsätze und Bücher zur deutschen Literaturgeschichte,* "Zwölftes Ergänzungsheft" of *Euphorion.* Leipzig/Vienna, 1922

417 Rost, Gottfried. *Bibliographie und Bibliograph. Eine Literaturinformation über Formen und Methoden der Bibliographie mit einem Ausblick auf die elektro-nische Verarbeitung bibliographischer Daten,* Bibliographischer Informations-dienst der Deutschen Bücherei, 10. Leipzig: [Deutsche Bücherei], 1966

418 Rudolf von Ems. *Willehalm von Orlens,* ed. V. Junk. Deutsche Texte des Mittelalters, 20. Berlin: Weidmann, 1905

419 Ruppel, Aloys. "Die Bücherwelt des 16. Jahrhunderts und die Frankfurter Bücher-messen." *De gulden passer,* 34 (1956), 20–39

420 Russell, Adolph. *Gesammt-Verlags-Verzeichnis des deutschen Buchhandels. Ein Bild deutscher Geistesarbeit und Cultur. Vollständig bis Ende 1880,* etc. 16 vols. Münster: Russell, 1881–93; index etc in vol. 0 (sic!) 1894

421 Sachs, Hans. *Werke,* ed. A. von Keller. 26 vols. Stuttgart: Literarischer Verein, 1870–; repr. Hildesheim: Olms, 1964

422 Saubert, Johannes the Elder. *Historia bibliotheca Noribergensis . . . Accessit . . . Appendix de inventore typographiae, itemque catalogus librorum proximis ab inventione annis usque ad A.C. 1500 editorum.* Nuremberg: W. Ender, 1643

423 Savage, Ernest A. *Notes on the early monastic libraries of Scotland; with an account of the "Registrum librorum angliæ" and of the "Catalogus scriptorum ecclesiæ" of John Boston of the Abbey of Bury St. Edmunds.* Edinburgh: privately printed, 1928 (repr. from Publications of the Edinburgh Bibliographical Society, vol. 14)

424 Scavenius, Petrus. *Catalogus auctorum qui suppresso vel ficto nomine prodierunt . . .* Part 2 of Placcius, *De scriptis,* q.v.

425 Scherer, Wilhelm. *Die Anfänge des deutschen Prosaromans und Jörg Wickram von Kolmar.* Quellen und Forschungen, 21. Strasburg: Trübner, 1877

426 –   *Geschichte der deutschen Literatur.* Berlin: Askanischer Verlag, [3]1921, [5]1929

427 Scheurl, Heinrich Julius. *Bibliographia moralis.* Helmstadt: Henning Müller, 1648

428 Schlawe, Fritz. *Literarische Zeitschriften 1885–1910.* Sammlung Metzler 24, 2 vols. Stuttgart: Metzler, [2]1965–73

429 Schlegel, [Carl Wilhelm] Friedrich von. *Geschichte der alten und neuen Litteratur.* Vienna: Schaumburg, 1813

430 Schmid, Johann Peter. *Catalogus von alten und neuen Büchern, welche um beygesetzten Preiß zu haben sind bey Johann Peter Schmid.* Berlin: C. L. Kunst, 1736

431 Schmitt, Franz Anselm. *Stoff- und Motivgeschichte der deutschen Literatur. Eine Bibliographie.* Berlin: de Gruyter, 1959, [2]1965

432 Schneider, Georg. *Handbuch der Bibliographie.* Leipzig: Hiersemann, 1923, [4]1930

433 Schomberg, Baron. *Bibliotheca selectissima, seu catalogus omnis generis librorum . . . Hi libri auctione publicè distrahendi venum exponentur die 11 et sqq. Novembris 1743 in aedibus Petri Mortier . . .* 2 vols. Amsterdam: Schouten & Mortier

434 Schottelius, Samuel. *Bibliographia historico-politico-philologica curiosa, quid in quovis scriptore laudem censuramve mereatur, exhibens, cui praefixa celeberrimi cujusdam viri de studio politico bene instituendo dissertatio epistolica posthuma.* Germanopoli (Frankfurt): no pub., 1677

435 Schottenloher, Karl. "Die Anfänge der neueren Bibliographie." *Festschrift Leidinger* (see Hartmann, Albert), pp. 233–40

436 – *Bibliographie zur deutschen Geschichte im Zeitalter der Glaubensspaltung 1517–1585.* 6 vols. Leipzig: Hiersemann, 1933–40; repr. Stuttgart: Hiersemann, 1956–58, suppl. (literature 1936–60), 1966

437 Schroeder, Felix von. *Die Verlegung der Büchermesse von Frankfurt am Main nach Leipzig.* Volkswirtschaftliche und wirtschaftsgeschichtliche Abhandlungen, 9. Leipzig: Jäh & Schunke, 1904

438 Schulte-Albert, Hans Georg. "Leibniz's plans for a world encyclopedia system." Diss. Case Western Reserve University, 1972

439 Schulte-Strathaus, Ernst. *Bibliographie der Originalausgaben deutscher Dichtungen im Zeitalter Goethes.* Münich: G. Müller, 1913

440 *Das Schweizer Buch.* Berne, 1943–; preceded by *Bibliographisches Bulletin*, q.v.

441 Schwetschke, Gustav. *Codex nundinarius Germaniae literatae bisecularis.* Halle: G. Schwetschke, 1850

442 *Science citation index; an international interdisciplinary index to the literature of the sciences,* 1961–. Philadelphia: Institute for Scientific information, 1963–

443 *Seminar. A journal of Germanic studies.* Toronto, 1965–

444 Shera, Jesse H. *Libraries and the organisation of knowledge.* Edited and with an introduction by D. J. Foskett. Hamden, Conn.: Archon Books, 1965

445 Simler, Josias. *Bibliotheca instituta et collecta primum a Conrado Gesnero, deinde in epitomen redacta & novorum librorum accessione locupletata, iam vero postremo recognita, & in duplum post priores editiones aucta . .* Zürich: Froschouer, 1574

446a – *Vita clarissimi philosophi et medici excellentissimi Conradi Gesneri Tigurini, conscripta à Iosia Simlero Tigurino . . . Item Epistola Gesneri de libris à se editis . . .* Zurich: Froschouer, 1574

– – see also Gessner, Konrad

446b Simonton, W. C. "Characteristics of the Research Literature of the Fine Arts during the Period 1948–1957." Diss. Illinois, 1960

447 Slater, John Herbert. *How to collect books.* London: George Bell, 1905

448 *Social Sciences Citation Index. An international multidisciplinary index to the literature of the social, behavioral and related sciences,* 1971–. Philadelphia: Institute for Scientific Information, 1975–

Sorbonne (library) – see Delisle, Léopold

449 Spach, Israel. *Nomenclator scriptorum medicorum.* Frankfurt: 1591

450 – *Nomenclator scriptorum philosophicorum atque philologicorum. Hoc est succincta recensio eorum, qui philosophiam omnesque eius partes quovis tempore idiomateve usq; ad annum 1597 descripserunt, illustrarunt, & exornarunt, methodo artificiosa secundum locos communes ipsius philosophiae,*

cum duplici indice, rerum uno, autorum altero collecta & digesta. Strasburg: Apud Antonium Bertramum, 1598

451 Spirgatis, Max Ludwig. *Die literarische Produktion Deutschlands im 17. Jahrhundert und die Leipziger Messkataloge.* Repr. from Sammlung bibliothekswissenschaftlicher Arbeiten (Halle: Haupt, 1901), XIV, 24—61

452 Spitzel, Gottlieb. *Sacra bibliothecarum illustrium arcana retecta, sive MSS theologicorum, in praecipuis Europae bibliothecis extantium designatio; cum praeliminari dissertatione, specimine novae bibliothecae universalis, et coronide philologica.* Augsburg: Apud Gottlieb Goebelium, typis Praetorianis, 1668

Stammler, Wolfgang — see *Deutsche Literatur des Mittelalters*

453 Stapf, Paul ed. *Handbuch der deutschen Literaturgeschichte, II. Abt. Bibliographien.* Berne: Francke, 1969—

454 Steinhoff, Hans-Hugo. *Bibliographie zu Gottfried von Straßburg.* Bibliographien zur deutschen Literatur des Mittelalters, 5. Berlin: Erich Schmidt, 1971

455 Stern, Adolf. *Lexikon der deutschen Nationalliteratur.* Leipzig: Bibliographisches Institut, 1882

456 Stock, Karl F. "Österreichische Bibliographien des 17. und 18. Jahrhunderts." *Archiv für Geschichte des Buchwesens,* 9 (1967—69), 207—16

457 Stolle, Gottlieb. *Kurtze Nachricht von den Büchern und deren Urhebern in der Stollischen Bibliothec.* Jena: Joh. Meyers Witwe, 1733—43

458 Struve, Burkhard Gotthelf. *Bibliotheca historiae literariae selecta.* Jean, 1704 [not seen], Jena: Ernst Claudius, [2]1706; etc

459 — *Bibliotheca philosophica.* Jena: Bailliar, 1704 [not seen] et seq.

460 — *Introductio in notitiam rei bibliothecarum.* Jena: Bailliar, 1710; etc.

461 *Subject index to periodicals* 1915— London: Library Association, 1919—; succeeded by *British Humanities/Technology Index,* 1962—

462 Sulzer, Johann Georg. *Eine allgemeine Theorie der schönen Künste.* Leipzig/Berlin: 1771, 1774; Leipzig, Weidmann, [2]1792—99

463 *Tägliches Verzeichnis der Neuerscheinungen des deutschen Buchhandels [Erschienene Neuigkeiten...]* — supplement to *Börsenblatt,* 1839— (Hinrichs) 1921— (Deutsche Bücherei)

464 Tanner, Thomas. *Bibliotheca Britannico-hibernica: sive, de scriptoribus, qui in Anglia, Scotia, et Hibernia ad saeculi XVII initium floruerunt ... Praefixa est ... praefatio, historiam literariam Britannorum ante Caesaris adventum, bibliothecae hujus schema, Bostonum Buriensem, aliaque scitu non indigna complectens.* London: Excudit Gulielmus Bowyer, impensis Societas ad literas promovendas, 1748, repr. Tucson: Audaz, 1963

465 Taylor, Archer. *The bibliographical history of anonyma and pseudonyma.* University of Chicago Press, 1951

466 — *Book Catalogues: Their varieties and Uses.* Chicago: The Newberry Library, 1957

467 — *Catalogues of rare books; a chapter in bibliographical history.* University of Kansas Publications, Library Series, 5. Lawrence, Kansas: University of Kansas Libraries, 1958

468 — *General subject indexes since 1548.* Philadelphia: University of Pennsylvania Press, 1966

469 –   *A History of bibliographies of bibliographies.* New Brunswick, N.J.: Scarecrow, 1955

470 –   *Problems in German literary history of the fifteenth and sixteenth centuries.* New York: Modern Language Association, 1939

471 –   *Renaissance guides to books.* University of California Press, 1945

472 Teissier, Antoine. *Catalogus auctorum, qui librorum catalogos, indices, bibliothecas, virorum litteratorum elogia, vitas, aut orationes funebres, scriptis consignârunt.* Geneva: Samuel de Tournes, 1686

473 Thelert, Gustav. *Supplement zu Heinsius', Hinrichs' und Kaysers Bücher-Lexikon. Verzeichnis einer Anzahl Schriften, welche seit der Mitte des neunzehnten Jahrhunderts, in den genannten Katalogen aber garnicht oder fehlerhaft aufgeführt sind.* Grossenhain/Leipzig: Baumert & Ronge, 1893

474 Thomasius, Christian. *Freymüthige, lustige und ernsthaffte, jedoch Vernunfft- und Gesetz-mässige Gedanken.* Halle, 1688–90 (title varies)

475 Thompson, James Westfall. *The Frankfort book fair: the Francofordiense emporium of Henri Estienne.* Chicago: The Caxton Club, 1911

476 Thou, Jacques Auguste de. *Catalogus bibliothecae Thuanae a clariss. W Petro & Jacobo Puteanis, ordine alphabetico primum distributus. Tum secundum scientias & artes à clariss. viro Ismaele Bullialdo digestus. Nunc vero editus a Iosepho Quesnel, Parisino & bibliothecario. Cum indice alphabetico authorum.* Paris: impensis directionis . . . 1679

477 Totok, Wilhelm and Weitzel, Rolf. *Handbuch der bibliographischen Nachschlagewerke.* Frankfurt: Klostermann, 1954, [4]1972

478 Totok, Wilhelm. "Die Nationalbibliographien." In *Bibliographie und Buchhandel*, q.v., pp. 107–23

479 Trefler, Florian. *Methodus exhibens per varios indices, et classes subinde, quorumlibet librorum, cuiuslibet bibliothecae, brevem, facilem, imitabilem ordinationem. Qua sanè peraccommodè, & sine multa inquisitione occurrat studiosis optata inventio, & lectio eorundem.* [Col] Impressum Augustae, per Philippum Vlhardum, 1560

480 Trithemius, Johannes. *Cathalogus illustrium virorum germaniā suis ingeniis et lucubrationibus omnifariam exornantium: dn̄i iohannis tritemii abbatis spanhemensis ordinis sancti benedicti: ad Jacobū Vimpfelingū sletstatinū theologum* [Petrus de Friedberg: Mainz, 1496?]

481 –   *De Laude scriptorum manualium.* Mainz: Petrus Friedberg, 1494

482 –   *De laude scriptorum. Zum Lobe der Schreiber*, eingeleitet, herausgegeben und übersetzt von Klaus Arnold. Würzburg: Fränkische Bibliophilengesellschaft, 1973

483 –   *Johannes Trithemius. In praise of scribes – De laude scriptorum*, ed. with an introduction by Klaus Arnold, tr. by Roland Behrendt, O. S. B. Lawrence, Kansas: Coronado Press, 1974

484 –   *Joannis Trithemii Spanhemensis primum, deinde D. Jacobi in suburbano Herbipolensi abbatis eruditissimi opera pia et spiritualia . . . a R. P. Joanne Busaeo redacta . . .* Mainz: Joannes Albinus, 1604

485 –   *Johannis Trithemii Spanheimensis . . . opera historica, quotquot hactenus reperiri potuerunt, omnia . . . Ex bibliotheca Marquardi Freheri . . .* Frankfurt: typis Wechelianis apud Claudium Marnium & heredes Ioannis Aubrii, 1601
      – see also Arnold, Klaus; Bestermann, Theodore

486   Van Hoesen, Henry Bartlett. *Bibliography, practical, enumerative, historical.* New
         York: Scribners, 1928
487   *Verzeichnis lieferbarer Bücher.* Frankfurt, 1971/72–
488   Vickery, Brian Campbell. *Information systems.* London: Butterworths, 1973
489   Vilmar, August Friedrich Christian. *Vorlesungen über die Geschichte der deutschen
         National-Literatur.* Marburg: Elwert, 1844
490   Voglerus, Valentinus Henricus. *Introductio universalis in notitiam cuiuscunque generis
         bonorum scriptorum.* Helmstadt: Henning Müller, 1670
491   Vogt, Johann. *Catalogus historico-criticus librorum rariorum.* Hamburg: J. C. Kisner,
         1732; [5]1793
492   Vorstius, Joris. *Ergebnisse und Fortschritte der Bibliographie in Deutschland seit dem
         ersten Weltkrieg.* Zentralblatt fur Bibliothekswesen, Beiheft 74. Leipzig: Otto
         Harassowitz, 1948.
493   –   *Der gegenwärtige Stand der primären Nationalbibliographie in den Kultur-
         ländern; zugleich ein Beitrag zur Theorie der Bibliographie.* Leipzig: Harrasso-
         witz, 1930
494   Walter, Elise. *Verluste auf dem Gebiet der mittelhochdeutschen Lyrik.* Stuttgart:
         Kohlhammer, 1933
495   Waterhouse, Gilbert. *The Yearbook of modern languages,* edited for the Council of the
         Modern Language Association. Cambridge University Press, 1920
496   *Webster's third new international dictionary of the English language unabridged.*
         Springfield, Mass.: G. & C. Merriam, 1965
497   Weinstock, Melvin. "Citation indexes." *Encyclopedia of library and information
         Science* (New York: Dekker, 1968), V, 16–40
498   Weitzel, Rolf. *Die deutschen nationalen Bibliographien. Eine Anleitung zu ihrer
         Benutzung.* Frankfurt: Buchhändlervereinigung, 1958, [3]1963
499   Weller, Emil. *Annalen der poetischen National-Literatur der Deutschen im 16. und
         17. Jahrhundert.* Freiburg: Herder, 1862–64
500   –   *Repertorium typographicorum. Die deutsche Literatur im ersten Viertel des
         sechzehnten Jahrhunderts.* Nördlingen: C. H. Beck, 1864–85
501   Wendt, Bernhard. "Der Versteigerungs- und Antiquariats-Katalog im Wandel von vier
         Jahrhunderten." *Archiv für Geschichte des Buchwesens,* 9 (1967–69), 1–88
502   Whitbread, Leslie G. "Conrad of Hirsau as a literary critic." *Speculum,* 47 (1972),
         234–45
503   Widmann, Hans. *Bibliographie zum deutschen Schrifttum 1939–50.* Tübingen:
         Niemeyer, 1951
504   –   ed. *Der deutsche Buchhandel in Urkunden und Quellen.* 2 vols. Hamburg: Ernst
         Hauswedell, 1965
505   –   "Leibniz und sein Plan zu einem 'Nucleus librarius'." *Archiv für Geschichte des
         Buchwesens,* 4 (1963), 621–36
      Widsith – see *Anglo-Saxon poetry*
506   Wiesner, Herbert & Živsa, Irena & Stoll, Christoph. *Bibliographie der Personalbiblio-
         graphien zur deutschen Gegenwartsliteratur.* Munich: Nymphenburg, 1970
      Willer, Georg – see *Die Messkataloge*
507   Wilpert, Gero von & Göhring A. *Erstausgaben deutscher Dichtung. Eine Bibliographie
         zur deutschen Literatur 1600–1960.* Stuttgart: Kröner, 1967

508   Wing, Donald Goddard. *A Gallery of ghosts: books published between 1641–1700 not found in the Short title catalogues.* New York: Modern Language Association, 1967

509   —   *Short title catalogue of books printed in England, Scotland, Ireland, Wales and British America, and of English books printed in other countries 1641–1700.* New York: Index Society, 1945–51; 2nd edition New York: Modern Language Association, 1972–

510   "Wissenschaftliche Forschungsberichte," ed. Karl Hönn. Gotha: Perthes, 1914–

511   Wittmann, Reinhard. "Die frühen Buchhändlerzeitschriften als Spiegel des literarischen Lebens." *Archiv für Geschichte des Buchwesens,* 13 (1973), 613–931; also separately [diss. Munich, 1971]

512   *Wöchentliches Verzeichnis der erschienenen und der vorbereiteten Neuigkeiten des deutschen Buchhandels.* Leipzig: 1843–1930 (supplement to *Börsenblatt*); succeeded by *Deutsche Nationalbibliographie,* Reihe A, q.v. and *Deutsche Bibliographie. Wöchentliches Verzeichnis,* q.v.
      Wolfenbüttel (library) – see Conring, Hermann
      Wolff, Hieronymus – see Augsburg (library)

513   *The World book encyclopedia.* Chicago: Field Enterprises, 1970

514   *The Year's work in modern language studies* (Modern Humanities Research Association), 1930–. London, 1931–

515   Zannach, Jakob. *Bibliotheca theologica, sive catalogus tam auctorum, quiin sacros biblicos libros veteris et novi testamenti in hunc usq; annum scripserunt . . .* Mulhouse: no publisher, 1591

516   Zapf, Georg Wilhelm. *Reisen in einige Klöster Schwabens durch den Schwarzwald und in die Schweiz im Jahr 1781.* Erlangen: J. J. Palm, 1786

517   *Zeitschrift für deutsche Philologie,* ed. E. Hoepfner & J. Zacher (1868–)

518   *Zeitschrift für deutsches Alterthum,* ed. Moriz Haupt (1841–)

519   *Zeitschriftenaufsatzkatalog,* ed. Deutsche Forschungsgemeinschaft: Bibliotheksreferat. Bonn-Bad Godesberg, 1962–

520   Ziegler, Jerome. *Illustrium Germaniae virorum historiae aliquot singulares, ex optimis, probatissimisque authoribus erutæ atque congestae . . .* Ingolstadt: per Alexandrum & Samuelem Weissenhornios, 1562
      Zürich (library) – see Hottinger, J. H.

Index

In addition to subjects this index includes the names of authors of bibliographical sources cited in the text and footnotes, the names of writers cited as examples from these sources, and the titles of works cited without author or editor. It does not include authors or titles of critical works cited.